LAVERSTOCK AND FORD

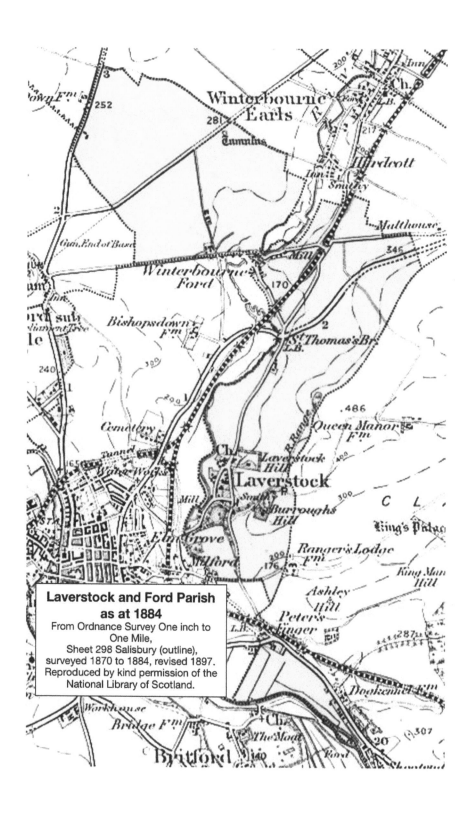

Laverstock and Ford Parish
as at 1884
From Ordnance Survey One inch to
One Mile,
Sheet 298 Salisbury (outline),
surveyed 1870 to 1884, revised 1897.
Reproduced by kind permission of the
National Library of Scotland.

Laverstock and Ford
Chapters from Local History

Sarum Studies 6

Editorial Team, Laverstock and Ford Research Group:
Bryan Evans, Jenny Hayes, John Loades, Ruth Newman,
Ken Smith, Sue Wight

Sarum Chronicle
Recent historical research on Salisbury & district

First published in the United Kingdom in 2019, on behalf of the Sarum Chronicle Editorial Team

How to contact us:
To order a copy, email ruth.tanglewood@btinternet.com
For other titles in the Sarum Studies series and for back issues of Sarum Chronicle please contact jane@sarum-editorial.co.uk with the words Sarum Chronicle in the subject line, or visit the website: www.sarumchronicle.wordpress.com

ISBN 978-1-9161359-0-1
ISSN 1475-1844

Designed and typeset by John Chandler

Front Cover:
Laverstock village under Cockey Down from Cow Lane and the Water Meadows. Drawn in the style of Edwin Young by Jenny Hayes.

Back Cover:
A group of glazed medieval jugs from the pottery kilns at Laverstock © The Salisbury Museum

Contents

Contents

Acknowledgements

Many Laverstock residents very kindly shared their memories and recollections of village life and these contributions are gratefully acknowledged. Unfortunately, restrictions on space mean that it has not been possible to include all of this valuable material.

Particular appreciation is extended to the following:

Laverstock and Ford Parish Council showed faith in our project and provided us with a generous grant to help funding.

Special mention is due to Jane Howells for her careful proofreading of the text, her valuable suggestions and constant support and encouragement.

The chapters have been greatly enhanced by Roy Bexon's preparation of the images and by his own photographs. Jenny Hayes' line drawings, maps and delightful bird's-eye view illustrations of the village have further created a visually appealing volume.

Claire Skinner, Steven Hobbs, Julie Davis and WSHC staff at Chippenham, Adrian Green and Megan Fowler at Salisbury Museum, and Salisbury Reference librarians have all been unfailingly helpful in fielding our queries and providing material.

Above all we owe enormous thanks to John Chandler who, with friendly patience, has taken time out of his hectic life to typeset and design this attractive book for us.

This 6th volume of *Sarum Studies* has also benefited from the expertise and advice of the current *Sarum Chronicle* editorial team, without whom this book would not have been published: Roy Bexon, John Chandler, John Cox, John Elliott, Jane Howells, Andrew Minting, Ruth Newman and Margaret Smith.

In addition, information, skills and time have been kindly provided by the following: Philip Annetts, Alan Clarke, Meryl and Philip Cleaver, Audrey Coggan, Hadrian Cook, Dave Cooper, Sharon Evans, Steve Hannath, Marti Hilliard, the late Gordon Hoskins, Tom Beaumont James, Brian Johnson, Christopher and Eileen Kirkup, David Law, Emily Naish, Joe Newman, Bill Osmond, Anne Parker, Sylvia Parrett, Amanda Richardson, Caroline

Rippier, James and Beth Robertson, Penelope Rundle, Peter Saunders, Pamela Slocombe, David Waspe and Christine Webb.

Tribute to Gordon Hoskins (1920-2019)

In the very last stages of producing this volume we heard of Gordon's death, aged 99. His evocative booklet *When the larks sang* has been quoted extensively in these chapters. His memories, whether oral or written, have provided inspiration, enhanced our writing and brought to life the Laverstock he loved when he first came to the village in 1937.

Ruth Newman

Abbreviations

HER	Historic Environment Record (https://services.wiltshire.gov.uk/ HistoryEnvRecord/Home/Index)
HMSO	Her Majesty's Stationery Office
MWI	Monuments in Wiltshire (prefix for sites recorded within the county HER website)
OS	Ordnance Survey
RCHME	Royal Commission on Historical Monuments (England)
SJ	Salisbury and Winchester Journal
ST	Salisbury Times
TNA	The National Archives
VCH	Victoria County History
VCH *Wilts* 1	Victoria History of the Counties of England, *Wiltshire,* vol 1 part 1 1957 edited Pugh & Crittall
VCH *Wilts* 2	Victoria History of the Counties of England, *Wiltshire*, vol 2 1955 edited Pugh & Crittall
VCH *Wilts* 3	Victoria History of the Counties of England, *Wiltshire*, vol 3 1956 edited Pugh & Crittall
VCH *Wilts* 4	Victoria History of the Counties of England, *Wiltshire*, vol 4 1959 edited Crittall
VCH *Wilts* 5	Victoria History of the Counties of England, Wiltshire, vol 5 1957 edited Pugh & Crittall
VCH *Wilts* 6	Victoria History of the Counties of England, *Wiltshire*, vol 6 1962 edited Crittall
WANHM	Wiltshire Archaeological and Natural History Magazine
WC	Wiltshire Council
WCC	Wiltshire County Council (currently Wiltshire Council)
WRS	Wiltshire Record Society
WSA	Wiltshire and Swindon Archive
WSHC	Wiltshire and Swindon History Centre

Bibliography

Drake, Vera, 1995, *Memoirs of a Laverstock resident from 1937 to 1990s.* (Extracts published in the Parish Newsletter) (Abb: Drake, 1995)

Grist, Kenneth, 2000, *Larks on Cockey Down,* ELSP in association with Cross Keys Press

Hoskins, Gordon, 1992, *When the larks sang,* privately published (Abb: Hoskins, 1992)

Parrett, Sylvia J, 1999, *Laverstock, from Victoria to the Fifties,* self published (Abb: Parrett, 1999)

Introduction

This project came about in December 2016 when a group of members of the newly formed Laverstock and Ford history group decided to form a smaller research body with the aim of producing a history of the village. It quickly became apparent that, given members' specific interests and knowledge, a full account of the parish was not viable. We could, however, create 'chapters from local history' which dealt with important aspects of the village. This we hope we have achieved, with different authors contributing a collection of varied topics, personally selected and independently researched and written.

The book has a general chronological theme with detailed sub-headings. It includes a more thorough history of the heart of the village than has ever previously been attempted. It cannot claim to be a complete history of Laverstock and Ford, but we hope, through the topics explored here, to stimulate the curiosity and enthusiasm of readers and perhaps inspire others to research further the village's past.

★★★

All English villages have unique characteristics but Laverstock has perhaps changed more than most. It is difficult for many to envisage the village of even 70 years ago and to reconcile it with today's busy through road, modern housing developments and a transient student population studying at the four schools.

This rural community was, and remains, set within a large parish which borders Alderbury and Britford in the south, to the margin of the Iron Age earthworks of Old Sarum. The locality stretches further north to include the First World War airfield, Longhedge and the Monarch's Way.

Nestling on the fringes of the royal forest of Clarendon, Laverstock, a village older than Salisbury, has a long and intriguing past. It has always maintained a separate identity from its large, expanding neighbour, separated crucially by the River Bourne and Milford Hill.

What makes the village so special? A postcard of 1914 described Laverstock as 'a lovely little spot with its thatched cottages'; idyllic before the planners and developers first arrived in the late 1930s. Older residents reminisce fondly of a cohesive community, of large farms, small workers' cottages and grand houses; a slower pace of life which has long disappeared. The neighbouring hamlet of Ford has also seen development but has retained its rural characteristics.

Some aspects of its past are well documented in contemporary records, others are more obscure. But much of the history around us can be explored and rediscovered. A successful, high status, medieval pottery industry brought economic benefits, while much later a progressive asylum ensured that in the field of mental health the village was firmly on the national map.

And despite the radical changes there is also continuity. Older houses and our one remaining thatched cottage cluster round the Green, once the centre of economic and social activity, while the church has remained the spiritual core of the village, possibly from Anglo-Saxon times.

Today the green lanes and early trade routes provide leisure and reinforce the semi-rural nature of the parish. We still have orchids and larks on Cockey Down while the River Bourne Community Farm, dating from 2010, has provided a new centre for both visitors and locals.

What we have tried to do is to recreate the 'lost' Laverstock and Ford. Oral memories have been vital to our understanding but equally we have responded to movements in society. The thread running through this story is of change. In recent years, with extensive boundary revisions and a fast expanding population, the village has shown resilience in retaining its own identity. It is different from the past but remains a diverse and vibrant community. Our ability to cope with the challenges of the future is strengthened by an understanding of the past.

The Setting
From tropical seas to downland: Laverstock geology
Ken Smith

It is a truism of physical geology that the look and nature of all landscapes are determined by their underlying rock structures. Laverstock is no exception to this rule.

The oldest surface rocks in Laverstock are those of the chalk, which date from the Cretaceous period, some 60-150 million years ago. Thus, in terms of earth history, the chalk can be considered a relatively recent deposit, even though it was being formed in the age of dinosaurs.

Chalk consists of innumerable tiny calcareous shells, or coccoliths. These small organisms lived in the warm waters of that time. It was during the Cretaceous age that the oceans covered a greater percentage of the earth's surface than at any time since. There is evidence that, owing to extensive volcanic activity, the atmosphere became warmer, the polar ice caps completely melted and dinosaurs roamed the Antarctic continent.

The chalk sea probably formed on the edges of a continental shelf where the water was no more than 100m deep. In this warm, relatively shallow water where Southern England now stands, huge layers of chalky sediment built up over millions of years. As the sediments compacted and began to form into rock, silica in solution (derived from sponge spicules) collected in layers and voids in the chalk. Eventually this hardened into flint layers and nodules of huge significance for our early ancestors. Some flints took the shape or impressions of fossils such as sea urchins in the chalk.

In time, other rocks were deposited on the chalk. These younger rocks are termed the Reading Formation and can be found in a small area on the top of Cockey Down. These remnants must have once formed part of a more widespread deposit on the chalk that erosion has stripped away.

Thus, the Laverstock area evolved, geologically, as a worn chalk surface covered in part by later deposits largely derived from the chalk, shaped and modified by the combined action of freeze-thaw, wind, water and gravity.[1] During the last ice-age, there were great glaciers to the north in the midlands. The Laverstock area resembled much of what northern Canada is like today. It would have been tundra with sub-arctic vegetation, such as sedges, grasses, moss, lichens and dwarf willow, rowan or juniper. The only animals would be those adapted to the harsh conditions; those of periglacial Laverstock included mammoths, reindeer, wolves, lemmings and arctic foxes.

The dry valleys, characteristic of the chalk lands, are likely to have formed during periglacial times, some 20,000 years ago, when the subsoil remained frozen throughout the year with only a few surface centimetres thawing. This meant that spring meltwater would not be absorbed by the normally porous chalk, but would run over the surface, gouging out valleys. Evidence for this exists in the periglacial detritus of small, worn and angular flints, broken chalk and clay/sand classified under the term 'head'. This can be found on the floor of dry valleys or as scree 'fans' below slopes.

Much of the village of Laverstock is built on this material, eroded, moved and deposited both by periglacial action and as water-borne valley gravel. The valley gravel is made up of broken or little-worn flints, sand, clay and chalk. It provides a good soil for arable crops and a secure foundation for buildings.

The medieval Laverstock pottery industry utilised some of these depositional materials to make the famous Laverstock ware seen in the Salisbury Museum. Evidence indicates that the nearest deposits of potting clay were found on Cockey Down or at Alderbury. Thus, it is likely that the clay originally formed part of the younger, Reading Formation deposited on the chalk.

The repeated erosional cycles controlled by water flow, ice, freeze-thaw and wind have resulted in a landscape with relatively thin soils on the hilltops and upper slopes. This made it possible for the Laverstock 'panda' to be produced in the 1960s, as a student prank, by removing the grass cover to expose the white chalk. Deeper soils containing more clay, sand and gravel are found on lower slopes, grading into gravels over-lain by river mud, clay and peat found on the valley floor.

Other uses for the local rocks of Laverstock might have included cob-walling. Cob was a mixture of trampled chalk, water, straw and either mud or animal dung. Surviving

A surviving cob wall in Queen Manor road on the Laverstock/ Clarendon border, photograph Jenny Hayes.

examples of this type of wall show a waterproof base of brick or mortared flints which are capped with thatch or tiles to throw off the rain.

Once covered in whitewash or some similar render, cob would serve for both cottage and garden walls. Today there are a few cob walls in the village but no cob walled dwellings. However, in centuries past, there may well have been several cob cottages in Laverstock.[2] There is good reason to think this to be the case, as building stone is in short supply in the village – owing to the geology – so, until brick became available, cob may well have been an alternative. There is a surviving wall in Duck Lane made from a variety of building materials: brick, chalk blocks, Chilmark stone (perhaps taken from Old Sarum) and flint. This too, indicates the scarcity of building materials in the village.

A wall in Duck Lane showing a variety of building materials, photograph Roy Bexon

It is possible that some of the buildings of Laverstock were constructed of Alderbury bricks although other local brick-makers were based at Clarendon, Downton and West Grimstead . Other sources of brick supply in the village are visible in the remaining gatepost leading to the house known as The Hill. This contains a substantial number of buff Fisherton bricks though red bricks are also present. At the turn of the 19th century, Fisherton brick was widely used in Salisbury.

For most of the time that the site of Laverstock has been settled, the village houses and buildings have been almost exclusively sited on the valley gravels. These provide firm foundations and are far enough above the valley bottom to avoid flooding by the river Bourne. Only during the 20th century and up to the present, have houses and other buildings, generally, been sited on the chalk or the valley alluvium.

Laverstock's past has helped to mould the village we see.

Boundaries:
the changing shape of the parish
John Loades

Fundamental to a study of Laverstock and Ford is determining its geographical area and the changes which have occurred over time.

As recently as 2017, there have been alterations to the boundaries of the civil parish of Laverstock and Ford. After a process of consultation, which included well-attended public meetings, Wiltshire Council considered three alternative boundary change proposals. The outcome was to increase the Laverstock and Ford parish area in the Bishopdown Farm vicinity.[3] This serves as a reminder that parish communities do alter and adjust to circumstances.

The existence of established communities both at Laverstock and Ford can be traced back at least to Saxon times. Clues to the origins of a location may often be found in the place name, with the derivation of Laverstock covered in the next chapter.

What emerges is that there has long been a settlement known as Laverstock along the Bourne valley, situated between the sites at Old Sarum and the later New Sarum to the west and Clarendon estate to the east, with the River Avon providing a natural southern limit from the point where the Bourne flows in at Petersfinger. Similarly, Ford has been the site of a crossing point of the Bourne dating back at least to Roman times, and is bounded to its north by the Winterbourne parishes.

Both the manorial system and the spread of Christianity during medieval times saw the establishment of parish communities centred on a local manor and a place of worship. The probability of Laverstock having its own church, linked to a local manor, during the Saxon and Norman periods is explored elsewhere *(see: Chapter 3)*. From these origins, a community would have existed with known boundaries with its neighbours, often confirmed by specific markers at key points.

Historically, Laverstock parish fell within the ancient hundred of Alderbury, bounded to its west by the Bourne and extending upstream to include the

Winterbourne parishes and as far as Idmiston. There are early records of three lost settlements in the Milford Bridge vicinity with two, Milford Pichard and Milford Richard, located east of the river and probably falling within Laverstock parish.[4] A further lost settlement, Mumworth, was located close to the confluence of the Bourne and the Avon in the Petersfinger area.[5] *(see: Chapter 4.)*

It is probable that there were minor adjustments to parish boundaries over succeeding centuries in response to local factors. For instance, there is a record of a proposal that three households within the hamlet of Ford be united within the Laverstock parish during 1650, as the Church authorities deemed them to be nearer to St Andrew's Church than to their assigned Winterbourne Gunner church.[6]

The 1841 Census showed Laverstock and Ford as being bounded on the east by Clarendon, on the west by Milford, on the north by Hurdcott and Winterbourne and in the south by Alderbury and the River Avon. A clearer picture of the extent of the ecclesiastical parish in the 19th century is provided both by early Series Ordnance Survey maps and by the 1842 parish Tithe Map. Before Laverstock's Tithe Apportionments commenced, the commissioners were involved in settling a boundary dispute with Milford, primarily relating to meadows bordering the Avon in the Petersfinger area.[7]

At this stage, natural features constituted the main boundaries, with the Bourne and Avon providing much of the western and southern features, and the ridge along the top of Laverstock Down defining the eastern border with Clarendon Park. In addition, the Petersfinger area south of the Southampton Road is shown on the Tithe Map as a 'detached' portion of Laverstock parish, predominantly consisting of pasture and water meadow. This was separated from the rest of the parish by the width of a single field that fell within Milford parish (Map 1).

At the other end of the parish, Ford was bounded on the north by the pathway now known as Monarch's Way as far west as Longhedge on the Amesbury Road and included the downs to the north of the Roman road through Ford, where Old Sarum Airfield is now located (Map 1). An anomaly relating to Ford hamlet is apparent from maps and records of the 19th century. Several households were located on the southern edge of the

The Laverstock Detached boundary sign with Alderbury, erected before 1884 on the old Southampton Road, by the turning to Shute End, beyond Petersfinger. Drawing by Jenny Hayes

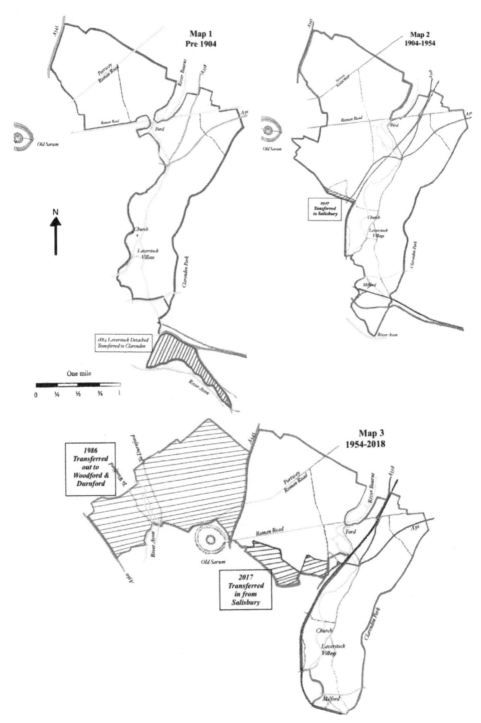

Parish Boundaries: snapshots from 19th and 20th Centuries, prepared by Jenny Hayes based on Ordnance Survey series.

Roman road and therefore fell into Milford parish, whilst two households situated opposite on the north side of the road were recorded within a detached portion of Idmiston parish. Other nearby properties were within Laverstock and Ford parish.[8] *(see: Chapter 5.)*

Reform of the parish system evolved during the 19th century, with the emergence of separate bodies to administer matters such as poor relief and sanitary districts. This process was consolidated by the Local Government Act of 1894, which created civil parishes as the first tier of administration. Like many others, Laverstock and Ford civil parish emerged with boundaries that no longer corresponded exactly with the ancient or traditional ecclesiastical parish.

The landscape in the vicinity had altered during the mid-19th century with the national surge in railway construction. Two rail lines were built adjacent to the parish, which merged at a junction located no more than half a mile west of Laverstock church and village, across the Bourne. The valley terrain resulted in embankments being constructed to accommodate the right of way, which inevitably influenced subsequent boundary reviews. Firstly in 1884, Laverstock Detached, south of the Southampton railway, was transferred to Clarendon Park civil parish, created in 1858.[9] (Map 1; Map 4 area 2.)

Further adjustments, prompted by the expansion of Salisbury, were recognised by the New Sarum (Extension) Order of 1904, when three segments of the civil parish of Milford Without were transferred to Laverstock and Ford (Map 2). The first shifted the parish's western boundary from the Bourne to the railway lines, following the track from the arched rail bridge close to Laverstock Bridge (Whitebridge), around the elevated curve of Laverstock Loop and along the London line to a point opposite the north side of London Road Cemetery. (Map 4 area 5.) This brought Cow Lane and the current River Bourne Community Farm within the parish. Secondly, the Bishopdown area from the London Road Cemetery northwards to the Roman road between Ford and Old Sarum was all now included. (Map 4 areas 6 to 9.) This alteration united all households within Ford hamlet into the same civil parish. Finally, a western section of Petersfinger was transferred to Laverstock, with the Bourne on its west, the Avon to its south, then following a lane beneath the rail track before proceeding along a pathway north east to join Queen Manor Road by Ranger's Lodge. (Map 4 areas 3, 4.) This southern area currently includes the Petersfinger sewage works, the adjacent Park and Ride car park and that part of Southampton Road retail park that lies east of the Bourne.

A small portion of the southern end of Bishopdown was returned to Salisbury in 1927 by an order of the Ministry of Health, possibly to facilitate an expansion of London Road Cemetery towards the current Crematorium (Map 4 area 6).[10] In 1954, a larger section of Bishopdown Farm was transferred to

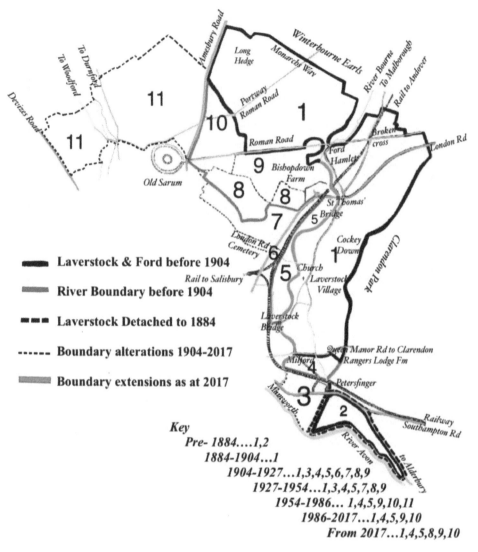

Key
Pre- 1884....1,2
1884-1904...1
1904-1927...1,3,4,5,6,7,8,9
1927-1954...1,3,4,5,7,8,9
1954-1986... 1,4,5,9,10,11
1986-2017...1,4,5,9,10
From 2017...1,4,5,8,9,10

Boundary Extensions and Movements, prepared by Jenny Hayes based on Ordnance Survey series.

Salisbury, including an area intended for council housing. (Map 4 areas 7, 8.) A northern part of this area subsequently returned to Laverstock and Ford in the 2017 boundary amendment. (Map 3; Map 4 area 8).

Also in the 1954 changes, Salisbury was allocated that portion of the Petersfinger area south of the railway that had been transferred from Milford fifty years earlier (Map 4 area 3). The southern boundary of the parish now follows the Southampton railway line from where it crosses the Bourne, eastward to the point where Milford Mill Road passes under the railway. Simultaneously, Laverstock and Ford gained the northern part of the abolished Stratford-sub-

Castle civil parish, incorporating into the parish a portion of land immediately north of Old Sarum about a mile in depth and extending some 2 miles west of the A345 Amesbury Road, across the Avon and as far as the A360 Devizes Road.[11] (Map 4 area 10, 11.)

This north-westward extension was reallocated in 1986, with Durnford and Woodford parishes receiving large portions to the west of Amesbury Road[12]. (Map 4 area 11.) A smaller triangular holding east of that road up to the Portway remained within Laverstock and Ford. (Map 4 area 10). This remainder includes the Beehive area with its current Park and Ride facility. Following the 2017 changes, the increase in area and households within the civil parish was recognised by subdivision into three wards: Laverstock and Milford; Bishopdown Farm; Ford, Old Sarum and Longhedge. [13]

In summary, what emerges clearly is that there is a 'core' part of the parish that has remained largely constant, illustrated in Map 4 as area 1.

The remaining peripheral and transitory parts comprise the Petersfinger portions shown as areas 2, 3 and 4 in Map 4 plus those sections of Bishopdown and Stratford-sub-Castle covered by areas 5 through to 11.These areas were largely rural and sparsely populated until modern times.

This evolution returns to the question: how is Laverstock and Ford best defined for the purpose of this study? The 'core' part deserves full coverage while for the peripheral areas, any activity of historic note is worthy of mention, even when it pre-dates transfer into or out of the parish.

Summary of Boundary Adjustments: Laverstock and Ford Parish					
Year	Tfr In	Tfr out	Legislation		Effective:
1884		2	To Clarendon Park, Local Government Board Order No. 18150		1884
1885			Minor transfer in: IdmistonNo 2 det.&W'bourneDauntseydet.		25/03/1885
1904	3,4,5,6,7,8,9		New Sarum (Extension) Order, 1904		09/11/1904
1927		6	Ministry of Health Order (New Sarum Extension), 1927		01/10/1927
1954	10, 11	3,7,8,9	New Sarum (Extension) Order, 1954		01/04/1954
1986		11	Salisbury (Parishes) Order, 1986 (Statutory Instrument 72/1986)		01/04/1986
2017	8		WC (Re-organisation of Community Governance) Order 2016		01/04/2017
NB: Refer to Map 4 for numbered areas transferred in or out.					

The population of Laverstock 1086-1800
Bryan Evans

Evidence for the population of Laverstock before 1801 (when the ten-yearly national census was introduced) must be sought in limited contemporary records and their interpretation. These include Domesday Book, medieval taxation returns, 17th century surveys carried out for political ends, and Parish Registers and Bishops' Transcripts. The following data and analysis draws on such records as survive for Laverstock, and it gives us some idea of population levels in the village in earlier times.

Domesday Book 1086

The Domesday Survey was not a census of the population, but was concerned with landholdings and values. There are two entries for Laverstock:

> The church itself holds Laverstock [Lavertestoche or Lavvrecestohes]. TRE ['in the time of king Edward', that is, Edward the Confessor] it paid geld for 2 hides. There is land for 3 ploughs. Of this land 1 hide is in demesne [lordship], and there is 1 plough. There are 6 villans [villeins] and 8 bordars with 2 ploughs. There is a mill rendering 7s 6d, and 18 acres of pasture. It was worth 100s; now £6. Of this land a fourth part has been 'put in the king's forest' (*in foresta regis est posita*).
>
> Særic holds Laverstock [Lavertestoche]. Gestr, his brother, held it TRE, and it paid geld for half a hide. There is land for half a plough, which (half-plough) is there. It is worth 10s.[14]

A villein (not a 'villain' in the modern sense) belonged to a class of peasants having the rights and privileges of freemen in their dealings with other peasants, but unfree in dealings with their lord. The standard land-holding of a villein was about thirty acres. Bordars and cottars ranked below villeins and above serfs in the social hierarchy. On average a bordar farmed about five acres of land, just enough to feed a family.[15]

It is generally agreed that Domesday only recorded heads of households, and so to work out the total population a multiplier is needed. How great should the multiplier be, and what is to be multiplied? (Besides close family a 'household' may have included elderly kin, servants, and lodgers.) The question of omissions must also be faced, for it is thought that Domesday may have concerned itself only with those who were directly responsible for paying taxes. If we take the total of fourteen villeins and bordars and apply a multiplier of 4.75 (a figure often used in work on medieval records), then take Nash's suggested omissions rate of 35 per cent we arrive at a total population of 102, in perhaps 20-25 households.[16]

The lay subsidy of 1332

The costly wars of Edward I and Edward III exhausted the resources of the crown, and those of Jewish moneylenders and Italian bankers. The crown was thus driven to seek tax revenue through so-called 'Lay subsidies', based on a proportion of each person's property. In 1332 Parliament granted Edward III a tenth of the movable goods of those laity living in cities and boroughs and on ancient demesne of the Crown, and a fifteenth of the property of rural dwellers. The 'fifteenth' (which would have applied to rural Laverstock) was to be based on the value of farm livestock and agricultural produce, but not agricultural implements, household goods, or food not for sale. Anyone whose movable goods were valued at less than ten shillings was to be exempt. This meant that cottagers and those living in the households of better-off husbandmen would have been below the tax threshold.

In Laverstock £2 12s 7d tax was collected, and we have the names of the twenty taxpayers, who included two women:[17]

John de Bouclonde	6s 8¾d	Thomas Swevynge	2s
John le May	4s 8½d	William Dure	2s
Alice la Yonge	4s 4¼d	Thomas Swevynge	3s 11d
William Orpedeman	4s ¼d	Maud Herynge	2s 8d
William Cole	12d	Edward Broun	12d
John le Ketere	3s	John le Bride	2s 10d
William le Bole	12d	Adam le Fishere	12d
Walter Serle	3s 4d	Thomas le Ketere	12d
John le Preost	18d	William Serle	3s
John Serle	18d	John Levesteman	2s

How complete might the assessors' lists be? In village communities where everybody knew everybody else, and each probably knew what neighbours owned and its quality, evasion would not have been easy. Thus the lists of taxpayers may well be more or less complete, and the valuations more or less accurate. However, this was not a census of the population, and to make an estimate based on the tax list we would have to make allowance for those whose property was below the minimum threshold. The resulting total would be of heads of households, to which the 4.75 multiplier would have to be applied. If we supposed that the twenty who paid the subsidy in Laverstock accounted for half the heads, an estimate of the whole population would be 190. If the taxpayers were two-thirds of the population, the estimate for the whole population would be 143. This lower figure would seem to fit better with the estimates for 1377 and 1524.

Poll taxes 1377, 1379, 1381

The Parliament of 1377 levied a poll tax to finance the war against France. The tax of one groat (4d) per head was levied on householders, wives, dependants and servants individually. The only exemptions were children of 14 years and under, beneficed clergy (who paid a separate tax) and mendicant friars (whose only support was the alms given them). In 1379 the minimum age was raised to 16, and the amount payable ranged from 4d to ten marks (a mark was 13s 4d). The levy of 1381 lowered the age limit to 15 and used a combination of flat rate and graduated assessments.

The most detailed returns to survive are those of 1379. However, they are less complete than the 1377 returns because there was widespread evasion. Such evasion was even more marked in 1381. Moreover, some of the 1381 assessments were destroyed in the Peasants' Revolt. (The poll tax is thought to have been one of the key factors in the outbreak of the revolt later in 1381.)

In Laverstock in 1377 sixty-three people paid the poll tax of 4d each, a total of £1 1s. The 'constable' for the collection in Laverstock parish was John Hulon, and the *probi homines* ('men of probity') were John Sheregold and Stephen Serle. Sadly, the list of the names of the taxpayers has not survived. For 1379 we do have the names of the 34 who paid (£1 12s 6d collected):

de Hugone Cheyne *armigero*	20s 0d	Ricardo Capmakere	4d
Thoma *servient' eius*	4d	Johanne Bakere	4d
Willelmo *s' eius*	4d	Johanne Colyn	4d
Johanne *s' eius*	4d	Jacobo Serle	4d
Alicia *ancilla eiusdem*	4d	Roberto Mulleward	4d
Thoma Swenynge *firm'*	18d	Alicia Carteres	4d
Nicholao *s' eius*	4d	Willelmo Cook	4d
Johanne Stretch	4d	Willelmo Huberd	4d
Johanne *filio eius*	4d	Ricardo Kyngeston'	4d
Johanne Orpodeman	4d	Stephano Wilkynes	4d
Alano Mason' *cementar'*	6d	Johanne Mancorn'	4d
Roberto Tannere	4d	Ricardo *s' eiusdem*	4d
Johanne Sheregold	4d	Willelmo Bole *travent'*	6d
Johanne Huberd	4d	Waltero *s' ipsius* Willelmi	4d
Johanne Mulleford	4d	Rogero Persones	4d
Johanna Palicers	4d	Johanne Sheregold	4d
Johanne Serle	4d	Johanne *s' rector' ibidem*	4d

(Latin *armigero* is 'Esquire'; *servient' eius* is 'his servant'; *ancilla eiusdem*, 'his maidservant'; *firm'*, 'renter, farmer'; *filio eius*, 'his son'; *cementar'*, 'mason'; *s' eiusdem*, 'his servant'; *travent'*, 'tranter, itinerant vendor'; *s' ipsius* Wllelmi, 'servant of the said William'; *s' rector' ibidem*, 'servant of the rector in that place'. 'Hugone Cheyne *armigero*' is presumably the Sir Hugh Cheyney who left property by his will of 1385 to fund a chantry at St Andrew's church for himself and his wife Joan.)

Taking the 1377 figure of 63 taxpayers, and multiplying by 1.5 to take account of the under 14s, brings us to a total population of 95. Guesses as to the evasion rate in 1379 vary so widely it is perhaps best not to risk making an estimate for that year. Note that if the figure of 143 is reasonable for 1332, and 95 for 1377, the fall might be accounted for by the Black Death of 1348-49. A recovery to a population figure of 111 in 1524 would fit in reasonably well with recovery rates elsewhere in the country.

Exchequer lay subsidy, 1524-25

Two questions arise here: How many people did not pay because they fell below the minimum threshold, or because they managed to evade the subsidy? Do the lists refer only to taxable males of 16 and above, or do they represent households? Only those assessed at under £1 a year in goods or wages were exempt, so a low exemption rate (say 6%) seems appropriate. As to evasion it has been said that the Tudor civil service was very successful in securing the due payment of money. The individual/household question has supporters on both sides. In Laverstock 22 men paid the subsidy. Allowing for 6% exemption gives us 23.4 households. Using a multiplier of 4.75 then gives us a population of 111.

The Protestation Returns 1641-42

After the Exchequer Lay Subsidy of 1524-5 the next headcount for which there is any surviving record for Laverstock is that related to the Protestation Returns made on the eve of the Civil War.

In May 1641, against a background of scares, plots, rumours, unrest in the army, and excitement among the populace of London, Parliament acted against fears that the Protestant reformation was in danger of being undone. A national declaration was drawn up, to which MPs and peers subscribed their names, each declaring, 'I, AB do, in the presence of Almighty God, promise, vow, and protest to maintain the true Reformed Protestant religion.' In January 1642, Speaker William Lenthall, in the name of Parliament, sent out a letter to the sheriffs of the counties, to the effect that all males of 18 years and above should take the oath. Every parish incumbent was to read the Protestation in church, then have each adult male parishioner sign, or affix his mark. This took place during February and March 1642. Not all local officials were assiduous in chasing up 'refusers' (Catholics) and other absentees, while in some parishes, women, temporary residents, or visitors were counted, but on the whole the returns are to be taken seriously.

In Laverstock 44 men took the oath.[18] If this figure is doubled, to allow for women, we have an adult population of 88. The Compton Census of 1676 suggests that there were no non-Anglicans in Laverstock during this period. We may therefore take 88 to be the adult population. Multiplying by 1.5 to allow for children making up one third of the population gives us a total population figure of 132.

The names of the Laverstock men who signed up were:

James Clarke *curat*	John Stent	Alexander Eastman
Rich Cirler *churchward*	Hugh Barnes	Xrofer Dew *jun*
Wm Dawlen *churchward*	Thom Williams	Nicho Whitear
Wm Brigge *overseer*	Simon Chaynie	John Soulfer
John Barnes *overseer*	Ambrose Moore	Francis Grey
George Acree	Roger Tennam	Thom Palmer
John Arnold	Daniel Wolley	John Willis
Nicho Arnold	Wm Peirce	Wm Hartford *sen*
Valentine Arnold	Henrey Peirce	Thom Hartford
George Williams	Wm Hutchins	John Harrowaie
Thom Beddyn	John Barnes	Thom Batchelour
Richard Cooper	Richard Spratt	Peter Tibballs
Xrofer Due *sen*	Austine Barnes	Robt Cullie
Thom Willes	Joseph Everett	Wm Noble
Ed'rd Shergoll	John Everett	

('Xrofer' is presumably short for Christopher. 'Shergoll' is perhaps Shergold.)

The Compton Census 1676

This census was the brainchild of the Lord Treasurer, Thomas, Earl of Danby. Danby was a member of the old Cavalier party, a strong upholder of royal authority. He was also a partisan of the established church, and he opposed toleration for Catholics and dissenters (nonconformists). In 1675 he introduced a Test Oath, to be taken by all holders of office or of seats in Parliament. All were to declare that resistance to the royal will was a crime, and they were to promise to abstain from any moves to change the government of church or state. Other statesmen opposed the measure, and even Charles II doubted its wisdom and practicability. Danby then ordered a return from every diocese of the numbers of Catholics and dissenters. He hoped thus to prove that their numbers were insignificant, and to overcome the royal scruples. The census takes its name from Henry Compton, Bishop of London, who was charged with organising the returns.

The bishops instructed their clergy to supply figures for the numbers of communicants of the Church of England in their parishes, then the numbers of 'papists', and 'sectaries' (dissenters). Incumbents should have supplied the total of those of 16 years and above (that being then the most common age for a first communion). However, some counted only the men, others counted the women as well, and others again added in the children. In her study of the census Anne Whiteman concluded that where women were included in 1676 the multiplier (to obtain an estimated population) should be 1.5, allowing for children making up one third of the population. The figure for Laverstock is 101. Seemingly this is the number of adult inhabitants, with no papists or dissenters.[19] Using the 1.5 multiplier gives a total population of 152. This seems to be more or less in line with figures arrived at for 1642 and 1721.

Bishops' Transcripts and Parish Registers

Parish Registers record baptisms, marriages, and burials. They were introduced in 1538, though for many years compliance with the law was patchy. In 1598 further regulation required every parish priest to supply, each year, a copy of the register entries to the archdeacon or bishop. These copies are known as Bishops' Transcripts.

W G Hoskins notes that burial statistics are of uncertain value as a basis for estimating population, as they may be affected by epidemics, harsh winters, and such. Neither can marriage statistics be so employed. To begin with, in a rural parish the number of marriages each year is too small to give satisfactory results. Furthermore, some parish churches seem to have been fashionable for marriages, thus attracting couples from outside the parish. Also, in a period of economic prosperity people may marry young, but in hard times might delay their marriage. It is, then, the baptism statistics that are the least unsatisfactory basis for estimating population. From the early 18th century nonconformity was spreading and we have to reckon with the fact that not all the children of the village would have been brought to the parish church for baptism. However, the Compton Census returns, and answers given to the 1783 questionnaire sent out by Bishop Barrington of Salisbury indicate that the number of nonconformists in Laverstock in the 17th and 18th centuries was very small.

For Laverstock baptisms we have Bishops' Transcripts for the years 1611–1726, though there are some gaps. The first decade for which we have a complete run of yearly figures is 1710-20. From 1726 the Parish Registers become available. The method for estimating population, as described by Hoskins, is to take the average number of baptisms over a period of ten years and multiply the result by thirty.[20] Can the method give us reliable figures? From the early 19th century we have census figures for purposes of comparison. The baptism figures for 1811-20 suggest a population of 291. We know from asylum records that there were 120 patients in 1815. This makes a total of 411, and the census figure for 1821 was actually 415 – very close indeed!

Summary of findings 1086-1800

Year	Popn. of Laverstock	Year	Popn. of Laverstock
1086	102	1731	180
1332	143	1741	195
1377	95	1751	201
1524	111	1761	294
1642	132	1771	333
1676	152	1781	363
1721	180	1791	363

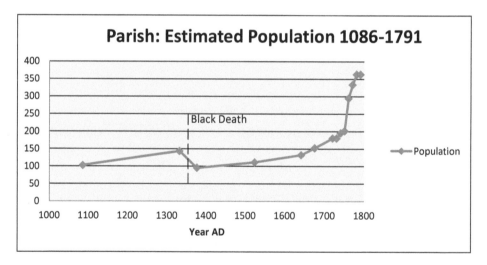

From 1801 we have the figures derived from the ten-yearly national censuses (see pp 216-17).

1   Freeze-thaw happens under periglacial conditions, when water turns into ice, expands and can shatter rocks or move material slowly down a slope.

2   'Kerrycroy' (Riverside Rd) dating from the mid 18th century was originally a cob cottage.

3   http://www.wiltshire.gov.uk/cgr 2016 order.pdf, accessed June 2018

4   Durman, R, 2007, SC *Milford*, Sarum Studies, 1 9

5   RCMHE, 1980, *City of Salisbury Vol 1*, Preface maps on pages xxx and xxxiii

6   Bodington, E J, 1919, 'The Church Survey of Wilts. 1649-50', *WANHM* 40, 398. It is uncertain to what extent these proposals by Parliament were implemented.

7   WSA, 1899/210, *Map relating to the boundary dispute between Laverstock and Milford, settled by the Tithe Commissioner. 1840.* Tithe Apportionments were conducted in all parishes in England during the 1840s to determine how the overall rentcharge was apportioned to individual landowners on the basis of identifiable pieces of land, and how much tithe had to be paid for each plot of land.

8   TNA National Census returns from 1841 to 1901 for Milford; from 1841 to 1881 for Idmiston. Two small detached sections within Ford hamlet, one of Winterbourne Gunner and the other of Idmiston, were transferred to Laverstock and Ford parish by a Local Government Board Order during 1885.

9   VCH *Wilts* 4, 351 footnotes (r) and (s)

10 Parrett, 1999, 8

11 VCH *Wilts* 6, entry for Stratford-sub-Castle, footnote 15. New Sarum (Extension) Order, 1954

12 The Salisbury (Parishes) Order, 1986. This Statutory Instrument also made two minor boundary adjustments affecting Laverstock and Ford; one by London Road near St Thomas's Bridge; the second at the south east corner adjacent to the Milford Mill Road railway bridge in the Petersfinger area.

13 http://www.wiltshire.gov.uk/cgr 2016 order.pdf, accessed June 2018 The Wiltshire Council (Re-organisation of Community Governance) Order 2016

14 Williams, A and Martin, G H, 2003, *Domesday Book, A Complete Translation*, 172, 196. When Domesday refers to number of ploughs it is referring to the taxable amount of land that can be ploughed by a team of eight oxen. Thus, land 'for half a plough' or four oxen means half a plough land. See glossary for other medieval terms.

15 Nash, Alan, 1988, 'The Population of Southern England in 1086: A New Look at the Evidence of Domesday Book', *Southern History* 10, 5

16 Nash, 1988, *Southern History* 10, 21

17 Crowley, D A (ed), 1989, *The Wiltshire Tax List of 1332*, WRS 45, 104-5

18 Hurley, Beryl (ed), and Newton, Joyce (assistant), 1997, *The Wiltshire Protestation Returns 1641-2 and Taxation Records for Warminster Division 1648*, Wiltshire Family History Society

19 Whiteman, Anne (ed), 1986, *The Compton Census of 1676, A Critical Edition*, Oxford University Press/British Academy, 124

20 Hoskins, W G, 1984, *Local History in England*, Longman, 200

Early Times
Bryan Evans

Laverstock in prehistory and the Roman era

The Salisbury area, including Laverstock, would have had much to offer prehistoric folk, with a mix of open woodland, scrub, downland grazing, along with the resources of the Avon and Bourne valleys, and with no mature wildwood to be cleared.[1] Moreover there would have been little competition for these resources. The population of Wiltshire in Mesolithic times (c9600-4000 BC in Britain) has been estimated at just 175.[2]

Various objects from prehistoric times have been found locally. A hand axe unearthed in Laverstock is listed in a gazetteer of finds from the Lower and Middle Palaeolithic periods, that is, from earliest times down to c10000 years ago.[3] Around fifteen round barrows (late Neolithic, c3000-2500 BC, continuing into the Bronze Age, c2500-800 BC in Britain) have been mapped at Clarendon. Three of these are on the crest of Ford Down at the northern end of Cockey Down, intentionally visible from the Bourne valley below.[4] An Early Bronze Age flanged axe is recorded as having been found in 1947 by a friend of a Bishop Wordsworth's schoolboy. The find site was a little to the west of Ford, and just north of the Roman road. It was bought for the school museum for 7s 6d, but has long since been lost.[5] At Castleford Farm a Bronze Age urn with cremated remains, possibly of a female aged between 20 and 35, was found in a chalk-cut pit during the construction of farm buildings in 1973.[6]

There is a group of 12 barrows, two ploughed-out earthworks, and adjacent ditches about ¾ mile north of Ford, alongside the Portway. Nearby is the tree-covered mound known as Ende Burgh or Hand Barrows. In plan it resembles a long barrow, but in profile it is more akin to a twin-barrow. There is little doubt that it has been much altered by ploughing, and it has been suggested that it was originally a cluster of three: a low bell barrow and two later ones built on opposite sides of it.[7]

A little way north of the parish boundary lies Figsbury Ring. It is thought that this was originally a henge monument of the Neolithic/Late Bronze Age periods, typically with a pair of opposed entrances. As a sacred site it may have served a wide area, including Laverstock. At some point it seems that a bank was thrown up round the outside of the site, then the material was later removed to strengthen the outer, Iron Age, rampart. Any remnants of the original bank were lost in subsequent ploughing. A number of such Late Bronze Age/Iron Age sites seem to have combined ceremonial and defensive functions.

Sorviodunum (Old Sarum)

In the Roman period Laverstock was in the hinterland of *Sorviodunum* (Old Sarum), a medium size Roman 'small town'. It was an important trading and transport hub, having a good network of roads, and river transport on the Avon. The Old Sarum to Silchester road (now the Portway) passed through the north-east corner of Laverstock and Ford parish. The Winchester road crossed the Bourne at Ford. There was probably another Roman road that went through the Bishopdown suburb, then across the Bourne, perhaps at Milford, and on towards the New Forest. Pottery from there and from the Wareham/Poole Harbour area, building stone, and lead from the Mendip mines would have passed through the Old Sarum hub. The local agricultural economy was based on sheep-rearing, and the growing of spelt wheat and barley. A few miles to the east the area boasted its own amphitheatre at Winterslow. This is now half ploughed away, but it would once have been about 340 feet in diameter.[8]

Cockey Down farmstead

From the top of Cockey Down the ground falls steeply to the narrow floodplain of the Bourne. This is chalk downland, with occasional patches of clay-with-flints. A reservoir was built on Cockey Down in the 1970s, and a pipeline was laid to Petersfinger. A number of inhumations were found at this time, and some late Roman pottery. Later work on this pipeline and another across to Bishopdown Farm, made further archaeological work possible.[9] This has produced evidence for three main periods of activity on the site: first of the Late Bronze Age/Early Iron Age, then the Late Iron Age/early Romano-British period, then the late Romano-British period.[10]

The first significant phase of occupation was represented by a large ditched enclosure (not quite circular) of the Early/Middle Iron Age, when there seems to have been a small rural agricultural settlement here. Within the enclosure there were two beehive-shaped storage pits. Among the finds were a loom weight or spindle whorl and pottery. This rural agricultural settlement seems

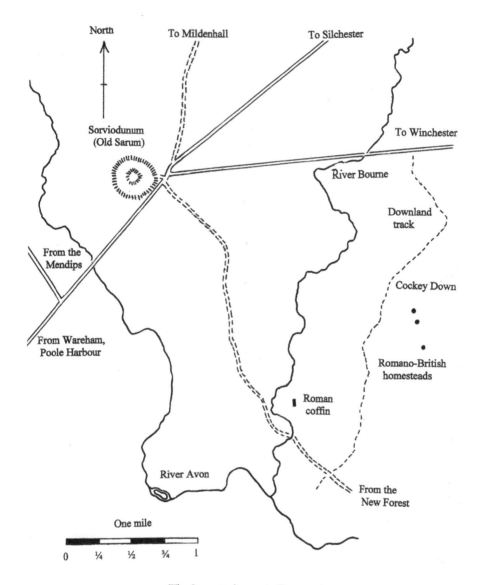

The Laverstock area in Roman times

to have been approached from the north-east along the ditched trackway seen on aerial photographs running along the crest of the Down.[11]

In the Late Iron Age/early Romano-British period (*c*100 BC–AD 150) the enclosure ditch was filled in, and a roundhouse built. Burials were also taking place, and the remains of at least 12 individuals have been found. Two of the graves contained skeletal material from two apparently separate acts of burial, one made directly above the other arguing for some form of close relationship between the two individuals. The first grave was opened some years after the interment to allow the second burial to be made, showing that the first grave must have been clearly marked, probably with some of the large flint nodules forming the upper fills of most of the graves. Radiocarbon dating carried out on three of the skeletons gave them Late Iron Age dates. Ages ranged from new-born children to older mature adults, with both sexes represented. This suggests a normal domestic cemetery of the period, associated with a small farmstead settlement and its field system.

The site was used for farming right through to the late Romano-British period when a corn drier was built. The corn drier (two pits linked by a trench) was found between the boundary ditches of the trackway already noted. The finds from the soil overlying the scorched chalk floor of the trench included a substantial portion of a Wiltshire greyware flagon, certainly of late Roman date. There were sherds of pottery from one fineware fabric and three coarseware fabrics.[12] Three fragments of late Romano-British brick and tile were recovered, as well as four iron objects (one of them a latch lifter), and two fragments of quern stone (one greensand, one quartz conglomerate). Bones of domestic animals, in poor condition, were also found.

In sum, the range of pottery found covers most of the period from 600-400 BC to AD 300-400. No pottery characteristic of the 3rd century BC was found. Was the site abandoned during that period, or simply moved to another part of the hill? The archaeology thus reveals a long-term settlement, and a community engaged in both arable and pastoral farming.
Other small, mixed farming communities have been identified in the Salisbury Plain area, including one at Bishopdown Farm/Pond Field. The results from Cockey Down add to the evidence for the presence of many small farmsteads scattered across the Plain in the Romano-British period.[13]

Roman coffin

The *Salisbury Times* of 4 June 1937 reported the finding of a stone coffin in Greenwood Avenue, Laverstock, some 18 inches to two feet below ground level. It was unearthed by workmen of the local building firm of Messrs W Forder & Sons, during work on new bungalows in the grounds of what had been the Laverstock Hall estate. According to a RCHME record of 2001 the workmen had been digging a trench for a sewer in the back garden of 29 Greenwood Avenue. The coffin was made from a solid block of Chilmark stone hollowed out for the reception of the body. It was aligned NNW to SSE, and the face of the person buried would have been towards the south. With the coffin were discovered unmistakable sherds of Romano-British New Forest pottery.[14] The coffin, which weighed nearly two tons, had been damaged at one side, and at the end, by the workmen's pickaxes before they were aware of its presence. Photographs, and a description of the coffin, were sent to an archaeologist[15] who confirmed that it was of the period of the Roman occupation.

The coffin was seven feet six inches long, with inside space of six feet. The ends were rounded, and the base was curved at the head and foot, giving it a shape not unlike a bath. The *Salisbury Times* reported that, 'When found, the coffin was covered with large broken stones, some of Chilmark stone, and many large flints. The

Roman stone coffin found during building work in Greenwood Avenue, Laverstock, 1937. Salisbury Times, 4 June, 1937

sides were also packed round with large flints. Possibly the broken stones at the top formed a cover for the body, and it is possible that at some time the grave was desecrated and stones broken in order to get at the body in the search for any valuables which might have been buried with it. Some few portions of human bones, very decayed, were found in the coffin.'[16] The reporter went on to say that the vicar of Laverstock (Rev Charles Pain) had been given the first opportunity to acquire the coffin for the churchyard. The writer closed with a few questions. What might be the date of the coffin? Why was this site chosen? The builders said that human bones and sherds of pottery had been found before, so perhaps there was an ancient burial ground nearby. But who had been buried here – surely it must have been a person of some importance – and where had he or she lived? We certainly have no means of knowing who. As to where, Old Sarum might be a possibility, though it is about two miles away. In the other direction there is Clarendon, where a concentration of Roman material has been noted at the eastern end of Gilbert's Copse. Quality building materials (limestone roofing slate, ceramic roof tiles, box flue tiles), and a range of building platforms, suggest there had been a villa here. Perhaps the person buried in Laverstock came from here, though it is about the same distance away as Old Sarum.

The coffin was removed to St Andrew's churchyard. When inspected in September 1937 it was found to contain several inches of water, meaning that there was a risk of damage from winter frosts.[17]

The latter history of the coffin makes sad reading. About 1952-3 the church asked the Blackmore and South Wiltshire Museum if they would like to have the coffin. Hugh de S Shortt, the Curator, wrote to Rev A G Barker in January

1953, telling him that the Museum committee felt unable to accept it. The reasons given were: the cost of removal, the lack of space for it inside the Museum, the poor condition of the coffin and the fact that it was 'without any real dating characteristics'. He suggested that it be allowed to remain where it was, preferably buried.[18] The church hardly had the resources to bury a two-ton coffin, so nothing was done. A generation later the true nature of the coffin was forgotten. It was taken to be an old horse trough, and in 1977, it was broken up, and the pieces used to help level the lower end of the churchyard.[19]

In sum, we know that there was a small human settlement here in Roman times, perhaps confined to the downland, with the valley floor too wet. We must be thankful for the evidence found, and hope that more will come to light in future.

The Anglo-Saxon period

Beginnings

The earliest known forms of the name 'Laverstock' are *Lavvrecestoches, Lavertestoche* in Domesday Book, 1086.[20] There are two parts to the name: Old English *lāverce, lāwerce* ('lark') and *stoc* ('place'). The second element is a very ordinary name for a place of habitation, and it is found widely across England. To begin with it was a 'stand-alone' name, so the village would originally have been simply 'Stoke'. But as time went on so many places were called 'Stoke' that something had to be added to their names if they were to be told apart. Hence we now have Winterbourne Stoke, Stoke Mandeville, Stoke-on-Trent and so on. Our village became known as the 'place where there are larks'.[21]

The skylark is a downland bird, and it is certainly possible that the village began life as a successor-settlement to the Romano-British farmsteads on Cockey Down, before a move to the valley floor. One known feature of Anglo-Saxon settlement history is what has been called the 'Middle Saxon shuffle'.[22] This refers to the shifting of settlements from upland sites to valley bottoms, roughly in the period 660-900. This may have come about through soil exhaustion, or through a number of small settlements coming together, perhaps with pressure from a great landowner such as the church.

Early Anglo-Saxon settlement in the Salisbury area

Anglo-Saxon burials of the pagan period have been found at a number of places in the Salisbury area, including Harnham Hill, Winterbourne Gunner and Petersfinger. It is thought that these cemeteries point to the existence of Anglo-Saxon settlements in the area by the early 6th century and possibly even before that.[23] But there is no evidence that any part of Wiltshire or Dorset was in Anglo-Saxon hands before the middle of the 5th century.[24]

Ten graves have been excavated at Winterbourne Gunner.[25] Among the finds were a throwing axe (*francisca*) of Frankish type, probably to be dated AD 450-525, a late Roman strap end, and a figure-of-eight buckle, inlaid with bronze wires, thought to date from the last half of the 5th century.

The site of the Petersfinger cemetery is on a slight natural terrace on the western slope of Ashley Hill. The cemetery was accidentally discovered during chalk digging by mechanical excavators in May 1948. More burials were found in 1951 when the chalk-pit was extended. The figures given in the *Victoria County History* are: 63 graves, 70 skeletons – 25 adult males, 20 adult females, 18 children (male and female) and seven doubtful.[26] One burial was of a warrior equipped with a fine Frankish sword, a spear and shield, and an axe which, in England, is a weapon nearly always associated with Frankish graves.

The Petersfinger finds of 1948/1951 were not the first to be uncovered in this locality. Just south of here many skeletons were exhumed in 1846 when a cutting was made for the South Western Railway. Two or three more skeletons were found some time later, when the line had to be widened, following a fall of chalk.[27] At nearby Dairyhouse Bridge, in 1860, a newly-dug gravel pit revealed sherds of Anglo-Saxon pottery and one complete bowl. In 1972 a stamp-impressed pottery sherd, probably of 6th century date, was found when some trenches were dug at Milford Farm.[28] Altogether, more recent work has revealed that the Petersfinger site may be much larger than was once thought. It is possible that there were originally two distinct cemeteries here perhaps serving two neighbouring communities, between the 5th and 7th centuries.[29] All three cemeteries show Frankish links, possibly spread from Kent.[30] As far back as 1853 Akerman drew attention to the close parallels between a semi-circular-headed brooch from Harnham Hill and another from Chessel Down on the Isle of Wight (where Jutish folk settled). This led to the conclusion that the early Germanic settlers in the Salisbury area were a mixture of Jutes and Franks moving up from Southampton Water.

To sum up, the Petersfinger and Winterbourne Gunner cemeteries are important as proving an Anglo-Saxon presence, with people from different ethnic groups, in the 6th century. The folk buried here may have been Germanic mercenaries and their families, the men being in the employ of the Romano-British authorities at Old Sarum. Both cemeteries are near strategic points, where roads leading to Old Sarum ford the River Bourne – at Winterbourne Gunner and at Milford.[31] An alternative suggestion for Petersfinger is that we have here a new political élite taking on 'Frankish' ethnic traits as a way of marking their status.[32]

Where was the community whose dead were buried at Petersfinger? It might be neighbouring Britford; the lost hamlet of Mumworth, near the meeting of the Bourne and Avon, has been suggested.[33] Another line of approach involves consideration of the boundary of Clarendon Park (see below). If the cemetery was sited in a border area, then the community served might be at Mumworth, or possibly Laverstock, but Britford would seem to be 'over the border'.

Two barrows on Ford Down

Two barrows were found on Ford Down during farming operations in 1964. One dated from the Early Bronze Age, though finds suggested that there had been an intrusive Saxon burial there, long since ploughed away. The other barrow was a primary Saxon barrow containing the skeleton of an adult male, buried with weapons and with a bronze hanging bowl containing crab apples and onions (remarkably preserved because of the infusion of copper salts into the remains). The date of the burial seems to be late 7th century, at the time when Wessex was being converted to Christianity. This burial, then, may mark a lingering pagan tradition.[34]

The Parish boundary

D J Bonney has noted that 69 pagan Saxon burial sites in Wiltshire (out of some 80 or so) can be located with fair accuracy.[35] He has drawn attention to the fact that 20 of these lie on parish boundaries, and a further nine within 500 feet of boundaries – a proportion far too high for mere coincidence. He goes on to explain that the majority of ecclesiastical parishes, from which modern civil parishes are derived, came into being during the 10th and 11th centuries. The boundaries of these parishes have survived very nearly unchanged from the 12th century almost to the present day. The ecclesiastical parishes were, in turn, based on earlier landed estates, which estates are first described in the land charters (effectively the 'title deeds') of the Saxon period. Bonney concludes that the presence of so many pagan Saxon burial sites on or near parish boundaries surely indicates that those boundaries were fixed as early as the pagan Saxon period. A J Goodier, after a statistical study of the evidence, acknowledges Bonney's findings, but says the link does not go back as far as the 5th century. Boundaries seem to have become more stable during the early Anglo-Saxon period, so that there are more 7th- than 6th-century burials on or near them. Different parts of the country produce different statistics, however.[36] Others have challenged this reading of the burials/boundaries evidence.[37]

In the case of Laverstock parish, if we begin in the north-west, and work round clockwise there is, first, a barrow just across the Salisbury to Amesbury road from Old Sarum Castle. There are two barrows near the northern

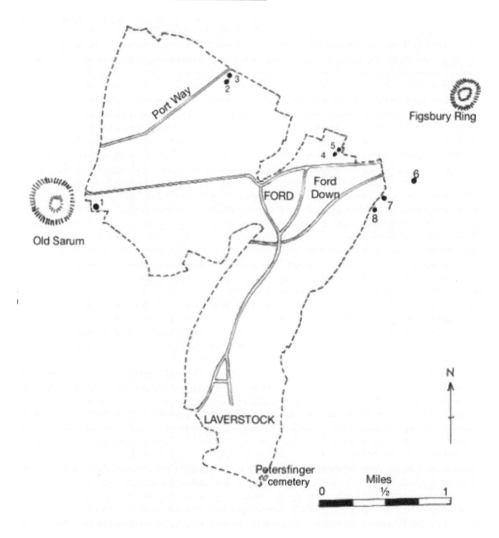

The use of prehistoric and Anglo-Saxon barrows as landmarks for the parish boundary.

boundary, close to the Portway, former Roman road from Old Sarum to Silchester. The two barrows on Ford Down are close to the north-east corner of the parish. John Musty notes that in the case of both these pairs of barrows 'the boundary appears to have been deliberately staggered to avoid the barrows or a former settlement area contiguous with them. Alternatively, the boundary might be following a Bronze Age ranch boundary no longer showing as a surface feature.'[38] There are two more barrows, across the London road and higher up the slope of Ford Down, close to the Hillcrest boarding kennels.[39]

Lastly, there is the 6th century cemetery at Petersfinger, straddling the boundary of the Clarendon estate. On an estate map of c1650 the outer park pale is of a striking near-circular shape, and the adjacent parishes seem to have been built around it. This suggests that the Park was earlier than the era of parish formation.[40] It would also imply that the cemetery was used as a boundary marker for the estate, then continued in use as a parish boundary marker.

An Anglo-Saxon Charter

There is an Anglo-Saxon charter included in the register held at Wilton Abbey, classified as S (for Sawyer) 543, or BCS (Birch *Cartularium Saxonicum*) 879. It describes a grant made in AD 949 by King Eadred to Ælfsige, his gold and silversmith, of one hide of land on the Isle of Wight and one 'æt Winterburnan' in the land of the Gewisse. ('Gewisse' was an early name that the West Saxons used of themselves.) The charter was written in Latin, but the description of the estate boundaries is given in Old English. The 'Winterburnan' boundary notes read:

> First from Byrhtferth's Low along the Burh Way to Beornwin's Stone, from the Stone along the Burh Way to the Stone Heap, then down along the burn as the Læfer shoots to the Old Lynch, then as the Læfer shoots to the deep ford's end, from the ford as the Læfer shoots to Chapman's Ford, from the ford as the Læfer shoots to the Horse Well, then as the Læfer shoots again to Byrhtferth's Low.[41]

Archaeologist Alex Langlands has suggested that the 'Winterburnan' of the charter was Laverstock.[42] His discussion of the boundary markers is interesting, but not without problems. To begin with he has to read the boundary clauses in an anti-clockwise way, whereas, as he readily admits, the overwhelming majority of Anglo-Saxon boundary clauses follow a clockwise direction. The first 'Burh Way' is identified with the south-north track along the ridge of Laverstock Down, heading towards the enclosure known as Figsbury Ring (hence 'burh' way). In fact, Figsbury was not, at least in origin, a burh or fort, but a Late Neolithic 'henge' monument, or sacred site, and it is perhaps more likely that the track was simply making for the Winchester to Old Sarum Roman road. A stretch of that road is then identified as the other 'Burh Way', and the 'Stone Heap' as possibly the remains of a stone pier of a Roman bridge across the Bourne at Ford. Would the same term, 'Burh Way', have been used of two such different roads as a ridgeway track and a paved Roman road? In fact, the wording seems to refer to two stretches of the same road. As for the name 'Winterbourne' this is a fairly common place-name. Ford was at one time 'Winterbourne Ford', and there are three other Winterbournes (Earls, Dauntsey, Gunner) a little way up the valley. Further afield, but still in the land of the Gewisse, there are Winterbourne Stoke and two Dorset clusters, one north-east of Dorchester, and the other to the west. And we know that the original name of Laverstock was not Winterbourne, but Stoke.

The suggestion of a link with charter S543 has been looked at before. G B Grundy was not convinced by the identification,[43] and, as already noted, neither was the English Place-Name Society. Darlington queried the identification,[44] though Finberg accepted it.[45] At the very least we have to conclude that the suggestion is not proven.

The Æthelwulf ring

This significant item of Anglo-Saxon jewellery was uncovered in Laverstock parish in the late eighteenth century and is now displayed in the British Museum. A contemporary report notes:

> March 22, 1781. Lord Radnor communicated a piece of gold found about August 1780, in a field near Salisbury in the parish of Laverstoke. By the account of William Petty the finder it appears to have been prest out of a cart-rut sideways, as it lay on the surface of the mould adjoining to the rut. It was carried down to Mr. Howell, a silversmith in Salisbury, who having proved it in the usual manner, gave the man thirty-four shillings for it, as the value of the gold, and from Mr. Howell lord Radnor purchased it. Its weight is eleven pennyweights fourteen grains, height one inch and a half, circumference two inches seven eights. The metal is as near as may be agreeable to the standard of the present English currency.[46]

The ring was inscribed 'Æthelwulf Rex'. Æthelwulf, the father of Alfred the Great, was king of Wessex 839-58, and before that king in Kent from at least 828.

The Æthelwulf ring found in a cart-rut in Laverstock in 1780.
© The Trustees of the British Museum

The ring is considerably crushed and distorted, no doubt reflecting the circumstances of its discovery. In the space above the inscription are two 'Trewhiddle-style' peacocks flanking a tree-of-life motif.[47] The fine ornament would certainly fit a mid-ninth-century date.

In recent years some local commentators have suggested that the finding of the ring in Laverstock is evidence that Æthelwulf himself must once have passed through the village and dropped the ring. However, this is really only a guess, and in the view of experts at the British Museum the ring was probably not the king's personal ring, but was given as a gift or as a mark of royal office.[48] It would still be pleasant to think that the man who lost the ring was someone from Laverstock who served the king, perhaps as a huntsman at some forerunner of the medieval deer-park of Clarendon. In truth, however, the ring might have been lost at almost any time between 858 and 1780, and we have no knowledge of the date or circumstances of the loss.

1   Powell, Andrew B, and others, 2005, 'Excavations along the Old Sarum Water Pipeline, North of Salisbury', *WANHM* 98, 277-78

2   Nash, Alan, 1988, 'The Population of Southern England in 1086: A New Look at the Evidence of Domesday Book', *Southern History* 10, 23

3   Roe, Derek, 1969, 'An Archaeological Survey and Policy for Wiltshire, Part I Palaeolithic' *WANHM* 64, 13

4   Beaumont James, Tom and Gerrard, Christopher, 2007, *Clarendon: Landscape of Kings*, Windgather Press, 20

5   Saunders, P R and Needham, S, 1977-78, *WANHM* 72-73, 170-72, 175

6   Anon, 1974, 'Wiltshire Archaeological Register for 1973, Bronze Age', *WANHM* 69, 185; Saunders and Needham, 1977-78, 173-7

7   Stone, J F S, 1935-37, 'An unrecorded group of barrows and other earthworks at Ford, Laverstock', *WANHM* 47, 406-11

8   Anon, 1960, 'Winterslow: A Roman earthwork', *WANHM* 57, 396-7

9   Anon, 2001, 'Excavation and Fieldwork in Wiltshire 1999' *WANHM* 94, 250-51

10 The Late Bronze Age would be c900-800 BC, the Iron Age c800 BC-AD 100, the late Roman period cAD 350-400.

11 Beaumont James, Gerrard, 2007, 26

12 Black Burnished ware from the Wareham/Poole Harbour area, New Forest Parchment ware, and coarse sandy grey wares from a number of sources.

13 Martin Trott, 1991, 'Archaeological Excavation on the Route of the Cockey Down to Petersfinger Main Pipeline, New Salisbury' *WANHM* 84, 116-19; Julie Lovell, with Sheila Hamilton-Dyer, Emma Loader and Jacqueline I McKinley, 1999, 'Further Investigations of an Iron Age and Romano-British Farmstead on Cockey Down, near Salisbury', *WANHM* 92, 33-38

14 Stevens, F, 'A Roman Stone Coffin at Laverstock', 1938, *WANHM* 48, 198-9

15 Captain E P Cunningham, FSA

16 Bates, H H, 4 June 1937, 'An old stone coffin. Interesting archaeological discovery at

Laverstock' *ST,* 5

17   Stevens, 1938, 199

18   WSA, 1324/57

19   Ray Thomas, church member, personal communication, 30 January 2011

20   The second spelling has the common scribal copying error 't' for 'c'.

21   Ekwall, Eilert, 1960, *The Concise Oxford Dictionary of Place-names*, 284, 290; Gower, Mawer and Stenton, 1970, *The Place-Names of Wiltshire*, English Place-Name Society XVI, 381-2. Attention has been drawn to Old English *læfer* meaning 'rush', 'bulrush'. This would give the meaning 'place by the reed-lined stream', which certainly fits the present location of the village (see Langlands, Alex, 2009, 'The past on your doorstep': community history and archaeology in Laverstock' *WANHM* 102, 308). However, the early spellings, in Domesday and throughout the Middle Ages, always include 'c' or 'k' as the final sound of the first part of the name, which means that *læfer* – with no 'c' or 'k' – is ruled out (Carroll, Jayne, University of Nottingham, personal communication, 10 October 2017, and see also Gower, Mawer and Stenton, 1970, xli).

22   The Middle Saxon 'shuffle' has been much discussed in Anglo-Saxon studies since the 1970s eg *Current archaeology* 291, 5 June 214

23   RCHME, 1980, *City of Salisbury* 1, HMSO, xxviii

24   Ellis, Peter (ed), 2001, *Roman Wiltshire and After*, WANHS, 215

25   Musty, John, and Stratton, J E D, 1964, 'A Saxon cemetery at Winterbourne Gunner, near Salisbury', *WANHM* 59, 86-109

26   Grinsell, L V, 1957. 'Archaeological Gazetteer' *VCH Wilts* 1, Part 1, 58

27   Moore, C N and Algar, D J, 1968, 'Saxon "Grass-tempered ware" and Mesolithic finds from near Petersfinger, Laverstock', *WANHM* 63, 103-5

28   Saunders, P R, 1975/76, 'Stamp-impressed sherd from Laverstock', *WANHM* 70/71, 129-30

29   Beaumont James, Tom, and Gerrard, Christopher, 2007, 37

30   Eagles, Bruce, in Ellis (ed), 2001, 218-19

31   Musty and Stratton, 1964, 104

32   Beaumont James and Gerrard, 2007, 39

33   RCHME, 1980, xxviii-xxix

34   Musty, John, 1969, 'The excavation of two barrows, one of Saxon date, at Ford, Laverstock, near Salisbury, Wiltshire', *The Antiquaries Journal* XLIX, part 1, 98-117. Anon, 1965, 'Ford Down, Bronze Age and Saxon Barrows', *WANHM* 60, 138

35   Bonney, Desmond J, 1966, 'Pagan Saxon burials and boundaries in Wiltshire', *WANHM* 61, 25-29

36   Goodier, Ann J, 1984, 'The Formation of Boundaries in Anglo-Saxon England: A Statistical Study', *Medieval Archaeology*, The Society for Medieval Archaeology, pub Taylor & Francis

37   Welch, 1985, cited in 2011, *Oxford Handbook of Anglo-Saxon Archaeology*, 280

38   Musty, 1969, *The Antiquaries Journal*, 113-4

39   See map in *The Antiquaries Journal*, 1969, 98

40   Beaumont James and Gerrard, 2007, 46. Bonney, 1966, 28xx

41   A 'low' is a barrow; a 'burh' a fortified place or borough; a 'burn' a river or stream; 'Læfer' is the name of the burn; 'lynch' refers to cultivation terraces on hill-sides, or to flat ground beside a river; 'chapman' is a trader, and 'well' is a spring.

42 Langlands, Alex 2009, *WANHM,* 102, 306-14. He returned to the subject in a talk given in Salisbury in 2015.

43 Grundy, GB, 1920, 'Saxon Land Charters of Wiltshire' *Archaeological Journal* lxxvii, 8-124, reviewed 1925 in *WANHM* 43, 123-25. Thompson, T R and Sandell, RE, 1963, 'The Saxon Land Charters of Wiltshire' *WANHM* 58, 444

44 Darlington, R R, 1955, VCH *Wilts* 2, 93

45 Finberg, Herbert P R, 1964, *The early charters of Wessex,* no 70, 43-4, 89-90

46 Anon, 1785, in *Archaeologia, Or Miscellaneous Tracts Relating to Antiquity* vii, 421

47 The 'Trewhiddle-style' referred to takes its name from the animal decoration of many of the artefacts in an Anglo-Saxon hoard of coins, and other gold and silver objects, found at Trewhiddle, near St Austell, Cornwall, during streaming for tin in 1774.

48 Webster, Leslie, and Backhouse, Janet (eds), 1992, *The Making of England: Anglo-Saxon Art and Culture AD 600-900,* British Museum Press, 268-69. Stone, L, 1955, 'Anglo-Saxon Art', VCH Wilts 2, 36-7, adds that the decoration shows connections with the Hanging Langford cross and with work of similar type at Kelston, Somerset.

The Medieval Age

The medieval church and its forerunners
Bryan Evans

The first firm references to a church in Laverstock are in records of the 13th century. In 1225 Bishop Richard Poore of Salisbury began a daily sung Mass of the Virgin Mary in his new cathedral, and he needed money for the stipends of the thirteen Vicars Choral. It is sometimes said that he appropriated Laverstock church for this purpose, but Colt Hoare tells us that this information came from an inscription that was once in the Chapel of Saint Mary in the Cathedral, which inscription, he says, 'seems to have been founded on imperfect information'. He adds that it is likely Bishop Poore was the founder of this mass, but it was Bishop Giles de Bridport (1256-1262) who augmented its revenues with the rectory of Laverstock, then estimated at the yearly value of ten pounds.[1] A further episcopal grant was made in 1265. Through these arrangements the Dean and Chapter of the Cathedral became the Vicars of Laverstock, and they appointed curates to work in the parish.

The first stone church

When might this church have been built? In the Middle Ages there were very few new foundations after 1150, and it seems that there may have been a spurt in church building between *c*1075 and *c*1125. The historian William of Malmesbury, writing at this time, said that one might see 'churches rise in every village'. It may well be that much of this work was the rebuilding in stone of wooden churches.[2]

There is one architectural clue as to the date of Laverstock's stone church. The archway leading into the porch of the medieval church still survives, it having been moved to the same position in the new church, in 1857/58. The archway is decorated in the style known as 'saw-tooth chevron', a feature of the so-called 'Romanesque' architecture of the period 1000-1200. Altogether, a date of 'about 1100' for the first stone church at Laverstock, seems reasonable.

A wooden predecessor?

It is not impossible that there was an earlier, wooden church in Laverstock, perhaps built in the period 850-1050.[3] At this time the local nobility were imitating the church-building of kings and lords. By the eleventh century one of the marks of a thegn (or local lord) was possession of a church.[4]

Can we go further back? Before any church buildings were put up it was a common practice to erect a standing cross with its own little thatched roof, and set perhaps in some kind of enclosure. Here a priest from the nearby minster church would preach, and celebrate mass from a portable altar. The village dead would henceforth be buried round this cross. 'There can be little doubt that in many English villages today the churchyard and church occupy ground on which originally stood a simple cross.'[5] For

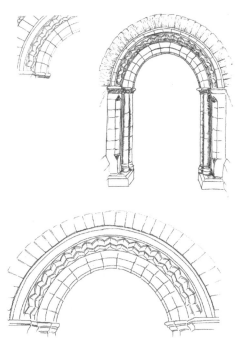

'Saw-tooth chevron' decoration of the arch at the entrance to the porch of St Andrew's church. Drawing by Jenny Hayes.

Laverstock the nearby minster in question was most likely either at Alderbury, the centre of the Hundred, or at Britford, which was probably the leading settlement in these parts in early and middle Anglo-Saxon times.[6]

This is probably as far back as we can go, as there is little evidence for Romano-British Christianity in south-east Wiltshire. It was a rural area, and likely to have been stubbornly heathen. As to the location of the church we may note that there was a tendency for religious communities to occupy sites overlooking waterways. And cross-road sites were favourable for gathering together a good number of tithe-paying households. Laverstock church is close to the river Bourne, and to the meeting of two old routeways now known as Church Road and Duck Lane.

Has the dedication always been to St Andrew?

There is no way to answer this question now, but one intriguing point concerns the alignment of the church. Morris notes the theory that churches were commonly aligned towards sunrise on the patronal day, a theory that was taken up by members of the Cambridge Camden Society in the 19th century and by others since.[7] St Andrew's church is in fact roughly aligned towards sunrise on 30 November, St Andrew's day.

The Middle Ages

We have little knowledge of Laverstock church in the Middle Ages, but some things may be inferred. The standard of teaching may have been a little higher than elsewhere, with the parish served not by a peasant-priest but by a Vicar Choral of the Cathedral. On the other hand he was probably often away, attending cathedral services or seeing to his duties at the Hospital of St Nicholas at Harnham. The Vicar Choral appointed to Laverstock often held the Mastership of the Hospital as well.[8]

Series of wall-paintings appeared in the 12th and 13th centuries. There might be portrayals of the death and resurrection of Christ, Doom scenes of judgment, scenes from the life of the patron saint of the church.[9]

The Black Death

The Black Death struck in 1348-49, coming first to Dorset. At the Augustinian Priory of Ivychurch, Alderbury, the prior and twelve of the thirteen canons died in the plague.[10] We have no direct evidence of it reaching Laverstock, though population estimates suggest Laverstock numbers fell by about a third between 1332 and 1377.[11]

Perhaps Henry de Lodelewe, curate at Laverstock, was a victim since his successor was instituted in 1349. Clergy were particularly likely to come into contact with the plague, through administering the last rites and conducting burial services.[12]

The Cheney chantry

The Black Death, and subsequent epidemics, brought home a sense of how short and uncertain life is. At the same time belief in purgatory (which began to take a hold in the 12th century) strengthened, also the belief that the time of one's sufferings there might be shortened through the saying of masses on earth. This belief was linked to growing reverence for the mass. Those who could afford to do so set up chantries.[13]

In his will, dated 1385, Sir Hugh Cheney of Laverstock directed the foundation of a chantry in the church at Laverstock, with daily service for the souls of himself and his wife, Joan de Woldeford. For the maintenance of the chantry he bequeathed a messuage and shops in the *Poletria* in Salisbury.[14] It is hard to imagine there being room for a chantry chapel in so small a church as St Andrew's, but in fact the chantry mass required no more than a priest, and room for a small altar within a consecrated building.[15]

The fire of 1410

One night in 1410 there was a sudden and serious fire which destroyed the church, the vicarage, and other neighbouring buildings. Bishop Robert Hallum (1407-1417) proclaimed the *Indulgencia pro reedificatione ecclesiae de Laverstoke*,[16] a general notification of an indulgence of forty days off purgatory promised to all who contributed towards the rebuilding of the church.

The canonisation of Osmund

We gain some glimpses into the medieval religious outlook of Laverstock people through the story of the canonisation of Osmund (Bishop of Salisbury, 1078-99). This long saga began in 1228, but made only hesitant progress until John Chandler (Bishop of Salisbury 1417-26), promoted the cause of Osmund. In 1424 three cardinals under warrant from the Pope began looking at the evidence for miracles wrought through the name of Osmund. There was the case of a girl at Laverstock who seemed to fall dead after being struck on the head by a quoit, but then came back to life. She afterward laid up the quoit at the bishop's tomb. Then, one John Combe shared in a game of 'playing at ball with great clubs' (perhaps some version of club-ball). The players fell out, and John Combe was badly beaten up and left blind and deaf. However, he was told in a vision to make a wax model of his head and shoulders and offer it at the bishop's tomb. This he did, and he was made whole again. Canonisation was settled at last in 1457, the long-drawn out process having cost £731 13s 0d.[17]

The pottery industry
Ruth Newman

U nderneath the present Potters Way and its immediate vicinity existed a substantial high quality medieval pottery industry. Following earlier finds of pottery sherds from the area,[18] the first kiln was discovered in 1958 when a new road was laid between Duck Lane and Queen Manor Road. This discovery was followed in the next five years by the excavation of a further nine kilns, potters' workshops and various pits.

The site at Laverstock was ideal, on the edge of Clarendon Forest and near Milford Bridge. The Bourne was just 300 yards/metres away and the kilns were found on the slope leading down towards the river. Potting clay was within easy access on nearby Cockey Down, Alderbury, and possibly from Clarendon ridge. Abundant fuel for firing the kilns came from the royal forest

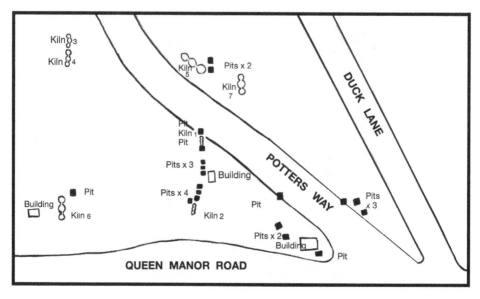

The Potters Way, Laverstock pottery site plan, redrawn by Jenny Hayes, 2018

and evidence found from the stokepits showed that ash, willow, hazel and birch were all burned. The kilns were constructed of a local chalk-clay mixture with flues leading to stokepits on each side.

Links with Clarendon

The pottery was also well located, on the overland route between the two major ports of Bristol and Southampton and crucially, on the main approach road between Salisbury and Clarendon Palace.

The royal household and their retainers were frequently in residence at Clarendon and became essential customers. The palace reached a peak in the 13th century under Henry III and the conversion to gothic splendour may well have attracted specialist potters into the area. Extravagant feasting meant a demand for the local ware: globular jars used for both storage and cooking and fine 'green-glazed jugs of baluster shape with rod and strap handles' used for ale or wine. Analysis has shown that most of the pottery excavated

A group of glazed medieval baluster jugs from the pottery kilns at Laverstock © The Salisbury Museum

from Clarendon came from Laverstock kilns.[19] These also served the needs of another royal palace, that of Winchester, where 2000 pitchers were purchased between 1268 and 1270.[20]

Growing demand from the city

Above all, and contemporary with Clarendon at its height, the new town of Salisbury just 1½ miles (2.4km) away provided an increasingly large and stable market. The move from Old Sarum inevitably created a need for housing and the city's growth from the 1220s meant that it became the most successful of the medieval new towns.[21] The demand for glazed roof tiles, decorated jugs and simple cooking pots from neighbouring Laverstock benefited both customer and supplier. Salisbury's expansion as a trading centre with its weekly Tuesday market from 1227 (and Saturday from 1315) meant that the city became the regional hub. Perhaps from Pot Row (*Potrewe*) at the eastern end of the Market Place, Laverstock wares would have made their way to nearby villages and further afield. Regional distribution of Laverstock jugs can now be plotted with some accuracy in southern England. Recent excavations have led to the discovery of pottery remains widely within the city, on the site of the Anchor Brewery off Gigant Street and in the Old George Mall. Laverstock wares accounted for about 90% of such medieval pottery fragments found in Salisbury and 'had an almost total monopoly of the local market'.[22] Finds have also emerged in Dorset and Southampton, at Wilton, Tidworth, and in the north Wiltshire villages of Highworth, Aldbourne and Cricklade.[23]

In 1973 a short-lived pottery kiln with products virtually identical to those found in two of the Laverstock kilns was found in Guilder Lane Salisbury, suggesting that the same potter probably worked on both sites. He may have come from Laverstock to establish a new kiln but later returned to his established community when the city enterprise failed to prosper.[24] Apart from this unsuccessful venture, no other medieval kilns have been discovered in the immediate Salisbury area.[25]

Evidence from the site means that it is possible to examine the life cycle of a Laverstock kiln. It has been estimated that a kiln was used for about five years and it may have taken up to 130 vessels in one firing. Possibly 2600 pots were produced in one kiln alone. Kiln 6 (see plan) was partly loaded with 13 jugs, several undamaged. The vessels in the bottom layer were inverted and stood directly on the oven floor and the stack was then built up like a pile of skittles, probably four to five layers high.[26]

In the first major report on the excavations in 1969, most of the pottery was dated to the 13th century with a possible short working life covering the years 1230-75, although there was also a reference to working potters in the vicinity in the 1320s. Wilelmus and John le Potter (probably from the Laverstock site) were able to remove brushwood from Clarendon forest for fuel between 1318-23.[27] Since this report was published further excavations in Salisbury indicate that the pottery had a much longer life span than at first recorded. Probably established in the late 12th century (some of the pits and buildings at Laverstock have been so dated), the wares were in use throughout much of the 14th century and perhaps even longer, although no local kilns later than the early 14th century have yet been discovered.[28]

The range of pottery

A wide variety of pottery was produced; the basic products were jugs or pitchers, the characteristic scratch-marked cooking pots and cauldrons (double handled jars). The jugs were often decorated with dot and circle stamps and spiral motifs becoming more complicated during the 13th century with foliage designs and ears of corn.

Laverstock jug, late 13th century. Buff earthenware with applied and brushed slip decoration; described as a kiln waster
© Victoria and Albert Museum, London

Household items included curfews (fire covers), lamps, two tiny oval money boxes (medieval 'piggy banks') and unusual aquamaniles.[29] Building materials saw decorated ridge tiles, drain-pipes, louvers, even a medieval chimney pot, all indicating a prosperous housing market. Some of the most exciting finds have been the rare face-decorated and anthropomorphic jugs, where the jugs are representations of the human form. Like the early stone masons in Salisbury Cathedral, it appears that the potter was given a free hand, enabling the design of the medieval ancestor to the Toby Jug.

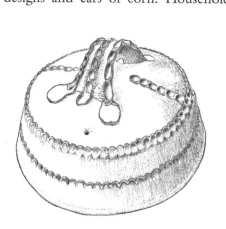

Curfew or fire cover displayed in the Salisbury Museum, drawing by Jenny Hayes, 2019

Anthropomorphic or face jug, humorous, crude face pottery © The Salisbury Museum

The heart shaped face is a further Laverstock characteristic with other jugs having a tubular spout between the eyes. These examples 'represent some of the finest achievements of the local potters at this period'.[30]

We know very little of the craftsmen involved but the high quality glazed ware and the distinctive jugs suggest at least one experienced potter. Research is ongoing and the site is currently thought to be more extensive than once believed. The lost settlements of Milford Pichard and Milford Richard (see 46-7) may have developed because of the expanding industrial complex and possibly housed the potters and their families within their small communities east of the Bourne. Pottery sherds have been discovered at the current Milford Farm, south of Queen Manor Road and further finds will help to determine the full extent of the site.[31]

Decline

Why did the Laverstock pottery disappear? There is no definitive answer. Clarendon Palace was still a royal residence in the 14th century and only began to decline from the mid-15th century although there is recent evidence from 'spoilheaps' on site of a wide range of imported wares.[32]

It appears to some extent that the local pottery was a victim of its own success as other regions began to copy its wares. Perhaps the competition encouraged a reduction in standards as seen in the early 14th century where the finish of the Laverstock jugs is less refined, as vessels of lower quality were churned out quickly in a move towards 'mass production'.

While Salisbury expanded as a manufacturing cloth town in the later years of the 14th century, the Black Death (1348-9) may well have affected smaller markets as both population and output declined. The epidemic was reported close to Laverstock, at both Downton and Ivychurch Priory in Alderbury and it is possible that the pottery site itself was directly affected.[33]

The answers to these queries may evolve as further excavations and tests are undertaken. At present we can be certain that the Laverstock pottery site is of national importance with significant implications for the regional medieval economy.

Clarendon and links with Laverstock
Ruth Newman

The powerful presence of Clarendon is scarcely recognised today. Here, on our doorstep, in the Middle Ages, were the largest deer park in the country and the greatest palace outside London.

Clarendon was an ancient landscape, developing from a Saxon hunting lodge into a pre-eminent royal estate. A place of government and power long before Salisbury Cathedral was built, it ensured its place in history in 1164 with the Constitutions of Clarendon and the growing conflict between Henry II and his Archbishop, culminating in Thomas Becket's murder in 1170.[34]

The palace reached its height under Henry III (1216-1272), who loved Clarendon and stayed regularly. Contemporary with the construction of Salisbury Cathedral, the great hall, royal apartments and wine cellar were all extensively rebuilt. High quality stained glass, elaborate tiles and interior decoration added to its high status.[35] From the Queen's Chamber views extended north where the deer grazed, toward Cockey Down.

Edward III (1327-1377) would have seen the new cathedral spire in the distance when he visited during the Black Death in 1349 'while the plague raged' just outside his park. After this, royal visits dwindled, apart from the sad stay of Henry VI who, in 1453, suffered a catastrophic breakdown at the palace.

Clarendon and Laverstock
Clarendon forest was extensive with its boundaries changing over time. The perambulations (beating the bounds) of Clarendon in the 13th and 14th centuries recorded the local boundaries, with Laverstock and Ford east of the

The view from the east with wine cellar in foreground and King's chapel beyond, at the height of the palace's gothic splendour, (with kind permission of Tom Beaumont James and Amanda Richardson)

Bourne, lying within the estate. By 1650 the area within the park had decreased with Ranger's Lodge gate (slaygate) becoming the boundary. Laverstock lies to the west with the Cockey Down chalk ridge to the north where you can still see parts of the massive bank and ditch of the outer park pale or boundary of 10.2 miles (16.5 km), designed to keep in the deer.[36]

Records suggest that the palace, park, and forest would have contributed to Laverstock's economy with demand for labour, especially through the thriving pottery industry. The local kilns, just on the boundary of the park, provided most of the palace's pottery in the 13th century and beyond, and this trade may well have partially accounted for Laverstock's relatively high population at this time.[37]

The close proximity of Laverstock and Clarendon brought both prosperity and conflict. The local forest courts from the mid-13th century enforced restrictions which affected Laverstock. Fines were levied for taking dead wood, and for dogs straying on to the king's land. Later in 1327 when the park buildings had fallen into disrepair, game was stolen including a buck by William Cole of Laverstock who brought heavy lifting equipment to remove it. Those accused argued that they were accustomed to taking the king's venison, but this was disputed.[38]

By 1500 Clarendon was ruinous and no longer a royal residence although the Tudors and early Stuarts continued to enjoy the hunting. In the mid-16th century, conflict became more common. Margaret York of Laverstock claimed that park officials had illegally enclosed her land. She persuaded her servants to resist the keepers and to hunt within the park and even invited local gentry to join her in opposition.[39] But during the 17th century, the number of deer declined and the park finally passed out of Crown hands in 1664.[40] Clarendon House, the fine early 18th century mansion, was built for Peter Bathurst whose engaging memorial may be seen in St Andrew's Church porch.

Clarendon only became a civil parish in 1858 and before that it was never recognised as such. Long after the decline of the palace, the estate fell into several parishes including Laverstock. Some residents

Clarendon, the garden terrace, much loved by Henry III and his Queen, Eleanor of Provence (with kind permission of Tom Beaumont James and Amanda Richardson)

could claim that they were in the 'liberty of Clarendon' and as such were in an 'extra parochial place' under the jurisdiction of the Dean of Salisbury. Thus it was that in 1827 David Rattey (Rattue) of Laverstock was entitled to marry Mary Erwood (Yerwood), of the Liberty of Clarendon, in the grandeur of Salisbury Cathedral.[41]

The llamas, both curious and friendly, help to keep down the shrubbery (photograph Amanda Richardson)

Clarendon, with its remote, ruined palace, remains a secret place. Llamas keep down the shrubbery, and a small group of 'Friends' weed tirelessly to maintain this very special neighbouring site.

1   Edwards, Kathleen, 1956, 'Cathedral of Salisbury', *VCH Wilts* 3, 168; Colt Hoare, 1837, *The Modern History of South Wiltshire* 5, 106

2   Morris, Richard, 1989, *Churches in the Landscape*, J M Dent, 147-8

3   It has been noted that 'In one church excavation after another, traces have been found of an earlier Saxon building', C Platt, 1995, *The Parish Churches of Medieval England*, Chancellor Press, 17

4   Morris, 1989, 92, 252-3. Turner, Sam, 2006, *Making a Christian Landscape*, University of Exeter Press, 151

5   Godfrey, J, 1974, 'The emergence of the village church in Anglo-Saxon England', in Rowley, Trevor, (ed), *Anglo-Saxon Settlement and Landscape*, British Archaeological Reports 6, 133-34

6   Tatton-Brown, Tim, 2009, 'Reconstructing the Medieval Landscape around Salisbury', *Sarum Chronicle* 9, 31; see also Table 7 in Turner, 2006, 67. St Peter's, Britford possibly dates to the 8th century.

7   Morris, 1989, 208

8   Grist, K, 1970, *Laverstock through the ages,* self-published, 7

9   Platt, 1995, 32, 35, 36, 124. In the case of Laverstock there might have been paintings of Andrew the fisherman, also his martyrdom on a 'saltire' or X-shaped cross. Small fragments of painted wall-plaster were found during the archaeological work in the chancel area, 2008.

10 Styles, Dorothy, 'Priory of Ivychurch', *VCH Wilts* 3, 292, 295. Brakspear, Sir Harold, 1934, 'Ivychurch Priory' *WANHM* 46, 435

11 Crowley, D A (ed), 1989, *The Wiltshire Tax List of 1332*, WRS 45, 104-5; Beresford, M W, 'Poll-Tax Payers of 1377', VCH *Wilts* 4, 306

12 Beaumont James, Tom, 1998, 'The Black Death in Berkshire and Wiltshire', *Hatcher Review* v (46), 11

13 A chantry was an endowment which paid for a priest to say masses for the souls of the founder and his family.

14 Jackson, Rev Canon J E, 1867, 'Ancient Chapels, etc. in Co. Wilts', *WANHM* 10, 290. The Poultry Cross seems to be meant, though *poletria* was a medieval word for a drove of young horses.

15 Morris, 1989, 365

16 WSA D1/2/7, folio 135/45

17 Anon, 1901, review of Malden, A R (ed) *The Canonization of Saint Osmund*, *WANHM* 32, 234-5. Farmer, David H, 1992, *The Oxford Dictionary of Saints*, 368

18 Medieval sherds (fragments of historic pottery) were first reported in 1940 and later in 1955 on allotment gardens; Musty, Algar and Ewence, 1969, 'The Medieval Pottery Kilns at Laverstock, near Salisbury, Wiltshire', *Archaeologia* Vol CII

19 Beaumont James, T and Gerrard C, 2007, *Clarendon, Landscape of Kings*, Windgather Press. Recent fieldwork (2004) at Clarendon has revealed 1,730 sherds of Medieval pottery.

20 Saunders, Peter, editor 2001, *Salisbury Museum Medieval Catalogue,* Part 3, Salisbury and South Wiltshire Museum

21 Newman, R and Howells, J, 2001, *Salisbury Past,* Phillimore

22 Mepham Lorraine, 2016, *WANHM,* vol 109, 153-6

23 Articles from *WANHM*, 2005, 177, 2008, 182, 2010, 182-3, 2013, 95,185

24 Algar and Saunders, 2014, A medieval pottery kiln in Salisbury, *WANHM*, vol 107,146-156

25 This excludes the mid-13th century tile kiln at Clarendon which produced superb inlaid tiles for the royal chambers.

26 Experiments in 1967 indicated that a kiln load might take up to 130 vessels, rather than the 50 first suggested. Musty *et al*, 1969; Musty, J, 1974, *Medieval pottery kilns*

27 Musty *et al,* 1969

28 Saunders, 2001

29 Water containers for washing hands during a meal, in the shape of an animal.

30 Saunders, 2001, 140. Many of the finds can be seen displayed in The Salisbury Museum alongside an excellent interpretive model.

31 Durman, Richard, 2007, *Milford*, Sarum Studies 1, 7, 15-16

32 Beaumont James and Gerrard, 92, 222, note 100

33 Recent research on thousands of test pits in East Anglia have indicated that a reduction in pottery sherds in medieval settlements may indicate the impact of the Black Death; from lecture by Carenza Lewis, November 2016, *Wiltshire settlements and the Black Death.*

34 The Constitutions were an attempt to limit the power of the church. Henry, at Clarendon, outwitted Becket, who fled from the site in tears and into exile. The Assize of Clarendon, 1166, led to the growth of itinerant justices and the development of civil law.

35 The circular tile pavement from the King's chapel was possibly the finest in Europe at the time. Beaumont James and Gerrard, 2007, 82

36 There were several deer leaps where the animals could leap in from outside the park but not out to escape – a walk-in larder!

37 Richardson, Amanda, 2003, *The Medieval Palace, Park, and Forest of Clarendon, Wiltshire c1130- c1650*

38 VCH *Wilts* 4, 427-431; Inquisition Post Mortem 1327 (information from Jenny Hayes)

39 Beaumont James and Gerrard, 112

40 In 1644 Clarendon was 'disparked' allowing the parkland to be used for other purposes. Edward Hyde, the Earl of Clarendon briefly owned the estate.

41 Information from Suzanne Eward, librarian (2009) Salisbury Cathedral; Heather Yeates (née Rattue).

From Larkestoke to Laverstock
Jenny Hayes

The descent of the Manor of Laverstock with Ford and Milford

(See Appendix I for Glossary of Medieval Terms)

What is a Manor?

After the Norman conquest of 1066, the estates of the old English aristocracy were re-allocated to the followers and allies of William of Normandy, as a reward for their past and future allegiance. A feudal system of tenure was established, whereby a hierarchy of lords held areas of land either from the church or the king, directly as tenants-in-chief, or as under-tenants. These lords of the manors were required to take an oath of fealty, swearing allegiance to the king, and paying homage to their immediate superior. Under feudal law, military service or cash *in lieu* was required by their overlord who may have held several manors.

The lord of the manor had specific rights and privileges, controlling law and justice on his estates.[1] A certain portion of land was for his own use, known as demesne land. The rest was allotted to peasants who were required to provide services for that land, or to pay taxes. They could rent small strips of land to grow crops, keep animals on common land, cut hay from waste land, and wood for fuel and building purposes. Hunting rights were specifically for the lord of the manor.

An estate or manor would typically include a mansion house for the lord and his family, agricultural land, woods, orchards, common pasture, meadowland, a mill, a village for the peasants, and a church. The manor house would have been an informal collection of buildings, including most importantly a hall, which served as the meeting place for village business, and where the manorial court was held.

Laverstock, Ford and Milford were located along the River Bourne, sandwiched between Old Sarum, which became a strategic military base for King William, and Clarendon Forest. The forest, in use well before the conquest, was found to be a suitable place for the king to muster his troops.[2] Early in the 13th century it was decided that another cathedral would be built on the bishop's land, between the rivers Avon and Bourne, south of Old Sarum. The route taken from Clarendon to the new, growing city of Salisbury was now west through Milford, instead of north west via the old Roman road to Old Sarum.[3]

Towards the end of the 11th century, the forest at Clarendon began to be defined as a royal park by King William's youngest son Henry I, and greatly improved under the direction of Henry II. The western boundary of the forest followed the rivers Avon and Bourne, from Bodenham bridge to Ford in Laverstock which remained at the edge of the forest well into the 14th century.

Both Laverstock and the eastern parts of Milford held lands belonging to the king's forest, and would eventually become part of the Manor of Laverstock.

In 1086 King William ordered a survey of all lands in England, known later as the Domesday survey.

Milford

At the time of the Domesday survey Milford had three Manors. The largest one was west of the River Bourne and held by the Bishop, whose manor stretched between the Bourne and Avon, south of Old Sarum and included the current Bishopdown area.

The two smaller Manors, later known as Milford Pychard and Milford Richard were on the east of the Bourne

The Manors of Milford, east of the River Bourne. From the Domesday survey 1086

1. Humphrey de L'Isle holds Milford.
Joscelin holds half a hide of land of Humphrey de L'Isle and it paid geld for as much.
In the time of King Edward, Saeweald and Saeweard held it.
There is land for one plough.
There are 6 cottars and 3 acres of meadow.
It was worth 15d now 7s.
Half this land is in the kings forest.

2. The Lord in chief is Wulfgeat
'the hunter for the King'
Wulfgeat holds half a hide in Milford.
There is land for 2 oxen.
It is worth 2s.
Half this land is in the forest

Domesday Survey of Milford Pychard and Milford Richard; Williams and Martin, Domesday Book, A Complete Translation 182 195

adjacent to Laverstock, containing land in the king's forest of Clarendon for which they were responsible.[4]

Milford Pychard

Milford Pychard was named after the Punchard/Pychard family who leased this land at the beginning of 12th century.[5]

Land tenure at Milford was greatly influenced by the vicinity of the king's palace and forest at Clarendon. It is not surprising therefore, that this small estate was held from Reginald de Dunstanville, one of the natural sons of King Henry I. Reginald had inherited Milford through his wife Adeliza, as one of the 27 manors held by her father Humphrey de L'Isle at the time of the Domesday survey.

Before 1216, Hugh de Punchard sold his lease to William Brewer, whose wife Beatrice de Vaux was reputed to have been Reginald's mistress. William was a major landowner, who founded Mottisfont Abbey and died in 1226. By 1242 Milford Pychard was held from the Dunstanville family by Gilbert de Milford.[6] His son Stephen de Milford (alias Wodefeld) is recorded as holding the mill and two virgates of land at Laverstock in 1250.[7] (See below, Laverstock: Wilton Abbey lands.)

Milford Richard

Richard de Meleford/Milford, son of Peter, is recorded as having the sergeanty for a quarter of Clarendon forest in 1198, for which he held a dwelling house and 30 acres in Milford. This had been held at the time of Domesday by Wulfgeat the 'hunter for the king'.

Richard's son, also Richard de Milford held this estate at his death in 1269 and also the mill with 16 acres at Laverstock from Stephen de Milford/ Wodefeld. Richard's grandson, Edmund de Milford passed the estate to his 24-year-old daughter Agnes in 1314. She then married Robert de Osgodby but had died by 1316.[8] Her kinsman Robert Cole granted the dwelling house and land in Milford Richard to Richard de Tudeworth and his wife Katherine.[9] Then in 1323, Richard Tudeworth bought the grant of the mill and nine acres of land from Milford Pychard.[10] These holdings came to Henry Burry, Bailiff of Salisbury, by 1327, held under the original terms from Richard de Tudeworth.

Laverstock and Ford

The Domesday survey (see 10) states that both the king and the church held land at Laverstock. A quarter of the forest belonging to the king came under the sergeanty of Laverstock, for which a house and 30 acres were supplied. The Abbey of Wilton held 240 acres.

Laverstock: The King's land

Jordan de Laverkestok or Larkestoke held the sergeanty of the forest in 1198.[11] His son Robert de Larkestoke continued the lease for the same service, also leasing a mill at Mumworth from the Prior of Ivychurch,[12] and 60 acres at Laverstock from Stephen de Wodefeld.[13] At his death in 1247 Robert's heir was his son Jordan de Larkestoke.

In 1304 Jordan gained permission to enfeoff Robert de Micheldever of the sergeanty of the forest, with the dwelling and land in Larkestoke. Micheldever then leased this land to Henry Burry of Salisbury, who was also leasing the lands now held from Margaret de Wodefeld, the widow of William, son of Stephen de Wodefeld.

In 1321 Micheldever evicted Burry from the king's land, for being part of an uprising against King Edward II, led by the Duke of Lancaster. In 1326 Queen Isabel led a second, successful rebellion, deposing her husband and executing many of his companions. Micheldever was a friend of Hugh Despenser, the King's favourite, who was accused of widespread criminality and was tortuously put to death in 1326 and Micheldever also executed.

Burry's land holdings and forester duties were restored to him by the Sheriff of Wiltshire in 1327, at which time he enfeoffed William Randolf, Bailiff of Salisbury, under the original terms from Jordan de Larkestoke.

Jordan de Larkestoke left two daughters, Avice and Petronella, who were still responsible for the sergeanty of the forest. By 1334 the sisters granted this office with the house and 30 acres to William Randolf. Besides the king's lands, he leased the lands previously held by Burry from the Wodefeld and Tudeworth families. As Randolf died without an heir in 1361, the Laverstock lands held from the crown reverted to the king, who granted them to Hugh Cheyne/Cheney. (see 34).

Laverstock: Wilton Abbey land

As mentioned above, Stephen de Milford/Wodefield held the mill and land at Laverstock in addition to Milford Pychard. His son William held Laverstock until 1310, when his wife Margaret was the Dame of Laverstock. Their heir, also William, married Joan, the daughter of Richard Tudeworth of Milford Richard (see above). Widowed, with a daughter also Joan, she is described as the Lady of Laverstock at the inquisition of her father's death, in 1354. Holding the Wodefeld lands from her husband, Joan had married Sir Thomas Farnhull by 1356. Her brother John inherited many of the Tudeworth lands including Milford, until his death in 1362, when these passed to his niece Joan Wodefeld, the younger.

The Descent of the Manor of Laverstock from 11th to 20th century

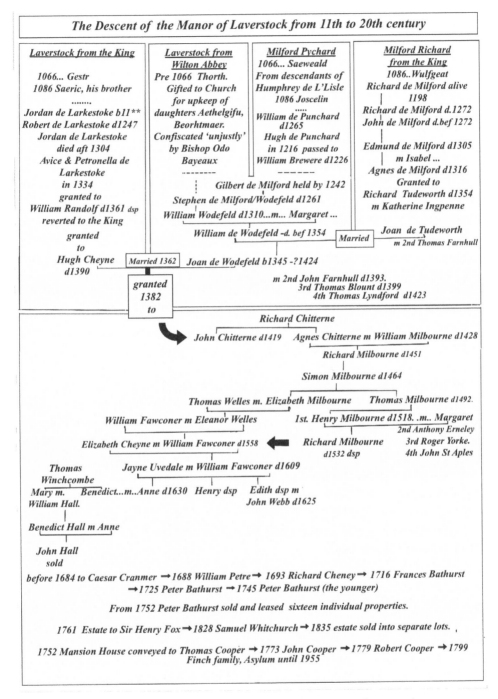

Laverstock from the King

1066... Gestr
1086 Saeric, his brother
....
Jordan de Larkestoke b11**
Robert de Larkestoke d1247
Jordan de Larkestoke
died aft 1304
Avice & Petronella de
Larkestoke
in 1334
granted to
William Randolf d1361 dsp
reverted to the King
granted
to
Hugh Cheyne
d1390

Married 1362

Laverstock from Wilton Abbey

Pre 1066 Thorth.
1066 Thorth.
Gifted to Church
for upkeep of
daughters Aethelgifu,
Beorhtmaer.
Confiscated 'unjustly'
by Bishop Odo
Bayeaux

Gilbert de Milford held by 1242
Stephen de Milford/Wodefeld d1261
William Wodefeld d1310...m... Margaret ...
William de Wodefeld -d. bef 1354

granted 1382 to

Milford Pychard

1066... Saeweald
From descendants of
Humphrey de L'Lisle
1086 Joscelin
.....
William de Punchard
d1265
Hugh de Punchard
in 1216 passed to
William Brewere d1226

Joan de Wodefeld b1345 -?1424

m 2nd John Farnhull d1393.
3rd Thomas Blount d1399
4th Thomas Lyndford d1423

Milford Richard from the King

1086.. Wulfgeat
Richard de Milford alive
1198
Richard de Milford d.1272
John de Milford d.bef 1272
Edmund de Milford d1305
m Isabel ...
Agnes de Milford d1316
Granted to
Richard Tudeworth d1354
m Katherine Ingpenne

Married Joan de Tudeworth
m 2nd Thomas Farnhull

Richard Chitterne

John Chitterne d1419   Agnes Chitterne m William Milbourne d1428

Richard Milbourne d1451

Simon Milbourne d1464

Thomas Welles m. Elizabeth Milbourne   Thomas Milbourne d1492.

William Fawconer m Eleanor Welles   1st. Henry Milbourne d1518. .m.. Margaret
2nd Anthony Erneley

Elizabeth Cheyne m William Fawconer d1558   Richard Milbourne   3rd Roger Yorke.
d1532 dsp   4th John St Aples

Jayne Uvedale m William Fawconer d1609

Thomas
Winchcombe
Mary m.   Benedict...m..Anne d1630 Henry dsp   Edith dsp m
William Hall.   John Webb d1625

Benedict Hall m Anne

John Hall
sold

before 1684 to Caesar Cranmer ➔ 1688 William Petre ➔ 1693 Richard Cheney ➔ 1716 Frances Bathurst
➔ 1725 Peter Bathurst ➔ 1745 Peter Bathurst (the younger)

From 1752 Peter Bathurst sold and leased sixteen individual properties.

1761 Estate to Sir Henry Fox ➔ 1828 Samuel Whitchurch ➔ 1835 estate sold into separate lots. ,

1752 Mansion House conveyed to Thomas Cooper ➔ 1773 John Cooper ➔ 1779 Robert Cooper ➔ 1799
Finch family, Asylum until 1955

From Larkestoke to Laverstock, The descent of the Manor of Laverstock

Wilton Abbey and the King's lands are held together

Now a considerable heiress from her Tudeworth and Wodefeld grandparents, 17 year-old Joan was married in 1362 to Hugh Cheyne. Since he held the the the King's lands of Laverstock, this marriage brought together the Abbey's land, the King's land and the two Milford estates.

In 1382 however, Joan and Hugh passed them to John Chitterne, a clerk later to become Archdeacon at Salisbury Cathedral. He was a prominent landholder of many estates in southern England, which he passed to his sisters, Christine and Agnes, when they married.

Hugh Cheyne died in 1390, Joan may then have married John Farnhull who died in 1393[14]. In 1394 she did marry Sir Thomas Blount, who was executed at Oxford in 1399 for his part in the conspiracy to assassinate King Henry IV.[15] Lastly by 1401 she had married Thomas Lyndford of Harnham. John Chitterne granted Joan and Thomas the lease of all her previous lands, including Laverstock for the rest of their lives. Thomas Lyndford died in 1423 but it is unknown when Joan died.[16]

Joan's estates were held from Agnes Chitterne who married William Milbourne of Witcombe, Somerset. Their son, Richard, was a verderer of Clarendon as early as 1422.

15th century

Joan's kinsman, Emund Dauntesey succeeded to many of her estates including Laverstock held from Agnes and William Milbourne; until his death in 1430. However Humphrey, Duke of Gloucester, the brother of King Henry V claimed Laverstock as being in the Honour of Gloucester. This was successfully contested by Richard Milbourne at the Inquistion of Humphrey's death in 1447.

Extracts from the Inquisition Post Mortem in 1447 of Humphrey Duke of Gloucester.[17]

In 1429 Edmund Dauntesey Esquire, was once seized in demesne as of fee of 26 messuages, 3 mills, 949a land, 53a meadows, 10a woods, £14 11s. 3d. rent, and rent of 1lb. Cumin, in Laverstock, Milford, Mummworth, Ford, 'New' Salisbury, Rollestone and Alderbury.

In 1429 he granted these to five under tenants, the rent and profit for Richard Milbourne. After Edmund Dauntesey died in 1430, Humphrey, Duke of Gloucester and Joan Stradelyng, Edmund Dauntesey's heir, entered these possessions, disseised and expelled them. The Duke died in 1447, his heir was his nephew King Henry VI. Richard Milbourne successfully petitioned the King as to his rights and those of the tenants which Humphrey had expelled. And so in March 1447 Richard Milbourne entered his properties.

Laverstock Manor descended in a direct line from Richard Milbourne, to his son Simon, and then to his son Sir Thomas Milbourne. Towards the end of the 'Wars of the Roses' (1455-1485), Thomas Milbourne joined the unsuccessful Buckingham rebellion, whose aim was to depose King Richard III in favour of Henry Tudor. This resulted in Henry Stafford, 2nd Duke of Buckingham, being executed in Salisbury in 1483. Thomas was among those who were attainted in November 1483, although pardoned the following April. Two years later, Thomas, a loyal supporter of the Lancastrian cause, was knighted just before the battle of Bosworth, where Henry Tudor defeated Richard III to become King Henry VII.

Sir Thomas died in 1492; his heir was his son Henry, who died in 1518. Henry's widow Margaret married a second husband Anthony Erneley. He held the lease of the Bishopdown part of Milford until his death in 1530, when their daughter Isabel, wife of Henry Uvedale, took up the lease. Margaret then married Roger Yorke as her third husband, and John St Aples as her fourth and was still living after 1550. Henry Milbourne's son Richard died in 1532 without a direct heir.

Laverstock Manor then passed to Richard's second cousin, William Fawconer of East Meon, Hampshire. His grandmother was Elizabeth, daughter of Simon Milbourne. William Fawconer's son, another William, succeeded to Laverstock Manor in 1558, marrying Henry Uvedale's sister, Jayne.

16th Century

The 16th century experienced the religious changes that became known as the Reformation.

The 1559 Act of Uniformity banned the catholic Mass and imposed a fine on those who refused to attend the new worship at their parish church. After 1581, refusing to comply with the new requirements, such as being a recusant, became a criminal offence; [18] fines and other penalties were increased and the education of Catholic children forbidden. It was treason to convert to Catholicism. [19] The Fawconers were unwilling to change from the old faith and so were subject to degrees of persecution as recusants.

The Fawconers held the Manor of Laverstock until 1609. It had been leased out latterly to a Mr Felton, who had offered a higher rent than it was worth, to gain possession of a recusant's property, with no intention of paying any rent. After leasing the property, Felton improved the land to a far higher value 'out of malice' and to the oppression of many tenants, but paid no rent and owed £380 in arrears.

For about five years from the beginning of this tenancy, the Mansion house was ransacked by Felton's wife and children. The ceiling had been torn down and even the locks on the doors had been sold. Any goods remaining belonging to the Fawconer family had been disposed of without payment. William Fawconer's nephew requested that he, as a Protestant, could be the tenant, paying regular rents. He suggested that Felton's goods should be valued and surrendered to pay the debt.[20]

17th Century

William Fawconer died in March 1609. He willed that the Manor of Laverstock should be left first to his son-in-law, Sir John Webb of Odstock, who held Laverstock until his death in 1625, and then to William's daughter Anne Winchcombe. However it went to her husband's nephew Benedict Hall. There followed a complex case in Chancery that depended on William's state of mind when he made his will. In the event, as Benedict and Anne were childless, William Fawconer's nephew, also William, lived there until his death in1645 when Laverstock Manor reverted to Benedict Hall.

The Halls were staunch Royalists as well as Roman Catholics. In 1645, during the Civil War, Benedict and his wife were forced from their homes, with their lands sequestered.[21] Benedict eventually recovered his estates in 1656, promising never to fight against Parliament again. He died in 1668. Before Anne died in 1684, she and her son John conveyed the Manor of Laverstock to Sir Caesar Cranmer. He in turn sold to William Petre in 1688, who sold to Richard Cheney of the Middle Temple, Inn of Court, in 1693.

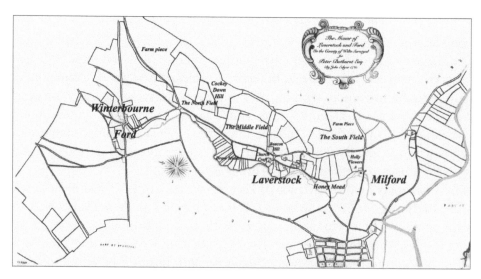

Map of The Manor of Laverstock & Ford drawn for Peter Bathurst in 1725, redrawn by Jenny Hayes

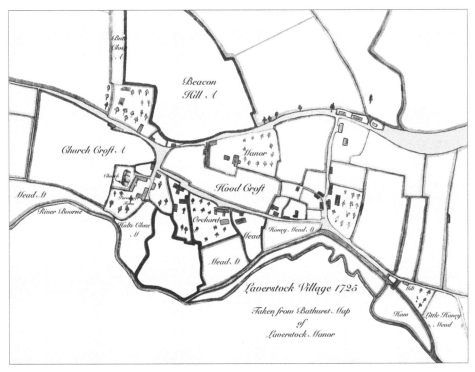

The Village of Laverstock taken from the 1725 Map of The Manor, redrawn by Jenny Hayes

18th Century

In 1716 Dame Frances Bathurst, widow of Sir Benjamin, purchased Laverstock Manor from Richard Cheney. Her son Peter had owned adjacent Clarendon Park since 1708.[22] The Manor comprised a mansion house, gatehouse, barns, stables, buildings, outhouses, courtyards, orchards and gardens, and were leased to William Hearst of the Close at that time, with provision for an under tenant.[23] Dame Frances died in 1723; her heir was her son Peter, who in 1725 commissioned a survey of the Manor of Laverstock and Ford (see above).

Peter Bathurst died in 1745;[24] his heir was his son, another Peter. Then began the gradual disintegration of the Manor. From 1752 onwards individual properties were conveyed either as freehold or leasehold, notably the Mansion house to Thomas Cooper of Salisbury[25]. In 1761 Peter Bathurst sold the remaining estate to politician Henry Fox, Lord Holland, son of Sir Stephen Fox of Farley, who founded the Royal Chelsea Hospital.[26]

The Mansion house, now Laverstock House, was sublet after the death of Thomas Cooper in 1773 and was acquired by his nephew Robert Cooper, on the death of Thomas' son and heir John who died in 1779.

In March 1775 an advertisement appeared in the *Salisbury and Winchester Journal* for the lease of Laverstock House 'in a pleasant healthy situation, an avenue leading up to the house, a good well laid out walled garden with coach house stabling and offices.' The lease was taken up by Infirmary surgeon Charles Curtoys, who established an asylum on this site in 1781. Laverstock House was sold after the death of Robert Cooper in 1799. It is probable that it was purchased at this time by the Finch family, who had been leasing the house (see 107-8).

19th Century

The remaining lands and farms belonging to the Manor of Laverstock were still in the possession of the Fox family in 1797. These lands were sold in May 1821, to Samuel Whitchurch, owner of 'The Whitchurch Brewery' in Milford Street. He died owning many properties in Hampshire and Wiltshire besides the Manor of Laverstock, which was sold in August 1835.

Local landowners who purchased Manor lands included Sir Wadham Wyndham, Ann Burroughs, Col Edward Baker, Thomas Blake, Richard and John Cooe and Dr William Finch.

Where was the Manor House?

Of the three large houses at Laverstock in the 19th century, The Hill was built in 1805, while The Hall was sold by Peter Bathurst, owner of The Manor in 1752. Laverstock House, later to become an Asylum therefore appears to be the 'Capital Messuage' of Laverstock. It remained as a private asylum until 1955 when it was demolished and Laverstock Park and Laverstock Park West were built in the grounds.

All that Manor or reputed MANOR of LAVERSTOCK and FORD in the County of Wilts about one thousand five hundred acres of land, and also that desirable and compact farm called FORD FARM situate at Laverstock aforesaid comprising three hundred and seventy seven acres of excellent Arable, Meadow, Pasture and Downlands with a newly erected farm house, good homestead and buildings together with seven cottages and gardens at Ford aforesaid, and the reversion in fee of two leasehold tenements at Laverstock aforesaid, within 2 miles of Salisbury adjoining the London road.

Beacon Hill Field situate at Laverstock in the occupation of Messrs Cooe and also the reversion in fee of six cottages and gardens at Laverstock comprising about 3 acres.

The Reversion in fee of two cottages and gardens at Laverstock aforesaid held by Sir James Burrough and Dr Finch on leases for lives.

All that piece of Freehold Meadow called Marsh Mead situate at Laverstock on the Southampton Road near Belmont. And the reversion in fee of an island in the River Avon called Saint Kitts Island

All that cottage called Holts situate at Milford near the Turnpike Gate on the London road now occupied as two tenements with the garden belonging..........

Sale of the Manor lands of Samuel Whitchurch, 1835: Devizes and Wiltshire Gazette, 3 September 1835

1   Newman, Simon, Manors of the Middle Ages. www.thefinertimes.com/Middle-Ages/manors-in-the-middle-ages.html., accessed 12/2018

2   Beaumont James, T and Gerrard C, 2007, *Clarendon, Landscape of Kings*, Windgather Press

3   Hutton, Edward, 1939, *Highways and Byways of Wiltshire*, Macmillan and Co, The valley of the Bourne

4   Mumworth Mill was situated at the confluence of Rivers Bourne and Avon, next to the meadows of Milford Pychard. Milford Richard lay east of M Pychard next to Clarendon, both bordered by Laverstock on north and Laverstock detached on south and were approximately 60 acres each.

5   Hugh de Punchardon of Heaton Punchardon in Somerset, son of William, grandson of Robert, was an undertenant but like all the Punchardons added their name to the lands which they leased; hence Milford Punchard or Pychard.

6   Gilbert de Milford also held a manor at Wylye from Walter Dunstanville in 1250, *Liber Feodorum* 1250-72

7   Sir Stephen of Milford, son of Gilbert, died holding land at Woodfalls assessed at 1½ hides and who in 1261, after his death, was called Stephen de Wodefeld (of Woodfalls) as was his son William.

8   TNA C143/90/3 6 Edward II

9   TNA C143/111/18. Richard de Tudeworth

10 Feet of Fines, 1323

11 Book of Fees, 1198-1242

12 Also known as Hederose.

13 IPM 34 Hen III

14 Joan is recorded as having the Manor of Winkton, Hants as dower from her husband John de Farnhull. IPM Thomas West 1401

15 History of Parliament 1386-1421, Blount, Sir Thomas

16 Joan died childless possibly in 1424, Kinsmen John Bokeland (Buckland) held Laverstock until 1428 when Edmund Dauntesey succeeded.

17 Mapping the Medieval Countryside project, http://www.inquisitionspostmortem.ac.uk/, IPM Humphrey, Duke of Gloucester.

18 Non-compliance with the perceived new faith.

19 www.genguide.co.uk/source/recusant-rolls-catholics/3, accessed November 2018

20 Calendar of the Cecil Papers in Hatfield House

21 Law to remove property temporarily from the owner, until legal claims were satisfied.

22 Beaumont James and Gerard, 2007

23 WSA 979/1, deeds relating to the Manor of Laverstock

24 Bishops court gave permission for a vault for the Bathurst family at St Andrew's church in 1748.

25 WSA 979/7 deeds relating to the Manor of Laverstock

26 WSA 979/1 deeds relating to the Manor of Laverstock

A History of Ford: part of the civil parish of Laverstock & Ford

Sue Wight

The hamlet of Ford appears to have been named simply for the placement of a river crossing, the current name being a contraction of the original documented title of *Winterburneforda*.[1] This describes the location and necessity for a fording place to cross a river (or bourne) during the winter, when the flow was more difficult to negotiate. Ford is approximately two miles in either direction from bridges on the River Bourne, at Milford to the south and at Winterbourne Earls upstream. Ford hamlet finally gained a road bridge to cross the Bourne in the 18th century, when a stone structure was erected to the east of the cross roads of the Roman road with Green Lane. This bridge still briefly deflects traffic to the south, away from the line of the Roman road, to form a junction with the lane from Ford Farm.

An earlier bridge built downstream at the Laverstock side of Ford carries the important London Road across the river. This is St Thomas's Bridge named after Thomas Becket who had visited King Henry II at nearby Clarendon Palace. This bridge allows road traffic to reach Ford and the farms and since 1932 also provides access to the local business of Boswell Brothers (Salisbury) Ltd.

There are many important historical markers around Ford, including clear evidence of a Roman road, still in use, which would have been established between 43 AD and 80 AD.[2] The route is delineated through the centre of Ford westward to the earthworks of Old Sarum. These man-made ditches date back at least to the Iron Age (about 400 BC), so the hillfort was in place long before the Romans arrived.[3]

Green Lane, which runs north from the London Road through Ford, keeps west of the River Bourne and then crosses the Roman road at right angles in the centre of the hamlet. This co-existence of roads supports the understanding

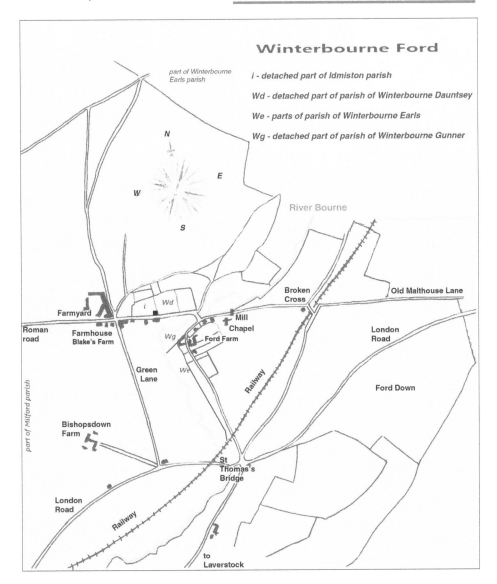

Ford c1881 (based on OS) showing the main locations
Sketch by S Wight, not to scale, 2019

that the Romans adopted existing local routes and improved them for their own purposes.

The earliest trace of habitation in Ford is from a Bronze Age burial discovered by chance in 1964 on Ford Down. There were two damaged barrows; on archaeological investigation one of these was found to include the remains of an ancient cremation, dating to the early part of the Bronze Age (approx 2500 BC).[4]

Within the Ford Down barrows there were two graves, but it was unclear whether one occupant was a young man or a woman. In the second barrow, however, were the skeleton and grave goods of a 'well-built man' from the 7th century Saxon period.[5] The grave of the Ford Warrior after excavation is shown in the illustration and has since been reconstructed in the Wessex Gallery of the Salisbury Museum. When the finds from the dig were examined, it was concluded that the grave goods (a bowl, a short sword called a seax, spear heads and other items) implied that this man had been buried following pagan ritual.[6] In the light of the known Saxon cemetery on the far south side of the parish, this individual probably lived during times of both pagan and early Christian influences. This Saxon grave is remote from the Petersfinger cemetery site, but it is unclear why.

Ford Laverstock Saxon Burial in situ during excavation, Ford Down, 1964. The Ford Warrior is on display in the Wessex Gallery © The Salisbury Museum

There is no mention of Ford in Domesday records. Evidence of human settlement in Ford after this time relies on information from documents, such as wills and maps, the oldest is a summary of rents in 1189.[7] In this source the resident is 'Johannes de Winterburneforda' who paid fees to Glastonbury Abbey in proportion to one meadow and a messuage. His rent was 16 pennies to the abbey and four chickens annually. The property is included under the manor of 'Idemestona' (Idmiston). The developing medieval hamlet of Winterburneforde[8] would have been based around that first farmstead with its waterside meadows and sheep. At some point the mill was built; originally a fulling mill driven by the water power of the River Bourne.

There have been numerous other archaeological finds within the Ford locality. Items of Bronze Age pottery, burial goods and prehistoric earthworks give strong evidence of human residence but detail of individuals is absent due to the lack of contemporary records.[9] There are also coins and fragments of jewellery dating back to the Anglo-Saxon period and medieval times.[10] These precious items may have been dropped by travellers through the area or by local wealthy people. The farming lands in Ford became valuable due to the rich sheep pasture on the meadows. Documentary evidence reveals the names of local people whose wealth was directly linked with land ownership. These include William Randolf, who in 1349 granted income to the nearby priory of Ivychurch from his land within Laverstock, Ford in Laverstock and Alderbury. On his death (1361 without issue) the land itself was granted to the priory.[11] The Glebe Terrier of 1616 was a survey of the lands which provided church income.[12] The details include Ford as well as Laverstock with a requirement for landowners to provide financial support to St Andrew's Church, itself in the care of the Cathedral. William Bragge was the farmer in Ford in the 17th century. His will, proven in 1667, states the lands he owned and monetary gifts to his family.[13] His is the earliest gravestone within St Andrew's churchyard in Laverstock.

By the 17th century Stuart and Commonwealth periods, the collective term of 'Laverstock and Ford' was in use. This seems to have become a convenient way to describe the locality for the purposes of formal church and government records. Due to this inclusion within the wider Laverstock community; baptisms, marriages and burials of Ford residents have usually taken place at St Andrew's Church in Laverstock. Children from Ford families attended Laverstock primary school from the beginning of formal education within the parish.

Ford Mill, a key functional building within the hamlet, has been on the same site since before 1361, when mentioned in the will of William Randolf. The mill is shown on sequential Ordnance Survey maps as sited on the line of the Roman road. This indicates that the mill and the attached living quarters were built on, or immediately adjacent to, the original Roman river crossing point.[14] The mill house was rebuilt, or extended, in 1783, according to a dated stone in the east end wall; no other records were located from this period. Perhaps this is when the first pair of grinding stones altered the chief product to flour. This also demonstrates the addition of cereal production to the local primary farm produce of wool. Detail from later 19th century documents show that regular maintenance was required to the mill building and the machinery; this was the responsibility of the owner rather than the tenant. Evidence following the Enclosure Act of 1820 shows the Ecclesiastical Commissioners as land agents on behalf of the Bishop of Salisbury who owned the mill property.[15] There was a damaging flood in the valley in 1841 after which repair work was necessary here as well as other riverside properties. Correspondence between the land agent and solicitors, referring to discussions with the tenant miller, provide an insight to the balance between professional relationships and responsibility for upkeep. The miller did succeed in securing funding for maintenance of the mill machinery and building in Ford, but nothing that might be described as unnecessary – the land agent declined to pay for fresh gravel for the path on one occasion.[16]

A second pair of stones was added to the mill in 1875/6 following the replacement of the original wheel (nine feet in diameter) with a new wheel 13 ft (4m) across. The local millwright recommended this change to make better use of the flow of the river.[17] This indicates that the Bourne was not merely a winter stream and power to the waterwheel was enhanced by improved channelling in the leat (water channel).

The first grinding stones were of Derbyshire millstone grit whereas the second pair was imported from central France. These heavy stones must have been transported from the French quarry to bring them for installation in Ford Mill, using cart, boat and possibly railway transport. To keep the mill working efficiently, the walls of the leat had to be maintained as well as all sluices and hatches, there are records of payments for this work.[18] There were also eel traps to prevent damage to the wheel and to capture this food supply. Later in the working life of the mill, labour saving sifting equipment was added reducing the laborious dusty work of separating and cleaning the raw flour.[19]

FORD MILL NEAR SALISBURY.

Colour postcard of Ford Mill and adjacent cottages. Griffin Mill Cottage is seen on the right.
Published by E F Newman, 91 Fisherton Street, Salisbury, approx 1900

The watermill remains here on the same ancient site spanning the river, with some restoration made to the original workings and it continues as a home. Across the lane is Griffin Mill Cottage; Griffin was the name of the mill tenants in each census from 1881 to 1911. The tail race in the picture seems to provide a good locality for various domestic birds, no doubt also supplying eggs to the villagers.

Ford residents of the Nineteenth century

This section considers people within the Ford community for whom we have evidence of residence and activities.

In February 1818 Charles Percy applied for a licence so that Methodist church services could be held at his home which was the property of Samuel Whitchurch esquire. On the application, the tenant Charles is described as a labourer and he was probably illiterate as he makes his mark (X) in place of a signature.[20] There are similar applications from residents of Hurdcott nearby and from the village of Winterbourne Earls, where building of a Methodist chapel and school room was approved in 1818.

Eventually Ford gained a Methodist chapel of its own, thanks to a grant for use of land for a building from the local landowning Wyndham family. It was constructed on the site of an earlier cottage, between the current properties of Undercliff and Down Cottage. A chapel is included in the 1842 tithe map and in the 1861 census survey it is recorded as uninhabited as it is not a dwelling.[21] It became known as St Francis' chapel after being transferred into the Anglican church. Later the dedication was amended to St Christopher. It is known to have been a corrugated iron chapel, painted green (20th century). However, the chapel was demolished in the 1980s and there are no remnants of the original building.[22]

Farmers, landowners and land usage

Seeking traces of other local wealthy families in Ford relies on documents related to farms and other assets; including wills, census returns and newspaper text of the 18th and 19th centuries.[23] The Blakes, Hunts and other landowning families have been influential within and beyond this parish over many years. The hamlet is referred to as 'the tything of Ford', indicating a small community. When the enclosures were agreed and mapped (1820) some exchanges were recorded between landowners. On the tithe map of 1842 there are numerous parishes shown having a continuing interest here. It seems that the holdings of landowners led to a mixture of nearby parishes being linked with various plots within Ford. The parishes of Idmiston, Milford and the Winterbournes are all represented.[24] The link with Idmiston dates back to the ancient manor lands here (1189), as above.

Local occupations can be construed from the enclosure map of 1820 and more detail becomes available in census returns from 1841.

In that year the farmer occupant at Ford Farm was Francis Nowlson with his wife, an adult son and two daughters Mary and Harriett.[25] As there is a direction in the will of John Blake (junior)[26] that the farm should be sold by auction on his death and that sale occurred in 1849, then Nowlson must have been a tenant farmer. This farm produced grain and wool, revealing the continuing presence of sheep. One of the brothers of John Blake junior, Thomas Blake, is described in his brother's will as the miller at Ford Mill. However, Thomas had left there by 1851, when the census shows the miller as James North.

By 1851 Ford Farm (380 acres) was held by farmer Edward Perry employing nine men and one house servant. In the census introductory description of the area the term 'Perry's Farm' is used.[27] In fact Francis Nowlson had died in 1848 and Edward Perry married the elder daughter Mary shortly afterward.[28] They had two small sons and Mary's sister Harriett was a visitor to the family on census night.

A second, separate farm of a similar size had also been established in Ford, later referred to as Manor Farm; it is possible that this was an extension of the manor at Laverstock. It is understood that this farm was north of the Roman road/Green Lane cross roads as the naming association lives on in Manor Farm Road, which leads west from here. In the 1851 census Edward Wansbrough was the second farmer in Ford, probably as a tenant, managing 370 acres with five labourers.[29] There was also some influence on land within the hamlet from Milford Manor, as Milford parish used to extend to Ford.

The 1861 census records the surveyed area as ... 'including Ford Mill, Gay's Farm (late Perry's) and 15 or 16 houses adjacent, situated in the hamlet of Ford belonging to the parish of Laverstock' . . .[30] Residents included members of the Cannings family, generally employed in agricultural roles. George Gay (aged 35) was the farmer of 370 acres, employing ten men and three boys. The farm staff listed includes three shepherds (Alfred Canning, Noah James and Thomas Lanham). Nearby, in contrast to the agricultural workers, four labourer employees of the new railway are recorded whereas John Best the baker probably lived and worked in the house now named 'The Hollies' using local flour from Ford watermill.

By 1871, the census locality was described as 'Mr Blake's Farm House and cottage . . . Ford Mill, Gay's Farm and 15 or 16 houses adjacent'. . . [31] John Best was still the baker and the miller was John Stone, who had a wife and five children. Some railway staff were resident with their families at Broken Cross cottages. One lodger there, aged 72, is the oldest railway labourer locally. This shows that men carried on working while they were fit to do so.

The occupier of Gay's Farm, Ford was George Gay, so we can deduce that

'Mr Blake's Farm' was occupied by the other farmer, Mr Good. The latter is recorded as farming 400 acres employing ten men and two boys. Mr Gay senior (aged 45) had moved and his farmer son George was at Gay's Farm, Ford, aged 18 years. This is rather young to be a householder, perhaps, but his sister Fanny seems to be in charge of the domestic side for him (along with a servant). George junior was now running the farm (371 acres) along with ten men and two boys.[32] Meanwhile his father was farming a further 470 acres (Bishop's Down Farm) mainly with sheep and a dairy herd. Another occupation shown in Ford is cordwainer (a shoemaker); James Dicketts with his wife and 4 children, so the growing hamlet was becoming more self-sufficient in trades and skills.

The Hunt family arrived at Ford Farm in 1873[33] and they are recorded in the census returns for more than three decades as they ran Ford Farm as tenants of Mrs King-Wyndham beyond James Hunt's death in 1914. The family tenancy continued through James' son Jeremiah (born 1878) until he purchased the property and land in 1920 from Mrs Campbell Wyndham Long.[34] Jeremiah Hunt was church warden at the little St Francis chapel, which was built on part of this land parcel.

Twentieth century residents

Jeremiah Hunt and his wife Kate had a son James William Pike Hunt while living at 'The Elms', the house built for them on their marriage in 1905.[35] This house still stands and was regarded as 'modern' by James W P Hunt's daughter Audrey when she was small, as it had an indoor toilet. This is in contrast with the 'old, large and cold' farmhouse, across the road, which Jeremiah and his young family had moved into after James senior's death in 1914. The families swapped accommodation in the 1930s, so Audrey had the opportunity to live in both houses. The younger James made many developments on the farm after the Second World War, including a pumped domestic water supply. He later gave a plot of land to the Laverstock school head teacher (Doris Belfield) to build a bungalow; 'Down Cottage' (1951). He was known as 'a staunch supporter of St Andrew's Church and of the chapel in Ford and was a governor of Laverstock primary school for many years'.[36]

Another interesting location nearby is Old Malthouse Lane (just beyond the edge of the parish). This runs uphill from Broken Cross as a continuation of the Roman road from Old Sarum. The route then crosses the London Road to travel toward Winchester. The malthouse here would process barley grain and send their malted products to breweries and makers of ale. The practice of diversification on farms is not new, as this malthouse establishment was later also the local knackers' yard and made glue and other products from retired horses.[37]

The railway provided opportunities for farms to send their produce further away from Salisbury and the growth and needs of city populations made for good trade. With the increasing demand for dairy and grain products there was significant potential for expanded farming and the development of farm-based businesses. The land in Ford was sufficiently fertile to support three separate farms to exist close by. The sheep flocks were exchanged for dairy cattle as milk was required in the towns and cities, transported by rail. There were some drawbacks to the arrival of trains though, as Audrey Coggan recalls being sent to run through crops to stamp out burning smuts from steam locomotives before they could start fires.[38]

Castleford Farm was not mentioned by this title in the 19th century censuses when landowners' names were consistently used for reference. Castleford farmhouse stands on the south side of the Roman road, close to the cross roads with Green Lane. It was owned by the Lodge family of Salisbury in the early 20th century and may have been part of the large Blake's farm nearby. The farmyard with associated land was later sold and new homes were established as The Steadings.[39] During building work here in the 1980s there were fresh archaeological discoveries. Finds recorded include food items associated with a Beaker burial.[40] In the late 20th century a county-wide project was undertaken concerning the position and extent of ancient farms.[41] The research from this thorough examination and recording of buildings and other markers has added more detail to the knowledge of Wiltshire agricultural sites including in this part of the county. Within Ford, as in other localities across the county, there were farmyards and barns placed at a distance from the farm houses (sometimes across parish boundaries). This has made it more difficult now to be clear on which agricultural buildings were attached to each farm.

In summary there has been steady utilisation of and residence within the land in and around Ford, right through from ancient times to the present day.

1   Henrici de Soliaco, 1189, *Liber Henrici de Soliaco, Abbatis Glaston,* [*An Inquisition of the Manors of Glastonbury Abbey,* of the year MCLXXXIX, from the original manuscript in the possession of The Marquis of Bath, Editor Jackson JE, Roxburghe Club publication, 1882, London]

2   Davies, H, 2008, *Roman Roads in Britain,* Shire Archaeology, Cambridge, 28

3   _http://www.english-heritage.org.uk/visit/places/old-sarum/history/, accessed March 2018

4   Musty, J, 1969, 'The excavation of two barrows, one of Saxon date, at Ford, Laverstock, near Salisbury, Wiltshire', *Antiquaries Journal*

5   WSA HER MWI various records for Ford, in the parish of Laverstock and Ford, ©
    Wiltshire Council, accessed March 2018

6   Musty, J, 1969

7   Henrici de Soliaco, 1189

8   Musty, J, 1969

9   WSA HER MWI Laverstock and Ford

10 WSA HER MWI Laverstock and Ford

11 'Houses of the Augustinian canons: Priory of Ivychurch' VCH *Wilts* 3, 289-295

12 TNA; *Glebe terrier of Laverstock and Ford,* 1616

13 TNA; *Prerogative Court of Canterbury and Related Probate Jurisdictions: Will Registers*;
    Class: *PROB 11*; Piece: *325,* the will of William Bragge of Ford, proven 1667

14 HMSO, OS, Sheet 1531, 164E 329N

15 WSA D24/18/7, bundle of papers referring to Ford Mill, Laverstock and Ford, 19th
    century

16 WSA D24/18/7

17 WSA D24/18/7

18 WSA D24/18/7

19 WSA D24/18/7 Cost estimates for improvements include installation of labour-saving
    sifting equipment (1875).

20 Chandler, J H, 1985, *Wiltshire Dissenters' Meeting House Certificates and Registrations
    1689-1852,* WRS, 40, entry number 876

21 1861 Census TNA RG 9/1315 f122

22 Coggan, A, 2014, personal communication with Bryan Evans

23 TNA; *Prerogative Court of Canterbury and Related Probate Jurisdictions: Will Registers*;
    Class: *PROB 11*; Piece: *1607*, the will of John Blake of Ford Farm, written 1792,
    proved 1818

24 Sequential alterations to parish boundaries have influenced records of land ownership
    and residency in census and other records. This has made absolute certainty about 19th
    century farm configuration very difficult. (see chapter 1 Boundaries)

25 1841 Census TNA HO piece 1164, folio 5

26 TNA; *Prerogative Court of Canterbury and Related Probate Jurisdictions: Will Registers*;
    Class: *PROB 11*; Piece: *2095,* The will of John Blake (son of John Blake) of Ford
    Farm, proved 1849

27 1851 Census TNA HO 107/1846 f396

28 Laverstock St Andrew's Church, parish records, (marriages), 1848, entry 42

29 1851 Census TNA HO 107/1846 f397

30 1861 Census TNA RG 9/1315, f122

31 1871 Census TNA RG 10/1952, f40

32 1871 Census TNA RG 10/1952, f81

33 Coggan, A, 2014

34 The Wyndham family had owned land in the parish since before the Enclosure Act of
    1820

35 Coggan, A, 2014

36 Coggan, A, 2014

37 Rippier, C, personal communication April 2018

38 Coggan, A, 2014

39 Rippier, C, 2018

40 WSA HER MWI Laverstock and Ford. Examples of Beaker pottery grave goods can be seen in the Wessex Gallery of Salisbury Museum. Items for the comfort of the deceased in the afterlife were stored in distinctive pottery jars, during the period 2900 BC -1800 BC.

41 WSA; Edwards, R and Lake, J; *Wiltshire & Swindon Farmsteads & Landscape Project*, 2014, English Heritage and Wiltshire Buildings Record

Piety and Poverty

The church through Reformation and Civil War

Bryan Evans

There is no direct evidence of Laverstock Church at this time, but it can hardly have escaped the upheavals going on everywhere else: the image-breaking, the whitewashing over of wall-paintings, the replacing of stained glass with plain. In 1547, at the beginning of Edward VI's reign, a Chantries Act proclaimed the appropriation of chantry assets. If masses were still being said for Sir Hugh Cheney and his wife, then the land and other property which paid for those masses would now have been forfeited to the crown. Confiscations of church goods also began under Edward VI. Many churchwardens responded to the threat either with pre-emptive sales, or by hiding vestments, images and plate. In 1552 a Commission was issued for the survey of those church goods still left, and to enquire into the embezzlement of such goods by 'certain private men.' The Commissioners noted that Laverstock had been left with a chalice of 9½ ounces.[1]

Edward died in 1553. Mary, his half-sister, came to the throne, and all Edward's church legislation was repealed. Altars, images and vestments all came back. Mary died in 1558, and the changes were reversed again as Elizabeth I sought to create a church that was still part of the 'Church universal' but also genuinely reformed. Adherents of the old religion now came under pressure to conform. At first the penalties were relatively mild – a 12d fine, for example, for failure to attend the parish church, and loss of office for failure to take the Oath of Supremacy.[2]

The pressures increased following Pius V's Bull of excommunication against Elizabeth (1570), and the first arrivals of Roman Catholic missionary priests from the Douai seminary in France (1574). In 1581 the fine for not attending church was increased to £20 a month, and because under common law there were twenty-eight days in a month, and thirteen lunar months in a year, the annual total was £260.

We have a local example of the impositions placed on Catholics in the 16th and 17th centuries. One William Fawkenor or Fawconer, of Laverstock, paid £734 in recusancy fines between Michaelmas 1593 and his death in 1608. This was the highest total paid by a Wiltshireman at that time.[3]

The Civil War

Many churches suffered grievously during the Civil War between King Charles I and Parliament, as both sides made use of church buildings as powder stores, prisons, or barracks. We have no record of Laverstock church being so used, but it did not wholly escape the troubles of the times. The Churchwardens' Presentments for 1662 note 'We present that we have not, as yet, a surplice nor a cup for the administration of the communion, both having been plundered from us in the time of the late unhappy wars, but will be provided of both as soon as we can'.[4]

The use of the Anglican Book of Common Prayer was forbidden, and it was replaced by the *Directory of Public Worship*, issued on the authority of parliament in 1645. However, there were clergy who adhered to the Anglican rite for as long as they could. In Laverstock Holy Communion was still being celebrated in accordance with the prayer book in 1646, and many were said to have gone there from Salisbury to take the sacrament after 'the old manner'.[5] In the end the Rev Francis Bayley was barred from preaching, and Francis Bushell was appointed in his place. This happened about 1649.[6]

Seventeenth century Churchwardens' Presentments

Churchwardens were required by canon law to present (report) anything that was amiss in the parish.[7] They were expected to report at least once a year, and usually twice (at Easter and Michaelmas) and at the time of visitation by the bishop or his representative. A wide range of subjects had to be covered, including the state of the church building and the churchyard; any improprieties in the conduct of services; moral offences such as adultery, drunkenness, ribaldry, Sabbath-breaking; not taking communion, not having children baptised, not paying church rates. The early Presentments can be informative, but as time went on the Churchwardens got into the habit of simply writing 'all's well'.

We have already seen that in 1662 the wardens had to acknowledge their lack of a surplice and a communion cup. That same year they had to admit that they did not have either the Book of Homilies, or the Apology (both by Bishop Jewel), 'nor ever had them to our remembrance'.[8] They went on to say, 'we have not had of late common prayer upon Holy days by reason of the long sickness of our Minister.' Three parishioners (Mr Vahan Friend, Mr Robert Friend and John Baker) were 'presented' as having refused to pay their church rates. The wardens stated that the parish clerk was unable either to write or read, 'but he is a poor man and for his dilligence in his office not to be blamed to our knowledge.'

In 1689 the wardens, Simon Williams and Richard Shoesmith, reported: 'We have duoly [duly] considered our oath and the articles given us in charge and do not at present know or find any person or thing in our Church or parish presentable save a generall neglect of our parishioners in not receiveing the sacrament according to canon and the want of a sermon every Sunday but having one but once in three weeks'.[9]

There had been a century and a half of upheaval in church and state. Now, for Laverstock, and, no doubt, much of rural England there were, on the one hand, no great moral lapses to 'present', but, on the other, little of the Word or sacrament to sustain spiritual life. This was how it would be for many years yet.

Society and poor relief
Bryan Evans and Ruth Newman

The labouring poor proved an intractable problem for those in authority during this period. In Laverstock, labourers, often living in tiny hovels, would have been hired seasonally for harvesting, woad growing and general cultivation. Unemployment and malnutrition were especially acute in Salisbury in the late 16th and early 17th centuries; bad harvests and economic depression saw the rural poor coming into the city in search of work and relief. Between 1598 and 1638, 600 vagrants were whipped out of Salisbury – the whipping post was in the Market Place – and returned to their parish of birth so that they would not be a burden on the city. So we find on

Beggar woman, 1602, from the Trevilian manuscript. The Folger digital image collection (LUNA)

6 April 1601 Cecily Musprett, daughter of Thomas Musprett of Laverstock, 'an idle person having no abiding place, is spared her punishment (whipping) because of her sickness. Passport to Laverstoke (sic) where she says she was born; 1 day assigned'.[10]

Rare glimpses emerge of 17th century village life from the disputes which are recorded in the Wiltshire Quarter Sessions. They might on occasions, investigate personal, civil disputes as in the following strange case in Laverstock, which perhaps reflected the uncertainty of life at the time.[11]

This concerned a family altercation in January 1650, between Anne Hutchins and her husband, both from the village. Anne informed the court that 'John Barnes of Laverstock husbandman, has persuaded her husband to depart from her and to live with Barnes and to allow her but ten pounds per annum towards the relief and maintenance of herself and two children, her husband having forty pounds per annum'. The justices were to attempt to end the difference between them, but the outcome is sadly unknown.[12]

At times of economic distress an increase in poverty normally meant a corresponding rise in expenditure. The burden of poor relief was the responsibility of the parish authorities[13] with revenue raised from local taxes. With high rates it was perhaps understandable that parishes might try to avoid responsibility to relieve those who could not prove their 'settlement' or established links to the parish. The Quarter Sessions also considered exceptional claims for relief and often acted with compassion.

In January 1654 the 'General Sessions of the Peace' were held at Salisbury. One case concerned a small house destroyed by fire in Clarendon Park where widow Prewet and her late husband had lived for 20 years. After the fire she and her children moved to Tibbols Lodge in the parish of Laverstock. It was ordered that Mary Prewet and her children should be allowed to stay in the lodge until the inhabitants of Laverstock 'shall show good cause to the court to the contrary,' namely, if they became a burden on the parish.

This is a reference to the Poor Law settlement orders over whether or not Laverstock was the responsible parish to support people who needed poor relief. Two of the justices were to look into the order and deal with any future settlement claim, possibly an attempt to protect a poor family now settled in the village.[14]

Later in the century, February 1685 (old style Julian calendar)[15] we find philanthropic clothier Nicholas Elliott paying 2s 7½d into the poor rate for Laverstock.

The Churchwardens' accounts also record relief payments to 'travelers' in 1687 and 1693, then a flurry of payments in the 1760s.[16] In April 1762, 6d was given 'toapass', that is, 'to a pass', referring to a poor man or woman having a pass that allowed him or her to travel without fear of arrest. On 19 August 1765, five seamen (discharged perhaps after the Seven Years War), were given a relief payment of 6d. In September of that year five men with a pass received 6d, and in October the same sum was paid to a woman.[17]

There is evidence of a poor-house in Milford; this may have been just a cottage or two, but it is possible that some Laverstock paupers were sent here long before the 1830s, with the neighbouring parish paying into the Milford poor rate system.[18] The problem of settlement was complicated legally with many claims and counter-claims. In 1820 the local JPs needed to decide whether 'a poor woman' was the responsibility of Laverstock or Milford parish. Who should support Rebecca Viney? She had 'resided in the Milford poor house for 15 years as a pauper. Before that she worked as a yearly servant to the late Mr Finch of Laverstock [House]. . . at the wages of five pounds per year and remained in such service about eighteen months, when she was received' into the Milford 'Poor House'.[19] No verdict is recorded.

The Settlement laws give us a glimpse into the hardships and insecurity suffered by those who could not prove their claim to relief. Parishes fought to avoid caring for a person without legal settlement. This was particularly true of often heart rending cases relating to the bastardy laws since no parish wanted to take on the additional mouth to feed. Ann Dew in 1820 was living in the parish of St Martin.[20]

> She declared on oath that on or about *21st day of January 1817* she was delivered of a *male* Bastard child within the said Parish of Saint Martin which is now living and is actually chargeable to the same. And the said *Ann Dew* . . . doth declare that *Edward Amor* late of *Laverstock* . . . *labourer*, had carnal Knowledge of her Body and did beget the said *Male* Bastard Child, of which she was delivered . . . and that the said *Edward Amor* is the true and only Father thereof and no other person whatsoever' (signed with her mark).

The Churchwardens' accounts

Further insights into village activities during this period can be gleaned from the accounts of the churchwardens. One of their duties was to make bounty payments for wildlife classed as 'vermin'. Tudor governments became concerned about food supplies and sought to eliminate unwelcome competition. The first legislation was enacted in 1532. Then under the 1566 Act for Protecting Grain parishes were enjoined to take up arms against various bird species, foxes, hedgehogs, otters, moles, polecats and badgers.[21] The heads, or eggs of bird species, had to be shown to the churchwardens who then paid for each a sum of money raised from parish rates.

The 'war on wildlife' seems to have reached a peak in the mid-18th century, and by the early 19th century it was drawing to a close although sparrow payments continued for several decades, providing a welcome bonus to supplement low agricultural wages. In Laverstock the 'war' seems to have been carried on somewhat erratically. Churchwardens' accounts survive from 1687, and these record payments in respect of stoats (2d each), hedgehogs (4d) and sparrows (6d for three dozen) until 1722. Then there is a break before payments resume from 1757 onwards. The otter (2s for one) first appears among the Laverstock bounty payments in 1732. But the 'pest' that seems to have been hounded most consistently was the polecat (4d each).

Surprisingly perhaps in the context of the time, the Churchwardens looked after not only their own community but also those far beyond the parish, showing concern for the wider world. In 1655 the Waldensians, a small Protestant group in northern Italy, suffered massacre, stirring horror throughout Protestant Europe. Oliver Cromwell proclaimed a fast and a relief fund for homeless survivors, with collections to be made in all churches. Laverstock gave 7s 8d. For comparison we may note that West Harnham gave 6s 8d and Stratford-sub-Castle £4 7s 0d.[22]

The available records for these years show considerable anxiety for the parish rates but, coupled with this, a genuine concern for the unfortunate, which stretches over two centuries.

1   Mackenzie, Rev E C Walcott (annotator), 1870, 'Inventories of Church Goods, and Chantries of Wilts', *WANHM* 12, 369

2   The 1559 Act of Supremacy restored Henry VIII's 1534 Act, which Mary had repealed. Elizabeth also introduced the Oath of Supremacy requiring anyone taking public or church office to swear allegiance to the monarch as head of the church as well as head of state. Catholics who refused to attend the parish church, and who also refused the Oath of Supremacy were called 'recusants'.

3   Trappes-Lomax, Brigadier T B, 'Roman Catholicism' VCH *Wilts* 3, 89n. In Old St Andrew's there was a memorial on the north wall of the nave to William Fawkener, of Westbury, Esquire (died 1644). This was not the recusant William, but his nephew, the son of Raphe (Ralph) Fawconer. See R Colt Hoare, 1837, *The Modern History of South Wiltshire*, 5, 109

4   Churchwardens' Presentments for 1662, WSA D1/54/1/3

5   Whiteman, Anne, 'The Church of England 1542-1837', VCH *Wilts* 3, 42, citing AG Matthews, *Walker Revised*, 382, 373, 370 (J Walker was the author of *Sufferings of the Clergy*, 1702)

6   Wordsworth, Rev Christopher, 'A list of clergy in Wiltshire, outed, sequestered, or silenced, 1643-1660', *WANHM* 34, 165, 173, 176, citing Shaw J, II., 547

7   Surviving records of presentments go back to the first quarter of the 17th century.

8   Richard Bancroft, Archbishop of Canterbury from 1604-1610, had ordered that the

Apology be placed in churches. This was the *Apologia ecclesiae Anglicanae* ('The Apology of the Anglican Church') by John Jewel, bishop of Salisbury from 1559-1571

9 Churchwardens' Presentments for 24 September 1689, WSA D1/54/12/3

10 Salisbury's register of passports for the early 17th century represents a unique record. Slack, Paul (ed), 1975 *Poverty in early-Stuart Salisbury*. WRS 30

11 Charles I had been beheaded in 1649 and many felt that their world had been turned upside down.

12 Slocombe, Ivor (2014), *Wiltshire Quarter Sessions Order Book, 1642-1654*, WRS 67, No 574

13 Normally the churchwardens and overseers of the poor

14 Slocombe 2014 No 927

15 Up to 1752 the year began on Lady Day, 25 March (the Annunciation) so February 1685 would have been the eleventh month of the year. The Gregorian calendar was adopted in Britain in 1752 and the year started on 1st Jan.

16 These were not travellers as in modern usage, but the destitute needing to travel back to their native parish where they could seek poor relief.

17 In 1697-8, payment was recorded for 215 'passengers' passing through Laverstock, possibly large groups of demobbed soldiers and sailors and those with settlement passes. Despite economic depression and concern about the poor, a recent Jacobite assassination attempt against William III, and the end of the nine years war against France, this seems an exceptionally high number, and remains a mystery. WSA 1324/25

18 The death was recorded in the *Salisbury Journal* (Dec 1822) of the former master of Milford workhouse. In 1836-7 the Alderbury Poor Law Union erected a workhouse on Coombe Road at Harnham, following the Poor Law Amendment Act of 1834. This covered 22 parishes including Laverstock and Milford.

19 G23 1/138 WSA, settlement order. The laws of settlement meant that a person was entitled to receive relief in their parish of settlement. This usually meant being born in a parish, or by marriage, but settlement could be gained by being hired for a year as in the case of Rebecca Viney.

20 WSA G23/1/145/119. The normal practice was to try to find the father and make him take responsibility. The bastardy orders were printed with gaps to complete the details (shown in italics).

21 Cragoe, Matthew and McDonagh, Briony, 2013, 'Parliamentary enclosure, vermin and the cultural life of English parishes, 1750-1850', *Continuity and Change*, 28, 29

22 *WANHM* 25, 112-118. The accounts also record for 1700 the collection of 10s 10d towards the redemption of British slaves in Morocco, toiling on building projects after being taken at sea by the notorious Barbary pirates.

Agriculture: a Time of Change

Innovation from the late 16th century
Ruth Newman and Ken Smith

The chalklands around Salisbury, including Laverstock, saw important advances in farming techniques in this period. The main profits came from corn growing within the open fields. Wheat, barley and oats were cultivated by peasants tending their strips, with one third of the land lying fallow every year, benefiting from the sheep that manured and enriched the soil. The more valuable wheat straw was also bound into sheaves for thatching. Horses, rather than oxen were used for ploughing on the chalklands. But changes were underway in Wiltshire particularly during the 17th century and many local farmers grasped the new opportunities in the river valleys around Salisbury.

Woad cultivation

One of the new crops cultivated in Laverstock was woad, a valuable rich blue dye for the Wiltshire cloth industry. From the late 16th century it began to be grown extensively on the surrounding chalk downlands, rather than imported. There were 59 growers in Wiltshire with a few wealthy merchants operating on a large scale in this very profitable trade with an increasing demand from the dyers. George Bedford, the elder, a wealthy Salisbury clothier, cultivated many acres of woad at Martin, and Cranborne Chase. When he died in 1607 his processed woad alone was valued at £400. He also owned a cloth mill at Laverstock possibly on the same site as the current Mill House. Here the blue dye was used and supplied to clothiers in both Wiltshire and Somerset. Those employed in the trade could be recognised specifically by their blue colouring and the unpleasant smell caused by the fermenting of the leaves to produce the dye.

Small areas of land in Laverstock were also used for the growing of woad despite a proclamation from Queen Elizabeth I in 1585 that the crop should be restricted because food production would suffer in times of hardship and inflation. She also believed that the smell 'infected the air'. Woad was a notoriously 'hungry' crop and was believed to exhaust the soil, with its cultivation depriving the sheep flocks of valuable grazing. On the other hand it was labour intensive and provided welcome employment for the village poor. In December 1585 Salisbury growers Thomas Marshall, haberdasher, and Robert Eyre, clothier, were cultivating land in Laverstock. Six acres of pasture, two acres of sheep down and a ten acre enclosed conniger (rabbit warren) had been turned over to woad with another two acres 'in the common fields of Milford'.[1] The importance of the crop gradually declined as new imported dyes became available, followed by artificial dyestuffs in the 19th century.

Nicholas Elliott's account book (1663-1726) records the importance of the village fields for Salisbury clothiers. The Elliotts owned property in Laverstock and neighbouring parishes and account books include the costs of shepherding and the importance of 'folding' the sheep flock on the land to fertilise it (see below). The soil depended on the sheep dung and large numbers were kept primarily to improve the arable crops. Elliott also refers to floated water meadows, and their widespread use was the most important agricultural innovation around Salisbury from the early 17th century.[2]

Water meadows and drowners

The meadows of Laverstock show clear sign of former irrigation. William Cobbett in the early 19th century noted how the upper slopes of the chalklands were used for grazing sheep whilst lower down the deeper soils allowed arable farming. On the valley floor the alluvial soils resulted in rich meadows.[3]

Skilfully managed, expensive watercourses, hatches and sluices permitted a thin film of river water (approximately two cm deep) to run over the field surface, warming the soil and depositing sediment. This stimulated grass growth by a number of weeks, giving early nutriment to ewes and their weaning lambs in the 'hungry months' of March/April. The sheep were also a source of valuable nitrogen. The flocks were 'folded' – temporarily fenced in, on the arable fields to manure them. Later in the year, the meadows produced one or sometimes two crops of hay for winter animal feed. More sheep further enhanced the crops of wheat, and barley for beer, and the success of the new system meant that it spread widely. When experts refer to an 'early agricultural revolution' in the 17th century, the Salisbury district including Laverstock played an important part in this progress.[4]

The hatches and channels used in the water meadow system were maintained and operated by skilled workmen known as drowners. A deed of 1801 gives detailed particulars of the Laverstock estate of the late Robert Cooper including instructions for 'clearing the watercourses used for the Watering and Drowning

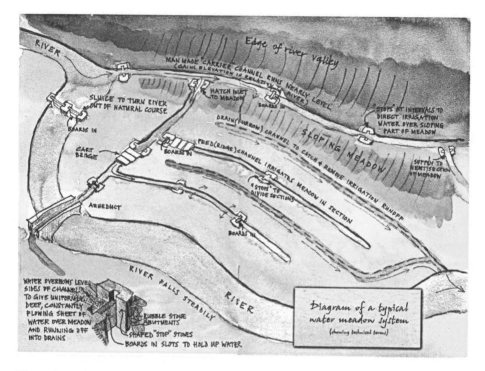

The following labels appear on the diagram:

RIVER

MAN MADE 'CARRIER' CHANNEL RUNS NEARLY LEVEL (GAINS ELEVATION IN RELATION TO RIVER)

Edge of river valley

SLUICE TO TURN RIVER OUT OF NATURAL COURSE

HATCH INLET TO MEADOW

BOARDS IN

'STOPS' AT INTERVALS TO DIRECT IRRIGATION WATER OVER SLOPING PART OF MEADOW

BOARDS IN

SLOPING MEADOW

DRAIN (FURROW) CHANNEL TO CATCH & REMOVE IRRIGATION RUNOFF

CART BRIDGE

BOARDS IN

FEED (RIDGE) CHANNEL IRRIGATES MEADOW IN SECTION

SUPPLY TO NEXT SECTION OF MEADOW

AQUEDUCT

'STOPS' TO DIVIDE SECTIONS

BOARDS IN

RIVER FALLS STEADILY

RIVER

WATER OVERFLOWS LEVEL SIDES OF CHANNEL TO GIVE UNIFORMLY DEEP, CONSTANTLY FLOWING SHEET OF WATER OVER MEADOW AND RUNNING OFF INTO DRAINS

RUBBLE STONE ABUTMENTS

SHAPED "STOP" STONES

BOARDS IN SLOTS TO HOLD UP WATER

Diagram of a typical water meadow system (showing technical terms)

The working of a water meadow system: from The conservation of water meadow structures by Mike Clark, © Hampshire County Council

of Part of the Premises . . . the late Mr Cooper kept the Hatches and Hatch wood in Repair at his own expense' while the Manor Farm buildings included a drowner's house.[5]

This procedure was cost-effective for much of the 18th and 19th centuries but the water meadows were gradually abandoned as corn/sheep farming became unprofitable with new artificial fertilisers and agricultural depression. Gordon Hoskins, in the late 20th century, wrote of one remaining hatch 'just above [Laverstock mill] . . . through which water can be diverted from the mill leat direct to the old river' but all the other hatches have been removed 'so the practice of drowning the meadows to give "an early bite" is no longer possible'.[6]

The enclosure award for Laverstock, 1820
Ruth Newman and Ken Smith

The term 'enclosure' is difficult to define but as a generalisation it involved the extinction of common rights; the classic three or four large open fields in strips with no physical territorial boundaries disappeared, and became plots of land in separate ownership with boundaries between people's land. Normally associated with parliamentary enclosure acts of the 18th and 19th centuries, it has been calculated that between 1760 and 1800 there were 2000 acts covering two million acres of land and this doubled by 1850.

One of the problems for the historian is that every village enclosure was different and often occurred over centuries. The process began by private agreement and became a widespread feature of the English farming landscape from the 16th century. Certainly in Wiltshire, and Laverstock is a good example, much land was already enclosed before the age of parliamentary acts, which were often just the final stage in a village's agricultural history. This more formal method (described below), was subject to outside scrutiny, very expensive and potentially controversial. No one doubted that the larger farmers benefited from this system which normally increased the value of their land. In Wiltshire the enclosure acts date from 1770 to 1869 reaching a peak in the first 20 years of the 19th century. Laverstock's act of 1818 (with its award two years later) came towards the end of this period.[7]

What did enclosures replace at Laverstock

There are few records relating to early enclosures but it appears that the open field system was under 'attack' in Laverstock as early as the 15th century as the following indicates: 'In 1441 a meadow called New Mead had been inclosed "under Laverstock", no doubt meaning in that part of Milford east of the Bourne'.[8]

The exact position regarding the open and common fields in the village before 1820 is unclear, even contradictory. Peter Bathurst's 1725 estate map of Laverstock and Ford (see 52), displays few obvious open fields.[9] The only conspicuous strips are seen in the water meadows, mainly to the west of the Bourne (between the current river and railway line), where either water-courses or hedges delineate different holdings. But much of Milford remained unenclosed in 1800 and, as shown on the Bathurst map, probably the land beyond Petersfinger, due south of Laverstock, known as 'Laverstock Detached'. The 1801 crop returns for Wiltshire refer to 'open fields [occupying] the greater part of the parish of Laverstock'.[10] A more detailed map drawn by Salisbury architect John Peniston in 1812 shows not only the water meadow divisions and the beginnings of the amalgamation of strips, but more obviously plots of land belonging to Edward Baker, one of the major landowners, dispersed throughout the unenclosed common fields.[11]

While it is impossible to assess accurately the agricultural state of Laverstock before 1820, the parliamentary enclosure map does clarify the new field holdings.

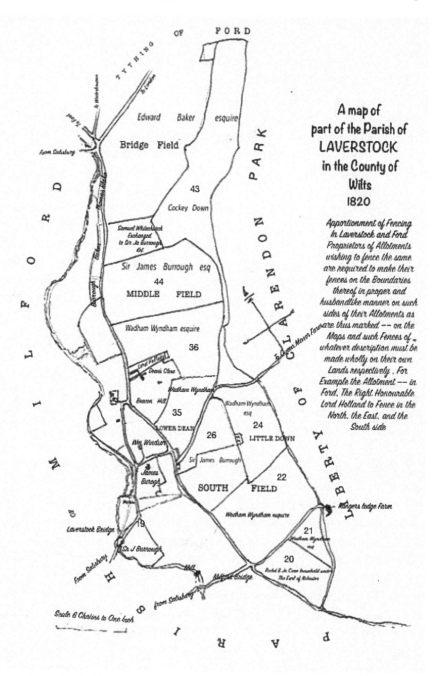

A map of
part of the Parish of
LAVERSTOCK
in the County of
Wilts
1820

Apportionment of Fencing
in Laverstock and Ford.
Proprietors of Allotments
wishing to fence the same
are required to make their
fences on the Boundaries
thereof in proper and
husbandlike manner on such
sides of their Allotments as
are thus marked -- on the
Maps and such Fences of
whatever description must be
made wholly on their own
Lands respectively. For
Example the Allotment -- in
Ford, The Right Honourable
Lord Holland to Fence in the
North, the East, and the
South side

The large, irregular fields shown on the 1725 estate map seem to correspond with
the three fields on the 1820 parliamentary enclosure map notably Bridge Field,
Middle Field and South Field. The apparent importance of these names might
be the result of their former status as open fields. The other smaller fields shown

in 1725 were possibly early private enclosures accomplished by individuals buying land from the lord of the Manor. Thus, the history of enclosure in Laverstock might reflect early exchanges among landowners and their tenants, perhaps from Tudor times, completed by parliamentary enclosure in 1820.

The timing of enclosure

Much land was enclosed during the wars against France (1793-1815) because of high prices and restrictions on imports, but this does not explain why many Wiltshire farmers chose to enclose in a period of post war depression with 'very considerable distress' for the labouring poor. The reduction in demand for foodstuffs and wool together with poor harvests might have been an incentive for some landowners to consider enclosure as a means of rationalising their land and raising rents. This could explain why Laverstock was enclosed within five years of the war ending as landed proprietors seized opportunities to extend their already considerable holdings.

The parliamentary enclosure at Laverstock

At some time in 1818, the decision to press ahead with a parliamentary enclosure act was made by the owners of the majority of the village land (probably just the few landowners in the parish mentioned below).

> An Act for inclosing Lands within the parish of Laverstock including the Tything of Ford' was passed on the 8th May 1818. It refers to 'divers Open and Common Fields, Common Meadows, Common Downs, and other Wastes' amounting to 1,211 acres. The following paragraph indicates those promoting the act. Lord Holland, as Lord of the Manor, was entitled to the *'Soil of the Commons and Wastes'* and *'Lord Holland, Sir James Burrough Knight, Wadham Wyndham Esq, Edward Baker Esq, Samuel Whitchurch Esq, Thomas Blake Esq, and others, are Proprieters of the Lands in the said Open and Common Fields . . . , and the lands of such Proprietors lie greatly intermixed and dispersed, and are otherwise inconveniently situate; and the Proprietors . . . are desirous that the* [fields etc] *should be divided and allotted . . amongst them proportionately according to the Value of their respective Estates.*

Each allotment should be enclosed and held *'in severalty'* (privately). Clearly, the few gentlemen farmers in the village were the instrumental voices behind enclosure and would be the key beneficiaries.[12]

The first public notice following the act appeared in the *Salisbury Journal* on 18 October 1818 by which time the three commissioners had been appointed. They visited the village with surveyor John Tubb from Fisherton, to decide on claims to the land. Meetings took place regularly for nearly two years 'at the house of Samuel Jones (the proprietor) called 'The White Hart Inn' (St John Street).

Notice of the forthcoming enclosure and the meetings were also announced on several consecutive Sundays in the parish church. These first statements of intent confirmed the rumours that must have been circulating in the village for months. At the meetings those whose homes and farms were affected by the act could present legal evidence of their rightful ownership. Many of the cottagers would have no such proof, their tenure being established by long custom rather than a legal framework, and potential loss of homes and livelihood must have caused great concern.

An enclosure award usually provided cottagers with alternative land in compensation for the loss of common rights, although often of poor quality and limited extent. The lower slopes of Cockey Down had already been amalgamated into Middle Field, and Lower Dean (field). It is just feasible that the narrow strip on the upper reaches of Cockey Down might have been provided for the village poor in compensation, but there are no examples of opposition to the Act; the fact that the award took only two years (compared with Mere's 14 years) implies that the large landowners' wishes were overwhelming. In contrast 60 very small tenant farmers of Mere who grazed their cattle on the commons gave 'notice that we dissent to . . . [the bill] for inclosing the commons. This would be hurtful to the inhabitants of Mere . . . and particularly distressing to the poor.' When the bill became law there were riots and the military was summoned.[13]

As far as can be determined the Laverstock commissioners acted scrupulously in looking at the 'rights and interests of the proprietors'. They posted their frequent meetings in the *Salisbury Journal* for weeks at a time, and gave opportunities for dissent. Just as the proceedings of planning committees today are open to public consultation, so the proposed 'allotments' were laid out for interested parties to see and to raise objections 'in writing'. Public and private roads, and footways were determined by the commissioners and described in comprehensive detail; they were widened, or diverted around the new fields. Main roads were to be a generous 50 ft wide (eg the Salisbury to Ford road), private roads 30 ft. New ditches, drains and watercourses were to be provided, plus a parish gravel pit on the lower slopes of Cockey Down.

The actual enclosure award was on 5 July 1820 affecting over 1000 acres, when boundaries were changed and any remaining common rights disappeared.[14] The map confirms the changes; the largest landowner remained Sir James Burrough with 227 acres. Thomas Blake gentleman farmer of Ford owned 212 acres but leased other fields including 101 acres from The Bishop of Salisbury.[15] Samuel Whitchurch, Edward Baker, Wadham Wyndham and Lord Holland among others all benefited from the reorganisation. Well connected brothers Richard and John Cooe increased their tenancies while William Windsor (described as a carrier) was left with two small allotments, one within the asylum grounds, the other to become the site of the Barracks. The exchanges reveal how the landowners used enclosure to their own mutual benefit. Small plots were added to larger fields eg James Burrough's 89 acre 'Middle' field gained the adjoining 15 acres from Samuel Whitchurch with a similar transfer in reverse. The complicated procedure proved beneficial to the participants increasing the efficiency of their holdings. None of this answers the query about the fate of Ned Pearce whose five acre croft was incorporated into Samuel Whitchurch's land in Ford. The bill for the whole process was £2275 16 shillings. This would have covered the fees and expenses of commissioners as well as the costs of surveying, mapping and all relevant paperwork. The landowners both had to pay these costs and were legally bound to fence their new allotments. In order to help cover his costs the bishop sold nine acres of land to Thomas Blake.

The importance of the watermeadows

The only obvious strips in Laverstock on the 1725 Bathurst map were the watermeadows. Their value was almost incalculable and this was recognised by the award. Sections of the meadowland were divided between the great landowners (see map). Those to the south of St Thomas's Bridge beside the River Bourne were clearly apportioned to Thomas Blake, Edward Baker and Sir James Burrough.

Possible effects of enclosure

It is difficult to reach conclusions about the impact of enclosure on Laverstock because little conclusive data exists. Probably, in the short term there may have been some disruption and hardship as a result of the changes in land ownership. We cannot determine the fate of the village poor but for the ordinary farming population, post-enclosure Laverstock was a challenging environment, although not solely because of the award. A few displaced agricultural workers may have found employment at the Asylum or left to find work in nearby Salisbury or further afield. Some possibly considered emigration which was being discussed in the *Salisbury Journal* at the time. Over a longer period, the effects could well have been positive with both greater agricultural productivity and more efficient use of the land. Whatever the results, enclosure changed the look of the landscape permanently. The rectilinear field patterns of enclosure as laid out by surveyors, shows itself as the chequer-board 'traditional' English countryside. It only serves to remind us just how artificial our 'natural' landscape really is.

Throughout the 19th century the numbers employed in agriculture in the village declined steadily and discontent surfaced quickly just ten years later with the agricultural labourers' revolt of 1830.

The Swing Riots of 1830
Ruth Newman

There is no reason to suppose that Laverstock agricultural labourers in the 1820s fared any better than others in south Wiltshire where wages were among the lowest in the country at seven shillings a week. Cobbett described the Wiltshire labourers as 'the worst used . . . on the face of the earth.'[16] The proximity to Salisbury probably provided little alternative employment in the pre-railway age, and domestic industries like spinning were declining. Local farmers had no incentive to increase wages or to provide accommodation.

The agricultural riots, the Swing Riots, took place in 1830, one of the most troubled years of English history as the movement for political reform was gaining strength. In the autumn a wave of riots in the rural south and east of England spread like wildfire as the agricultural labourers rose in revolt with 3000 incidents reported.[17] Many were near starving, illiterate, underemployed, and suffering the effects of terrible harvests in 1828 and 1829. Low wages provided the underlying causes of the riots but the actual spark came with the introduction of the new threshing machines which took away the guaranteed winter work of manual threshing. The new machines became the symbols of the labourers' misery and the main targets for destruction.[18]

The riots began in Kent in August 1830 but by November had spread through Wiltshire and reached the Salisbury area with threshing machines attacked in many of the local villages. There is no evidence of involvement from Laverstock or Ford labourers although they must have followed events closely as fellow workers from Idmiston, Odstock, and Alderbury were active. There were probably no threshing machines in the village but nearby at Bishop Down Farm, unrest occurred and it is possible that men from Laverstock were drawn in by the contagious element of the mob.[19] '*On Tuesday last (23rd) the citizens of Salisbury were considerably excited by the information that a party of rioters, [possibly 500] after destroying a threshing machine of Mr Colbourne's of Bishop Down's Farm, were proceeding, armed with bludgeons, iron bars and portions of machinery they had broken, towards this city, for the purpose . . . of destroying the iron foundry of Mr Figes. Mr Wyndham of the College placed himself at the head of the Special Constables and supported by a detachment of the Salisbury Yeomanry met them at the entrance to the town*' (near the Greencroft). The mob charged but was driven back, 22 rioters were arrested with 17 committed to the County Gaol. There was a real sense of crisis as the Guildhall was put under guard all night, but the local riots continued culminating in the violent 'battle of Pyt House' in the parish of

Agriculture: a time of change

The photograph shows part of the threshing machinery. In the 1830s this was small, usually horse powered and consequently easy to destroy.

Tisbury.[20] By early December the riots had been quelled but 2000 awaited trial in the country as a whole. The largest trials took place in Wiltshire at Salisbury Guildhall in January 1831. In all, 339 prisoners were brought before the court, mainly accused of machine breaking, and the sentences were harsh. Two men at Salisbury were sentenced to death, although later reprieved, but 150 were sentenced to transportation, for periods of at least seven years with little hope of return, including rioters at Idmiston who had demolished Charles Blake's threshing machine.[21]

One of the curious and frustrating factors about the trials is the omission of all references to Bishop Down Farm even though a threshing machine was destroyed and the mob was threatening Salisbury. What happened to the 17 local rioters committed to Fisherton gaol 'for further examination'? Perhaps farmer Colbourne chose not to press charges or it was simply regarded as an isolated incident with no arson involved or demands for money? The trials and sentences were reported in great detail but there is no evidence of how the agricultural labourers in Laverstock and Ford felt about the uprising. It is unlikely that they had security in their jobs but they might have feared reprisal from the great landowners if involved. Perhaps they lacked a motivational skilled leader who might have persuaded them to act? The 1841 census records 53 persons involved in farming in the village, a substantial number. Did they secretly support their fellow workers' protests? We shall never know, but local riots would have been watched by the villagers with a variety of emotions.

Several years later Mr Colbourne's Bishop Down Farm was advertised in the *Salisbury Journal* with 'a very important sale of farming stock.'[22] The scale of his enterprise was apparent, including 900 pure Southdown sheep, 12 cart horses, 200 acres of arable, a great deal of machinery and significantly 'a capital 4-horse power thrashing machine'. Was this perhaps the replacement for the one destroyed in 1830?

In the aftermath, there is nothing to indicate any pay rise for the local agricultural labourers. An account book of 1847-50 kept by John Blake of Ford records farm expenditure, and his labourers' wages. Common jobs were grass mowing, hoeing, reaping oats or wheat, and mowing barley, while beer money was a necessary expense for outdoor work. Many villagers' names are identifiable eg in 1849 Reuben Mullins earned just 16 shillings for two weeks work while a 'boy' earned five shillings. The shepherd earned 18s for the fortnight, his wife adding just an extra two shillings.[23] The grind of agricultural poverty still existed cheek by jowl in the mid 19th century with those living in the great houses of the village.

Manor Farm
Ruth Newman

The 1841 census records 60% of those in employment involved in farming in Laverstock and Ford. This percentage declined in the 19th century with agricultural depression, mechanisation and greater diversity of employment. Farm labourers continued to leave the land in the new century, especially single men. But agriculture remained an essential component of the village economy until beyond the Second World War.

Manor Farm was the principal farm in Laverstock (originally known as Laverstock Farm) and long predates the others. The farmhouse is a well preserved mid-17th century building.[24] To a great extent the exterior is unchanged with its attractive limestone and flint chequers and tiled roof, with the porch and northern (kitchen) extension as late 19th century additions.[25] But the farmhouse today has lost its land and outbuildings, except a barn and the cowman's cottage. The latter, attractively restored and known in 2019 as White Cottage was the home of James Cable, carter on the farm, who lived here in 1901 with his wife and six children.

In 1820 the farmhouse belonged to Edward Baker, but by 1842 the tithe map shows the Manor Farm 'with outbuildings and yard' in the ownership

Manor farmhouse, a well preserved 17th century building, with the cowman's cottage on left.
Photograph, c1911, private collection

of Ann Burrough, with tenants as John and Richard Cooe. Following the brothers' deaths in the 1840s, a notice appeared advertising the impressive sale of Southdown sheep comprising '519 capital Ewes, 200 Lambs and 10 Rams', an indication of the importance of the water meadow system in the village.[26] Indeed, there is evidence that Manor Farm included 'a drowner's houfe' as early as 1799.[27] In 1870-1871 it was briefly tenanted by Elisha Parsons who had previously farmed with his father at Roche Court. He was appointed overseer of the poor for Laverstock in 1870 but his renown was short-lived when he was declared bankrupt in October 1871.[28]

The influential Blake family owned the farm for much of the 19th century. Following Charles Blake's death the 'valuable freehold estate' was sold in May 1888 for £4000; 'comprising capital farm residence, extensive homestead and 156 acres of sound land' with the normal mix of arable, 'fertile meadow' and pasture.[29] A further sale of Laverstock and Ford farms in 1895 is perhaps indicative of the difficult times for agriculture at the end of the 19th century as large scale foreign imports of first wheat and later refrigerated meat flooded the market, reducing agricultural profits.

Manor Farmhouse itself was occupied in 1901 by 62 year old Thomas Rose, born in Dorset to a farming family. He was the father of ten daughters and just one son, the ninth child, Benjamin (1877-1961). On his arrival in Laverstock he was living with his wife Mary, two daughters and his son who worked for him. Thomas died in 1907 and by the following year William Lywood (older brother to Albert at New Farm) was running his business from Laverstock Farm Dairy advertising for a 'respectable youth' for a milk round.[30] The rising demand for liquid milk meant that increasingly farmers switched to dairy production.

By the 1920s James Keevil of Manor Farm was probably responsible for taking the milk from Laverstock for sale in the 'Cathedral Dairy', London Road (currently Estcourt Road) owned by J C Keevil and Son.[31] The Keevil family lost their son Ernest in a motor accident near Portsmouth in 1921, and as an Army officer he was given a military burial in St Andrews Church. Subsequently, ill health forced James Keevil into retirement and in 1926 the expanded Manor Farm was put up for sale advertising 184 acres (freehold), excellent pasture, arable and downland. The farm's permanent pasture covered most of Laverstock Down, and the area now occupied by the schools. The farmhouse was described as having 'modern conveniences, and four excellent cottages', price £5,500, 'one of the cheapest farms in the Salisbury district', a reflection again of economic depression and agricultural decline.[32]

Contemporary with the Lywoods at New Farm was Herbert (Bert) Latham. Born and raised in Lacock, he bought Manor Farm in 1927 and remained there until his death in 1965. It remained central to village life in the first half of the 20th century. As recorded elsewhere in the 1920s (see 203), children collected fresh milk daily and the cows processed twice a day through the village to fertile fields on the edge of the Downs where currently (2019) nearly 2000 students study.

The land was sold in the 1960s for building. Manor Farm's 'home pasture' of two meadows was transformed into Riverside Close and Willow Close and school playing fields became Elm Close.[33]

New Farm
Ruth Newman

New (Manor) Farm Laverstock was so called because in September 1865 a destructive fire destroyed Henry Cooper's 'old' farm house, occupied by his bailiff, and situated near the Green (see 131-2). The 'living farm' included the land up to St Thomas's Bridge, and Cooper, a solicitor from Castle Street Salisbury, built a house for his bailiff in Bridge Field, over ½ mile to the north towards the London Road.[34] Cooper owned the house only briefly, selling it in 1868 as a going concern.[35] By 1871 Mrs Jane Lear, 36 years old, and recently widowed, was head of a 150 acre farm, employing two men and a boy.

New Farm, photograph Roy Bexon, 2018

NEW FARM, LAVERSTOCK.
One and a-half Mile from Salisbury.

MR. JOHN WATERS is favoured with instructions from Henry Cooper, Esq., (who is relin-
quishing the Farm), to SELL by AUCTION on the Premises,
on MONDAY, MARCH 30, at One o'clock,—The under-
mentioned

FARM IMPLEMENTS, &c., viz. :—

3 iron-arm waggons, 3 carts, 7 coulter corn drill, Rawlings'
3 coulter turnip and manure ditto; Tasker's iron 18 inch
double cylinder roller, grass seed machine, two-wheel presser,
winnowing machine, scarifier and turnip cutter; 3 iron and 5
wooden harrows, pair of iron drags, 2 Tasker's ploughs,
wooden roller, water barrel on wheels, pair of broad wheels
with iron axles and shafts, chaff cutter, 40 corn sacks, 2 corn
bins, wheel-barrow, barn and dairy utensils, sheep troughs
and cages, hurdles, 2 pair of trace and 1 pair of thill harness,
small shepherd's house, four-wheel phæton, &c., together with

A HANDSOME YEARLING HEIFER,

and a BLACK HORSE, quiet to ride and drive in double
and single harness.

Catalogues ready. **[4083**

Sale of farm, March 1868 (Salisbury Journal)

Albert Lywood (1852–1927) was the farmer at New Farm in 1911. He knew the village having spent part of his youth at St Andrew's School when his father, George, was a substantial market gardener in Laverstock, managing 50 acres and employing five workers. The Lywoods were resident farmers here for many years in the 20th century through two world wars, with Albert's son Alfred (1888–1959) listed in the 1939 Register. Hence, locally it was often called 'Lywood's Farm' to avoid confusion with Manor Farm. The farmhouse is an impressive double fronted house, set back from the road, with a mixture of Georgian and Victorian elements. Probably built in the early 1860s it is old fashioned for its time with windows and doors which have a distinctly earlier 'feel'. A 1920 sale catalogue refers to 'a good residence', with a two stall nag stable, coach house and cow house plus 'three excellent underground cellars'. The largest of these still possesses a long butcher's rail with hooks; intriguingly Albert Lywood was working as a butcher and cattle dealer in Fisherton in 1901, so possibly brought that trade to Laverstock with him. The 1920 auctioneer's catalogue also describes a typical medium dairy and corn farm of 162 acres, (let to Mr Albert Lywood), a mixed area of arable, pasture and productive meadows. Most of the riverbank meadows on the west side of the current

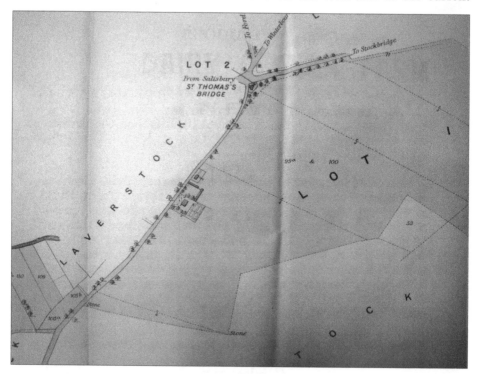

1920 auctioneer's catalogue showing site of farm (lot 1) and also tollhouse cottage at St Thomas's Bridge (lot 2) WSA 776/111

Church Road belonged to the farm and stretched from below St Thomas's Bridge to just south of the church.[36]

A further public auction of the 'exceptionally useful Mixed Agricultural freehold Farm' was held by Woolley and Wallis during the war in March 1943. Of the 155 acres, 90 were arable, 'suitable for mechanical cultivation', 21 pasture, 17 meadow down and 27 meadows abutting the River Bourne. The land was portrayed as being 'in fine heart' and 'capable of increased production in Milk and Corn'. In many ways the details were similar to the sale of 1920 but as well as the agricultural details, the 'long Road Frontages with Important Development Values' were stressed, perhaps a sign of the future for the village.[37] Following the sale of the farm, the stock and machinery were auctioned including the dairy cows and a 1938 Fordson tractor. In July 1943 an advert appeared from T Cook, Netherhampton, Salisbury for a foreman for New Farm 'able to control and arrange work for a small staff', and T and R T Cook were the listed farmers at New Farm until the 1970s.[38]

During the war a home guard unit was stationed in the stable or carriage shed. Later the farm contained a dairy unit and piggery and the house was divided into two flats. In 1996 it was bought and restored by Doctors James and Beth Robertson and remains a private residence.[39]

Laverstock Mill
Ruth Newman

Laverstock Mill was mentioned in the Domesday survey but it is not known whether this was on the current site in Riverside Road. The brickwork and masonry of the present building date to the late 17th century but the house is effectively of the early 19th century, much altered and recently restored.

The miller was an influential member of the community and the mill a focus of village life, occasionally playing a vital role in local history. During the 1627 outbreak of the plague, one third of the population of Salisbury was said to be 'sick of the famine . . . and to look as . . . pale as death'. The Mayor, John Ivie, coped with the catastrophe as the rich fled the city, but fearful of mass starvation he requested Mr Limming of Laverstock to send 'one quarter of wheat and a quarter of barley ready ground for the poor . . . he having a mill of his own to do it, which was accordingly sent'.[40]

By the early 18th century the mill certainly stood on its present site and is shown on Andrews' and Dury's 1773 map of Wiltshire as 'Laverstock Mill manufactory'. Peter Bathurst's 1725 map shows both the line of the original river and the mill leat. The 'river' alongside the road leading from the village

View towards Laverstock Mill c1911, showing both the mill leat (foreground) and original river, just visible

to the Mill House is actually the leat constructed to provide a head of water to drive the mill wheel. The river, much reduced in size, joins the leat below the mill, the water flowing over the sluice which was built to replace the original hatches.[41]

The Blake family, long associated with mills at Ford and neighbouring Winterbourne Earls, also owned Laverstock Mill. Daniel Shergold is listed as the miller in Pigot's commercial directory of 1830.[42] He died in 1833 and his widow Sarah immediately announced that it was her 'intention, with the Assistance of her SON, to continue the business'. The new widow had more to contend with than milling when, just a few months later, she was the victim of a forced entry and robbery at the mill.[43]

By 1841 the young John Sutton was the residential miller, renting ten acres of land from Ann Burrough. In January of that year floods in the region were widely recorded as torrential rain fell on frozen ground, with devastation and three deaths in the Shrewton/Tilshead area. In Salisbury the whole of the Close and Fisherton were flooded. Laverstock experienced its own tragedy when Hezekiah Collins and John Sutton set out to examine the situation at 'Six Hatches' on the river Bourne. Laverstock Mill Bridge (on the site of the current Whitebridge) had already been swept away. Collins lost his life on the 16th January attempting to assist the miller draw the hatches, and his body was found in an 'eel stage' by Sutton the following day. He was buried in St Andrew's churchyard, his untimely death recorded in the parish register.[44]

Sutton, left a widower by 1847, continued at the mill until the 1860s. By 1861 the scale of his business had expanded; as a miller and farmer he employed five men and three boys. His life was not uneventful; he suffered the theft of a 'live ferret from a box' on his premises and more seriously a fire started by a tramp in 1863, burning stacks of straw, barley and hay ricks in his yard opposite the asylum. The 'borough engine' and fire brigade came from Salisbury, neighbouring thatched cottages were saved and fortunately Sutton's stock was insured.[45]

The papers of the Blake estate 1863-1909 provide details of the sale of the mill in 1868 with six acres of valuable water meadow adjoining.[46] The sale described a very desirable water corn mill with convenient dwelling house attached – 'an excellent opening for a good baking business'. The stock included 20 sacks of barley, 200 new flour bags, weighing machine, beam, scales and weights, 'five dozen hurdles, boat, pole and oars . . . Apply to Mr. Edwd. Blake, Manor Farm, Idmiston'.[47]

Philip Goddard was the 'miller and fellmonger' in 1871, employing four men. Ten years later sons Frank (17) and Alfred, just 14, were described as fellmonger and miller respectively.[48] Despite the family enterprise, including another son Charles advertising as coal merchant and potato salesman, we next find Philip in 1888 in the bankruptcy court with his household furniture and mill 'effects' being sold by auction.[49]

In 1907 Edward Blake died and the mill was sold. He left considerable debts including one to Mrs Frances Kellow, builder and undertaker, The Green Laverstock, WSA 776/940 (papers of Blake estate)

Mr. Edward Blake, deceased.

LAVERSTOCK AND EAST GRIMSTEAD,

⁂ WILTS. ⁂

Important Sale of **WATER GRIST MILL**, with Fishing Rights, **RESIDENCE** and Accommodation Meadow Land.

PARTICULARS, PLAN AND CONDITIONS OF SALE

OF THE

⁂ FREEHOLD ⁂

WATER GRIST MILL,

Situate at Laverstock, One Mile from Salisbury,

With Valuable Fishing Rights, and Accommodation Water Meadow Lands, known as *"Laverstock Mill,"* together comprising an area, according to the Tithe Map, of

5A. 3R. 5P.,

or thereabouts, now and for many years in the occupation of members of *the Blake Family*, immediately adjacent to, but outside the Borough Boundary, possessing *Extensive Frontages* to the Laverstock Road, and being *within easy walk* of the Centre of the City, especially suitable for *early development*; together with

THE SMALL FREEHOLD

RESIDENTIAL ❧ PROPERTY

⁂ SITUATE AT EAST GRIMSTEAD, ⁂

About two Miles from Dean Station, and five from Salisbury, with Accommodation Dry Pasture and Arable Lands, containing an area, according to the Tithe Map, of

13A. 0R. 13P.

well placed in the *Village of East Grimstead*, and including the Comfortable Detached

Freehold Family Residence,

With Productive Garden, Enclosed Yard, Range of Cow Houses, Stabling, Piggeries and Paddocks, as now in the occupation of *Mr. Joe Crutcher* on a yearly Tenancy, and which

---

WATERS & RAWLENCE

Have received Instructions to Sell by Auction, in *Three Lots*, at their Rooms, Canal, Salisbury, on

Tuesday, April 16th, 1907,

AT 3.30 P.M.

Printed Particulars, with Plan and Conditions of Sale, may be obtained of the Auctioneers, Canal, Salisbury, of

Messrs. MACKRELL, MATON, GODLEE & QUINCEY, Solicitors, 21, Cannon Street, London, W.; or of Messrs. WILSON & SONS, Solicitors, Salisbury & Wilton.

Sale of Mill 1907, WSA 776/940

The Blake family, father and son, then reoccupied their mill although Harry Blake (son), corn miller, faced a difficult, widely reported, paternity claim. He denied being the father of the child but was found guilty and ordered to pay five shillings a week towards maintenance. His father, Edward Blake, refused to pay 'a farthing' towards his son's costs.[50] The Blakes remained in residence until 1907 when Edward Blake died and the mill was sold. He left considerable debts including one to Mrs Frances Kellow, builder and undertaker, The Green Laverstock.

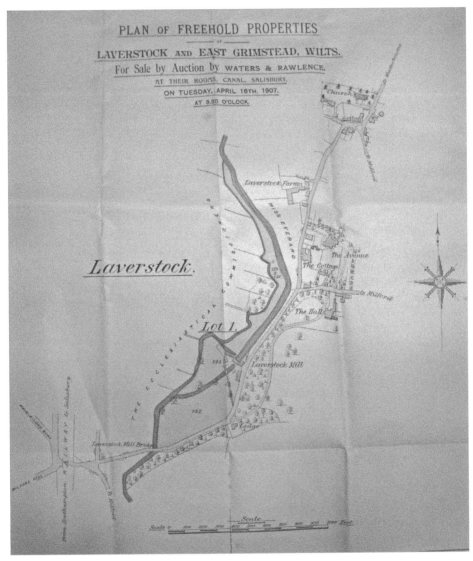

Plan, 1907, sale of mill, clearly showing the mill leat and the River Bourne, WSA 776/940

Described as a freehold water grist mill with important fishing rights and water meadows 'for many years in occupation of the Blake family', it was sold for £1,300.

As far as is known the mill was no longer active after 1907. On the 1925 Ordnance Survey 25 inch map of Laverstock a 'pump house' is shown on the mill site whereas in 1901 the mill is clearly depicted with sluices and an aqueduct. The mill house today has become a characterful private residence with spacious grounds between the leat and the river.

1   Bettey, Joseph, ed, 2005 *Wiltshire Farming in the 17th century*. WRS, 57; Bettey, Joseph, 'The cultivation of woad in the Salisbury area', *Textile History*, 9, 1978, 112-117

2   Bettey, Joseph ed. 2005

3   Cobbett, William, *Rural Rides*, Penguin books 1983, 298-303

4   Kerridge E, 1954, 'The floating of the Wiltshire Water Meadows', *WANHM*, 55, 108-18

5   WSA 727/2/10

6   Hoskins, Gordon, 1992

7   Sandell, R E,(1971), *Abstracts of Wiltshire Inclosure Awards and Agreements*, WRS 25

8   VCH *Wilts* 6, 92

9   WSA 727/13/15L. Estate maps like that of Bathurst's were drawn up by the landowner for his own use and may not include details of fields.

10 Henderson, H, 1951,Crop returns for Wiltshire, 1801, *WANHM* 54, 86

11 WSA 451/354/H

12 The plots of land 'allotted' were always known as 'allotments'.

13 Baker, T H, 1897, 'Enclosure in Mere', *WANHM* 29, 260-262

14 The actual award was the final measure; it was legally binding and allotted the various plots of land.

15 Bishop John Fisher, Constable's patron

16 **Cobbett, William, *Rural Rides*(1830), Penguin Books 1983, 320**

17 The leader of the riots was the mythical 'Captain Swing' who signed threatening letters to farmers and landowners.

18 The threshing machines were not the large steam powered machines of the 1850s but small horse or water powered machines which were easy to destroy.

19 The day before, two machines had been destroyed at Idmiston and one at Winterbourne Gunner and it is possible that the same people were involved.

20 *SJ*, 29 November 1830 4. Pyt House was the home of unpopular landlord, John Benett where one of the rioters was killed by the yeomanry. Such extreme violence was rare.

21 *SJ* January 1831

22 *SJ* 26 October 1836

23 WSA 1214/8 (farm labourers' wage book)

24 The building is shown clearly on the map of the manor of Laverstock, Peter Bathurst's survey 1725. WSA 727/13/15L

25 Tenders were invited for repairs and alterations at Laverstock Farm House by Fred Bath, well known Salisbury architect and builder. *Salisbury Times*, 14 June 1890

26 *SJ* 22 Aug 1843

27 *SJ* 20 May 1799 (local auction following the death of Robert Cooper). The drowners were the skilled workmen employed to maintain and operate the hatches and channels used in the water meadow system (for further information see 75-6)

28 *SJ* 21 Oct 1871

29 *SJ* 19 May 1888, *Devizes and Wilts Gazette*, 14 June 1888

30 *SJ* 24 Oct 1908, 3 Dec 1909

31 Parrett, Sylvia, 52

32 *Western Gazette* 19 Feb 1926

33 Hoskins, Gordon, *When the larks sang; Drake, Vera,* 1995

34 Bridge Field had been part of Edward Baker's freehold farm until 1862 and at one time part of the manor lands.

35 *SJ* 21 March 1868

36 WSA 776/111, Hoskins, 1992

37 *Western Gazette* 26 Feb, 26 March 1943

38 *Western Gazette* 30 July 1943, Kelly's Directories of Salisbury, 1953,1971

39 Additional information on New Farm kindly supplied by Dr James Robertson.

40 Newman, R & Howells, J, 2001, *Salisbury Past,* Phillimore, 41-46

41 Information supplied by Gordon Hoskins. In particularly wet weather the original river can be seen beyond the leat.

42 Rogers K and Chandler J 1992, *Early Trade directories of Wiltshire,* WRS, 47, 88

43 *SJ* 5 Aug 1833, 19 Aug 1833, 30 December 1833

44 *SJ* 25 Jan 1841, *Hampshire Chronicle* 25 Jan 1841

45 *Hampshire Advertiser* 7 July 1849, *Hampshire Advertiser* 4 April 1863

46 WSA 776/940

47 *SJ* 14 Dec 1867, 10 Oct 1868

48 A fellmonger was a dealer in hides or skins.

49 *SJ* 21 July 1888

50 *Devizes and Wiltshire Gazette* 3 Oct 1889

Routeways and Travel within Laverstock and Ford

Sue Wight

Within the parish there are many tracks of ancient origin. Bronze Age finds provide evidence of early man living and working across the Bishopdown and Hampton Park areas and in Ford as well as on Cockey Down.[1] People then would travel many miles on foot to trade goods, share information and skills and to link with others at social gatherings. The ancient trackways within our parish provided travel routes across the downs, between early farms and settlements as well as facilitating access to ceremonial sites such as Figsbury Ring and Stonehenge.[2] The presence of a river valley in our locality provided fresh water for man and his animals but access was challenging across the seasons so that fording places were necessary. In time bridges were constructed to improve reliability and safety at river crossings.

The massive earthworks at Old Sarum created in the Iron Age would have been a focal point for early paths to access that settlement.[3] Later the Romans utilised and improved local routes including the track from Winchester; some of this is still in use today (see 56). They also added the Portway which cuts through the modern day Old Sarum residential part of the parish.[4] This trade route arrives from Silchester in the north east and continues via Wimborne to the sea at Poole.

The continuous development of farming practices with the necessity to move flocks, harvest crops, distribute materials and access land, led to a rich network of lanes and tracks. Many of these can be identified by field boundaries, ancient hedges and green lanes. Routes from higher, dry ground to reach river crossings were essential for travel, whether on foot, on horseback or by cart. After the Normans arrived and further developed Old Sarum with stone and ditch fortification, there would have been many travellers and craftsmen with building materials, food supplies and other goods for the court. There would also have been regular traffic between

Clarendon royal hunting lodge and Old Sarum with its new Norman castle and the original cathedral. During the time the deer park at Clarendon was set out (12th century) and the medieval pottery was established in Laverstock (13th century) there were two (or perhaps three) regularly used wading points on the River Bourne. These were at Winterbourneford (Ford hamlet) in the north and at Milford in the south, the latter is still referred to as the medieval bridge. The third probable site of a ford would be at St Thomas's, where a bridge was later constructed. Together these ford crossings imply that there was substantial traffic accessing key sites and settlements.

The primary road through Laverstock village keeps to the east side of the river. The road system through the village later became less important for long distance travellers and was predominantly just in local usage, both social and commercial. Milford bridge and the associated Clarendon Way (Winchester to New Sarum) provided the more regular route from the east, to reach the growing city around the new cathedral (primary building completed 1258).[5]

It is difficult to determine when the name of the river crossing at St Thomas's was adopted. From other structures similarly dedicated, the title was possibly added in the mid-1200s, after the reburial of the remains of St Thomas.[6] The first substantial bridge (which probably upgraded a ford) was known by this name in the mid-16th century.[7]

Post medieval

Road usage for social, commercial and military purposes continued to increase during and after Tudor times with greater use of horses and carts. The local geology was not hard stone, but soft chalk which broke up easily. Damage to track surfaces in bad weather from all modes of transport would have made travel hazardous, particularly due to floodwater and mud. Any delays to travellers and coaches or damage to vehicles on poor roads could affect carrier profits and create dissatisfied customers. A pressing need arose therefore to improve road surfaces for coaches, delivery of goods and all travellers using the highways.

During the mid-16th century responsibility for the upkeep of roads was delegated by Act of Parliament to the parishes of the time.[8] Laverstock parish was designated to keep in good order the section of the London Road within the parish which led to the key river crossing at St Thomas's Bridge. It seems that the tasks were poorly managed as charges were lodged against the parish due to poor maintenance.

The Quarter Session records for Wiltshire show two associated cases; in 1647 it is stated that it is unclear locally where responsibility lay for upkeep of Milford Bridge - Milford and Laverstock parishes were ordered by the court to resolve the issue. Then in 1652 William Stragnell of Laverstock complained that he had paid a fine that had been levied against the villagers following an indictment for 'decay of several highways within the parish'. He asked the court to direct that the 'charge ought to be borne by the whole parish'. He was granted an order for 'an equal rate to be made on all the inhabitants of Laverstock for the repaying of Stragnell the sum of forty seven shillings'.[9] At that time this was a considerable sum of money.

The Monarch's Way is a long-distance path which follows the route taken by King Charles II in 1651 to escape from his enemies, ultimately taking a ship to France. His cross country route relied on sympathisers hosting him and providing transport, as much of the journey was undertaken on horseback. The king stayed at Heale House in the Woodford valley while travelling locally. His eastward path took a route roughly following the northern margin of the parish, then turned north to cross the River Bourne in Winterbourne Dauntsey.[10]

The business of travel

Turnpike or toll roads were introduced across southern Wiltshire from the mid-1700s amid reports of accidents due to poor surfaces, including an incident of a coach overturning into the River Bourne at St Thomas's Bridge in 1754 just after the Turnpike Trust for this route was established.[11] Mapping of the major routes across the countryside also gathered pace, with Salisbury an important interchange.[12] With the proximity of the city and key links across the countryside, Laverstock residents would have seen the establishment of this toll system along the local roads which still connect with Amesbury, London and Southampton.

The Sarum and Eling Trust (1753-1871) primarily cared for the major roads between Southampton and Salisbury with an extension north east to Lopcombe Corner at the county boundary with Hampshire. The trust erected three toll houses within the first year of business.[13] These were at strategic positions and two were built locally; one was close to St Thomas's Bridge, on the London Road just south of the junction with Green Lane and near the entrance to Bishop's Down Farm.[14] At the time this was within Milford parish and there are references to this turnpike as Lopcombe or

Lobcombe Gate. The other local toll house dating back to 1753 was at Petersfinger on the south east boundary with Clarendon Park.

By 1841, a turnpike gate was added to the east of St Thomas's Bridge by the junction of the London Road with the Laverstock to Ford road.[15] The position of the London Road turnpike can be seen to secure fees from travellers in and out of Salisbury city from numerous directions, by whichever route.

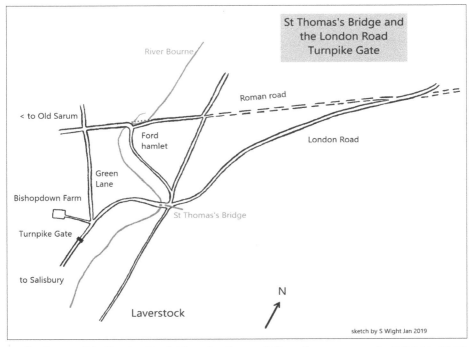

Sketch map of the London Road, Turnpike Gate and Green Lane, not to scale, S Wight, 2019

The Marlborough and Salisbury Trust extended the management of roads and collection of tolls to the north of Old Sarum earthworks in about 1835.[16] The brick and flint tollhouse cottage here was positioned in the fork between the roads to Amesbury and Marlborough (the Roman Portway). The 'Beehive' cottage still exists with little external alteration (a Grade II listed building) and vintage way-markers remain nearby although the road junction has been moved to the north.[17]

Toll gates were added and repositioned along turnpike routes for the collection of fees, which were determined by Act of Parliament. No records have been located of the toll charges within Laverstock parish, but advertisements by the trust for the letting of the business of toll collection reveal the net profit in 1799.[18] Other similar tariffs are recorded, with fees for animals being moved to and from market as well as for all horse-drawn vehicles.[19]

Numerous and regular stagecoach services were established between cities, market towns and ports with Salisbury as a key interchange on many routes.[20] Frequent coaches passed through the parish, for example the famous Salisbury Flying Machine (departed the city each night for London) and the Telegraph (or Royal Mail) coach with a guard on board, between Salisbury and Portsmouth via Stockbridge and Winchester.[21] Chandler cites the level of activity in 1839 as 49 commercial coaches each week along the London Road in each direction, carrying over 37,000 passengers per annum. Private coach travellers added about a further 14,000 people in that year.[22] This was a considerable level of routine traffic, with plenty to observe and a need to avoid wheels and horses' hooves.

The turnpike system was in use in this part of Wiltshire for over a century with local toll collectors shown in some of the census records. In 1851 John Farley was the tollgate keeper on the London Road, apparently at St Thomas's Bridge, he then moved to the Petersfinger tollhouse on the Southampton Road by 1861. At this southern toll gate in 1851 was James Hiscocks while Frank Stokes had taken over the role at St Thomas's Bridge by 1861.[23]

The river crossing at the south of the main village originally known as Laverstock Bridge allows direct access to the city. Sited nearby and downstream of Laverstock Mill this bridge seems to have been a later addition to local communication routes but was in place by 1811.[24] Damaging floods in 1841 caused the original structure to be broken up and washed away. (see 90) The iron-framed replacement bridge (now called Whitebridge) was installed soon afterwards and confirmed this as the principal village route to the city.[25] Laverstock Road proceeds westward from the bridge to the crest of Milford Hill where it also joins Shady Bower and Milford Hollow. The latter track is the route of the Clarendon Way long-distance path downhill to reach Milford Bridge. Regular traffic in the 1800s would have been on foot, by cart, horse-drawn carriage or on horseback.

Modernisation and development

There had been ambitious plans in the late 18th century to bring modern transport systems to Salisbury from Southampton with a canal system via Petersfinger, to culminate at Milford.[26] Engineering work commenced and south-eastern sections of the canal became operational. However, this project failed due to poor management and a lack of custom, leading to bankruptcy. There are still a few traces of these excavations visible but the Salisbury section beyond Alderbury was never completed.[27]

The new attraction for investment from the 1830s to replace canal building was the innovative rail transport system or 'permanent way'. Investor and landowner interests helped to ensure that Acts of Parliament were secured that licenced substantial growth of railways across the country. Parliamentary approval for the building of a railway to Salisbury from London (via Basingstoke) was first granted in 1840, but disagreements between rival rail companies caused delays.[28] The first line to reach Salisbury (1847) approached from Bishopstoke (Eastleigh). Construction commenced from Andover toward Salisbury in 1848 after revisions to the plans, having been originally licensed for completion within two years. There were many additional problems and the line finally opened in 1857, initially for goods and then also for passengers.[29] Train services from London to Salisbury via Andover still follow this trackbed which utilises the contours of the valley of the lower river Bourne. Originally, this line only came as far toward the city as the old Milford station. This had been built earlier as the terminus of a branch line of the London to Southampton railway route, but the Milford station buildings were badly damaged by a fire in 1858.[30] The arrival of a railway system to service the Salisbury locality was comparatively late and initially was poorly received.

Following the establishment of the railway within the parish, local occupations recorded in the next census (1861) reflect tasks associated with how railways were run in those early days. Employment in roles such as look out man or gang labourer (supervisor) came with tied accommodation in railway cottages, usually close to the tracks. However, the navvies who built the line are not generally found in standard census records due to the timing of construction (between census years) and their temporary accommodation, owing to the mobile nature of the work.[31] The groundworks required extensive landscaping, with teams of navvies employed to construct the railway bed to the specific design of the engineer. Valley contours had to be straddled with bridges to provide a manageable gradient for the heavy locomotives and freight. To achieve this a considerable tonnage of earth was moved to create cuttings and embankments, and all of this was conducted *by hand*.

The first railway cottage at Broken Cross (on the north-east side of Ford hamlet) was built in 1857 at a cost of £190 by a private builder (William Gue of Andover).[32] In the census of 1861 local railway workers are shown at their home addresses but this does not include the Laverstock signal box, as it is a place of work, not residential. This first signal box is believed to have been a timber structure with a simple rail switch mechanism.[33]

The London and South Western railway company (LSWR) later extended the line from Andover further toward the city through a large, freshly-cut tunnel to terminate at the new Fisherton Street station (built 1859).[34] In due course a newer signal box, close to this busy tunnel and junction, took control for all lines approaching the city from the east and the old Laverstock signal box was taken out of use.

The emergence of massive earthworks and the innovative engineering associated with the coming of the railway provided work for many manual labourers. However, the village residents will have seen this new landscape emerge to completely change the south and western aspects of the locality. The tunnel excavation and track extensions created the Laverstock Loop or Triangle. The rail tracks still have this shape alongside Cow Lane, raised up from the water meadows on embankments and permit a locomotive to change direction without a turntable or to bypass Salisbury station altogether (especially useful for freight). The major re-landscaping also allowed the contemporary establishment of allotments nearby and above the tunnel (just beyond the parish boundary), providing an important resource for a working man to grow fruit and vegetables as food for his family.

With the 1850s railway development the track bed had to cross the river and the associated marshy ground that was prone to flooding. Some of this land had been managed water meadows, so not only was the line created but the existing drainage systems needed revision. In addition to the primary brick bridge carrying the line across the Bourne and the London Road close by, there are numerous small bridges across culverts and lanes. When travelling the line nowadays these are not readily visible, but all the engineering design, planning and construction had to take account of the underlying geology and water courses in order to be built on solid ground.

Motorised travel

The addition of motor transport from the early 20th century had a huge impact on the speed and comfort of travel. In the early days of cars there were various hazards and awkward bends near bridges were frequently problematic. In his memoirs, Arthur Maidment recounts spending time at the St Thomas's river crossing, telling of the humpbacked stone bridge, built at an angle of 45 degrees to the approach road.[35]

The brick building of the St Thomas's tollhouse can be seen in the image. There was another smaller building at the tollbar, which by the 1930s was used as an RAC shelter, with the aim of reducing the pace of drivers approaching the bridge via 'Three Mile Hill' (the London Road).[36] Audrey Coggan, at this time growing up in Ford, remembers that 'Mr Crouch was the RAC officer. He was a big man with a big moustache, and he grew marigolds in the little patch of ground by his RAC box. He would put up a hand to try to slow motorists who were speeding down the hill from the London direction. Not everyone took notice, and he would sometimes be exasperated - from time to

St Thomas's Bridge, about 1900, postcard in private collection

time a car would end up in the river'.[37] Traces of the tollhouse here have been lost since this time.

Bicycles have seen various phases of popularity since their introduction. In the first half of the last century they were used in Laverstock as much for delivery of groceries, laundry and other goods as for social travel and to reach work. There are also parish residents who enjoy horse riding and still use the local lanes and byways. Twenty first century students can travel to the Laverstock schools using the locally provided cycle routes and some walk along the ancient paths.

The roads remain busy with local and commercial traffic, however the green lanes, byways and footpaths that were once minor roads still have leisure and amenity value and reinforce the heritage and rural aspects of the parish locality.

1   WSA HER MWI records for the parish of Laverstock and Ford © Wiltshire Council, accessed March 2018

2   https://www.english-heritage.org.uk/visit/places/stonehenge/history/permanent-exhibition/, accessed September 2018

3   http://www.english-heritage.org.uk/visit/places/old-sarum/history/, accessed March 2018

4   OS sheet, 2011, *Roman Britain, historical map and guide*, Ordnance Survey

5   Chandler, J, 1983, *Endless Street*, Salisbury, Hobnob Press, 127

6   http://www.canterbury-archaeology.org.uk/becket-shrine/4590809614, accessed October 2018

7   Chandler, J, 1983, 300 refers to Leland c 1540

8   Parliamentary Act of 1555 introduced 'statute labour' of four days supervised work on

the highway per householder per year, this was increased to six days in 1563; http://www.oxfordreference.com, accessed October 2018

9   Slocombe, I (ed), 2014 *Wiltshire Quarter Sessions Order Book, 1642-1654*, WRS 67, cases 286 & 780

10 http://www.monarchsway.50megs.com/about.html, accessed October 2018

11 Chandler, J, 1980, *Stagecoach operation through Wiltshire*, Salisbury, South Wiltshire Industrial Archaeology Society; Minutes of the Sarum and Eling Trust, WRO 1316/4, July 1754

12 http://www.visionofbritain.org.uk/maps/, accessed July 2018

13 Haynes, R and Slocombe, I, 2004 *Wiltshire Toll Houses*, Hobnob Press, 30

14 WSA Andrews' and Dury's maps, 1773 and 1810

15 Haynes and Slocombe, 2004, 85, 86

16 VCH *Wilts 4*, 262

17 Haynes and Slocombe, 2004, 49, 50

18 *SJ* December 1799 *Notice of auction for lett of collection of tolls at toll gates,* Sarum and Eling Trust

19 'Roads', in VCH *Wilts 4*, 254-6

20 https://www.georgianindex.net/horse_and_carriage/coaching.html, accessed October 2018

21 Garman, E M, 2017, *The Public Houses and Inns of Salisbury*, Hobnob Press, Warminster, item 216

22 Chandler, J, 1983, 137

23 1851 Census TNA HO 107/1846 f388; 1861 Census TNA RG 9/1315 f122; accessed July 2018

24 OS Map 1811, Sheet XV in Margary, H, 1980 *The Old Series Ordnance Survey Maps of England and Wales, Vol III,* Lympne Castle, Kent

25 RCHME *Salisbury* vol 1, 1980, 52 (20)

26 Chandler, J, 1983, 131

27 Alderbury and Whaddon Local History Research Group, 2000, *Alderbury and Whaddon, A Millennium Mosaic,* 110

28 Nicholas, J and Reeve, G, 2004, *Main Line to the West, part one, Basingstoke to Salisbury,* Irwell Press, Bedfordshire, 121

29 Nicholas and Reeve, 2004, 127

30 Nicholas and Reeve, 2004, 94

31 Many of the heavy labourers were previously involved with cutting canal *navigation* ditches.

32 Nicholas and Reeve, 2004, 89

33 Nicholas and Reeve, 2004, 89

34 History section in https://historicengland.org.uk/listing/the-list/list-entry/1242134, accessed July 2018

35 Maidment, A, 1990 *I Remember, I Remember*, Baverstock Books, Westbury, Wiltshire, 179

36 Haynes and Slocombe, 2004, 51

37 Coggan, Audrey, 2010, personal communication with Bryan Evans

Laverstock House Asylum

Ruth Newman

A kindly tradition,
175 years of mental health care

**Much of this article was originally published in
Sarum Chronicle 13 (2013)**

Salisbury held a unique position in the care of the mentally ill. Two private asylums, Laverstock House and Fisherton Asylum (later the Old Manor hospital), meant that there were more psychiatric patients here than anywhere else in the country outside London. Despite conflicting evidence they seem generally to have been progressive and well run, contradicting the views often associated with such early 19th century institutions with blood letting and physical restraint. An emphasis from the late 18th century on the concept of 'moral management' (treatment through kindness and reason) was practised at Laverstock.[1] By 1850 it was generally believed that lunatics were best treated in certified, protected 'asylums' – places of security and shelter.

Salisbury's asylums, just outside the city boundary, were run by members of the Finch family for many years. The early history of Laverstock House is uncertain although it is probable that the original manor house was on this site (see 53-4). Often, dubiously described as a private 'mad house' since the mid 18th century,[2] it was certainly between 1770-1772 a centre where patients could be inoculated successfully against smallpox before Jenner's vaccination from 1796.[3]

The early years

The period from the 1770s until the mid-19th century saw a rapid expansion in provincial mad houses. The Lunacy Act of 1774 stated that private houses had to be licensed and inspected regularly with the number of

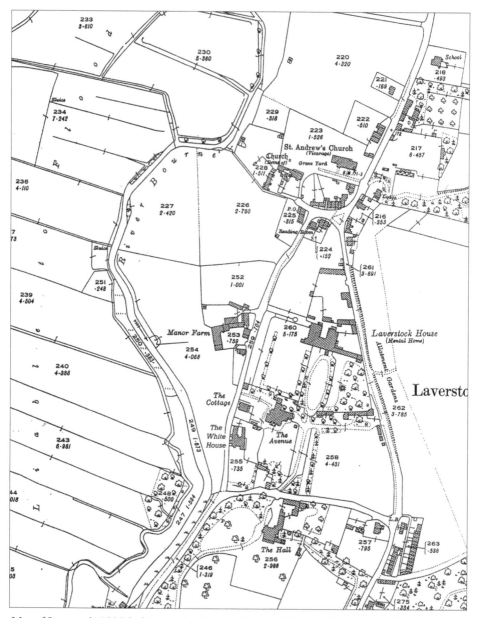

Map of Laverstock 1925 looking north, showing the mental home and the doctors' houses within the asylum triangle

patients recorded. Originally there were three categories of patients: private patients, disruptive paupers from the workhouses where payment was made by the parish, and criminal lunatics, guilty but insane and paid for by the Home Office. Laverstock never received the last category but Fisherton Asylum took considerable numbers only declining after 1863 with the opening of the

Laverstock from the air looking south, showing the old asylum triangle bordered by Duck Lane, The Avenue and Riverside Road, photograph by Joe Newman, 2008

specialist Broadmoor Hospital.

Laverstock House was advertised for lease, with its extensive grounds, in 1775, 'convenient for a genteel family'. In 1780 Charles Curtoys, a London surgeon practicing at the Infirmary, advertised the 'House' for 'unfortunate people labouring under that deplorable malady INSANITY'. It was opened for patients in 1781; nearly 175 years later, in 1955, Laverstock House Nursing

Home for Nervous and Mental Disorders, closed.[4] William Finch, practicing at nearby Milford, was the founder of a dynasty of asylum owners, and although a non-medical proprietor, claimed as early as 1779, 'great success in curing people disordered in their senses' asserting that all have been 'discharged perfectly well'.[5] He moved from Milford in 1784, taking over from Curtoys, and the following advert in the *Salisbury Journal* of that year is one of many promoting the asylum. "William Finch . . . has removed to Laverstock House where he receives . . . lunatic patients. The House is delightfully situated on an eminence about one mile from Salisbury . . . with every other accommodation for ... any lady or gentleman needing such a retreat'.[6]

Humanity was the watchword rather than restraint and Finch's obituary (December 1798) praised him as a man 'much respected for integrity and humanity'.[7] In his will he left his son William 'an additional yearly sum of 30 guineas to purchase medicines . . . [to carry] on my said business.' Two of his 14 children became doctors, Laverstock House passing to his son, Dr William Finch (1776-1848), who later in 1813 established Fisherton Asylum. Dr Finch quickly stressed his medical credentials, with his mother, Caroline in charge of the 'domestic part of the house'.[8] She sought to attract more females proposing that she received 'at her NEW HOUSE, at Laverstock, FEMALE LUNATICS ONLY, giving the best possible relief and comfort to her patients'.[9]

There is no evidence to confirm the first William Finch's success in curing all his patients. A register of patients for Laverstock is available from 1797 to 1955. Whilst not a comprehensive record in its early years it provides valuable evidence on the patients admitted, the length of stay, and condition when they left. Many recorded patients were long term. The second person in the register in 1797 was a 40 year old Frenchman, M Darins. He was committed by the government, a 'foreigner', at the time of the French wars, possibly regarded as a threat to national security. He died in 1830, having spent 33 years in the asylum.[10]

After the 1828 Madhouses Act, new certificates were required, signed by two doctors which should have avoided possible collusion between the family and local doctor. But these certificates of admission and removal for the patients often raise queries. 18 year old Julia Saunders from the Isle of Wight was placed in the asylum by her father on 6 September 1834 and 'removed [by him] therefrom on the 20th day of October 1834. Cured', posing the question as to why a young girl was so confined for just six weeks.[11]

Occasional incidents come to light which were reported in the national press. In 1816, one of the passengers in the Quicksilver mail coach failed to escape to the safety of the inn after the leading horse was attacked by a lioness at 'The Winterslow Hut' (later 'The Pheasant Inn'). He survived to give a report

Statement and Order to be annexed to the *Medical Certificates,* authorising the Reception of an Insane Person.

The Patient's true Christian and Surname at full length.................................... *Julia Saunders*

The Patient's Age.................................... *18*

Married or Single.................................... *single*

The Patient's previous Occupation (if any)......... *none*

The Patient's previous place of abode.............. *Fern Hill, Isle of Wight*

The licensed House, or other place (if any), in which the Patient was before confined.................. *none*

Whether found Lunatic by Inquisition, and date of Commission.. *no*

Special circumstance which shall prevent the Patient being separately examined by two Medical Practitioners.. *none*

Special circumstance which exists to prevent the insertion of any of the above particulars.......... *none*

SIRS,

Upon the Authority of the above Statement, and the annexed Medical Certificates, I request you will receive the said *Julia Saunders* as a Patient into your House.   I am, Sirs, your obedient Servant,

(Signed)   Name...................................... *Samuel Saunders*

Occupation (if any)........................

Place of Abode .... *Fern Hill, Isle of Wight*

Degree of Relationship (if any) to the Insane Person............. *Father*

To Dr. FINCH and Mr. LACY,
    Proprietors of Laverstock House, Wilts.

FORM OF MEDICAL CERTIFICATES.

I, the undersigned, hereby certify, that I separately visited and personally examined *Miss Julia Saunders* the Person named in the annexed Statement and Order, on the *sixth* day of *September* one thousand eight hundred and thirty *four* and that the said *Julia Saunders* is of unsound Mind, and a proper Person to be confined.

(Signed)   Name...................... *Rob. Bloxam*

Physician, Surgeon, or Apothecary.. *Surgeon*

Place of Abode.................. *Newport Isle of Wight*

I, the undersigned, hereby certify, that I separately visited and personally examined *Miss Julia Saunders* the Person named in the annexed Statement and Order, on the *ninth* day of *September* one thousand eight hundred and thirty *four* and that the said *Julia Saunders* is of unsound Mind, and a proper Person to be confined.

(Signed)   Name...................... *John Weaver*

Physician, Surgeon, or Apothecary.. *Surgeon*

Place of Abode .... *Salisbury*

Medical certificate and (overleaf) removal, Julia Saunders 1834, WSA A1/563

We William Finch MD, & James Lacy of Laverstock House, hereby give you notice that Miss Julia Saunders, of Fern Hill, in the Isle of Wight, a Patient in the Licensed House situate in Laverstock, was removed therefrom by her Father, on the 20th Day of October 1834. Cured.

Dated this 20th day of October 1834.

Finch & Lacy

To the Clerk of the Peace of the County of Wilts.

to the newspapers, then collapsed and spent the next 27 years in Laverstock Asylum. 'He is now, Dr Finch thinks, an incurable patient.'[12] Some years later *The Times* reported that an aspiring suitor to the young Queen Victoria who 'conceives himself to be king of several countries' managed to elude the royal guard and 'gained access to the Palace'. A warrant was issued 'but as his insanity was manifest, and his connections highly respectable . . . he has been placed in the asylum of Dr Finch of Laverstock.'[13] A further patient in the 1830s, John Welch, was an ex slave owner from the West Indies.[14]

The account of Thomas Campbell

A fascinating account from the 1820s gives an impartial view, the only contemporary record of a family member being placed into the asylum. Thomas Campbell, the Scottish poet,[15] was faced in the early 1820s with the dilemma that his only son, Thomas Telford Campbell, aged 18, was becoming increasingly disturbed. Campbell senior discovered Laverstock and decided to place his son in the establishment. His praise was fulsome;

> I have put him into Dr. F's hand, implicitly . . . Everything is open at all times to inspection.'[16] Campbell described a not altogether comfortable visit which he and

his wife made in October 1822. 'We came to a garden terrace . . . A female [patient] dressed like a nun, was parading . . . By and by, a poor man came out - a pauper patient - limping and hanging his pallid head . . . we heard a dismal howling, but very soon discovered that . . . Dr. F. keeps a pack of hounds for his patients to hunt with. But the momentary belief of its being the voice of human beings, made one's blood run cold. At last, we came in full sight of a beautiful house and spacious grounds . . . the black man who opened the outward gate, I have since understood to be an excellent creature.

They were met by Dr Finch and his wife, who did much to allay their fears. The Campbells spent the day at the asylum with their son, enjoyed dinner with the Finches and 'two very well-behaved patients'. The 'black man' was a reference to John Hillier, the well known cook to William Finch, described in the 1841 census as a 'man of colour'.[17]

Campbell was not completely satisfied with Laverstock Asylum and withdrew his son. After a year at home, further difficulties saw the son's return in November 1824, Campbell adding, 'the more I think of [the superiority] of Laverstock, the more mitigated I feel by my poor boy's misfortune'.[18]

Laverstock Asylum within its extensive grounds, photograph c1900, WSA 3433/1/38

'Moral Management'

An undated prospectus for 'Laverstock House Retreat' (probably 1824) stresses the improvements to the accommodation, facilities for the 'most compleat separation of *Male from Female patients*' with apartments subdivided according to 'station in Life'. Earlier 1815-16 reports praised Laverstock as one of the finest private asylums in existence. With 120 patients . . . [there was] 'not a single patient in a strait jacket . . . Every possible kind of amusement was provided for them; billiards, cards, books etc in doors; cricket, greyhounds, riding on horseback and in a carriage, out of doors'. Dr Finch worked to keep the patients busy to keep their mind off their illness. He kept individual records for each patient and the type of treatment adopted. This included the infamous 'rotatory' chair which spun patients round causing vertigo and vomiting. Described as 'most useful as the pain it excites takes the patients' minds on to it rather than the disease', but generally, under the Finch family, there was a desire not to resort to such mechanical devices or seclusion.[19]

The prospectus and every advert stress the lack of coercion. 'Sympathy' and 'kindness' were fashionable words in the treatment of mental illness in the early 19th century. Finch also emphasised the 'careful selection of servants' and the importance of advances in medical treatment, with impressive figures to endorse his preventative measures.[20]

Even before 1815 pleasure grounds were laid out at Laverstock for the patients, based on the idea of a country estate with nine acres for 'superior patients' and about one acre for paupers. Much attention was placed on a restful environment. Magnificent ornamental trees which date back to the first half of the 19th century still survive, including a rare grafted manna ash.

Following the 1828 Act, asylums were visited four times a year and minutes kept. 'Visitors' could set at liberty persons who they considered to be improperly confined. A copy of their minutes of May 1835 reported that they were 'satisfied of the insanity of the whole. Not a single doubtful case'.[21] The October 1842 report further noted the generous patient/staff ratio; '128 patients attended by 18 men and 25 female servants . . . Dr Finch has added two padded cells, one for male and one for female pauper patients'.[22]

Rare grafted manna ash; garden of author, photograph by Joe Newman

Buildings

Plans exist for both 1829 and 1844 following alterations to the asylum. The later general plan shows the 'buildings and premises', including the institution within its landscaped grounds, the chapel, several doctors' cottages, an extensive cricket pitch and a large kitchen garden and drying area for laundry. The house

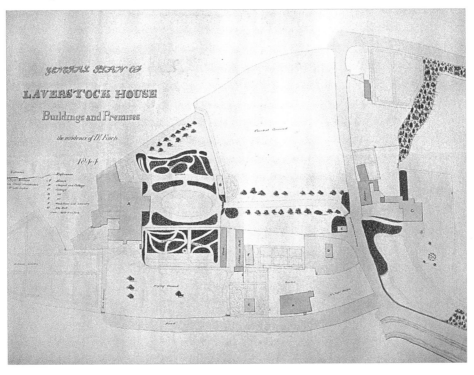

1844 plan of the asylum and landscaped grounds, WSA A1/562/6

opposite the main entrance was 'The Hall', the private residence of Dr Finch. The detailed plan of the asylum for 1844 includes the padded cells mentioned above, a brewhouse, granaries, the paupers' yards, 64 bedrooms and 19 privies/water closets.[23]

The importance of religion was recognised but from 1829 a purpose built chapel in the grounds was dedicated to St Christopher, 'a very neat and Commodious Building'. Some patients regularly attended St Andrew's Church in the village and were buried in the parish churchyard normally with just initials on their headstones.[24] Whilst an increased emphasis was placed on the healing powers of religion the management was careful to exclude those suffering from religious delusions.[25]

Fees

There are few references to charges at Laverstock. In an early example of care in the community, 'patients are attended by Mr Finch, at their own houses; and careful and experienced servants sent in cases which will not admit a removal'. This appears to be the case not just for the wealthy. Bills were sent to the churchwardens and overseers of the poor at Britford in 1808-9 for Jane Tinham, the wife of Joseph, 'a labourer and poor person'. She was 'so far disordered in her senses that it is dangerous for her . . . to go abroad and that . . . for her safety some proper person should be provided to take care of [her] during her lunacy'. A bill for £12 3s (£12.15p) for the year from Easter 1808, included board, medicine, visits and attendance on her at Britford. A later charge was made for her coffin and 'laying out'.[26] A further bill to the overseers at Longbridge Deverill was for the 'Board, Lodging and mending etc of Benjamin Wheeler' for nine months in 1813-14 at 14 shillings (70p) a week. The total costs were £29 10s (£29.50p) considerably more than maintaining pauper lunatics in the community and therefore they were only sent to asylums when unmanageable.[27]

The fees for private patients varied according to their wealth and status.[28] Thomas Campbell wrote of the fees varying from two to ten guineas a week. He wanted to do what was best for his son but 'could not afford to place him among [those] who paid at the rate of five hundred a year.'[29]

Pauper lunacy

Wiltshire was an important centre for pauper lunacy. Most came from outside the county, Laverstock taking considerable numbers of females from the Isle of Wight workhouses. As a result the local asylum became one of the largest provincial licensed houses in the country with over 100 patients for the first 50 years of the 19th century, reaching a peak of 135 in 1841, but with provision for 50 paupers and 100 private patients. The 1847 'pauper dietary' appears generous by the standards of the time eg for dinner '½lb hot meat, beef or mutton with vegetables, 1½ pints of beer and on Sundays ¼lb suet pudding'. Women had the same as men 'but in rather less proportions' though with vast quantities of tea. The pauper men worked in the gardens and farm whilst the women worked in the kitchen and washhouse. Patients thus employed were 'allowed two extra pints of beer daily with snuff and tobacco and have their meals in the kitchen with the servants'.[30]

By 1845 every county was required to build a pauper lunatic asylum and Laverstock's pauper intake ended when such patients were removed to Roundway Hospital in 1851, the county Asylum at Devizes. The census of that year showed that Laverstock had 83 private patients, 44 male and 39 female (120 including staff).

The Asylum within the community

A delightful report from the *Salisbury Journal* reveals how Dr Finch saw the asylum as part of the wider community in the post 1832 Reform celebrations. *'On Saturday last, the village of Laverstock . . . was all life and gaity, owing to an invitation . . . by Dr Finch and Mr Lacy, to the inhabitants of the parish to an excellent supper . . . Two hundred and ten sat down . . . under an avenue of trees, in the outer grounds of the Asylum ... A band of music was in attendance, and after supper, dances were introduced, whilst the elders smoked their pipes, and the children diverted themselves on the green ... Gothic lanterns tastefully hung amongst the trees. It is impossible to imagine a scene of greater happiness.'[31]* Villagers for their part saw the 'House' as providing employment; in 1881 for just 43 patients, staff included Dr Manning as medical superintendent, a matron, three cooks, six nurses, four housemaids, four laundresses, four male hospital attendants and a gardener. Most of these came from Laverstock or nearby and this continued well into the 20th century.[32]

Later history

Dr Finch died in 1848 with the business passing to his widow, Mrs Mary Finch, assisted by John W Finch Noyes and Dr Hewson.[33] The involvement of the Finch family at Laverstock ended in 1854 following Mary's death but continued at Fisherton into the early 20th century. From the mid-19th century Laverstock was no longer at the forefront of mental health care, but the institution with up to 70 private patients remained one of the country's largest private hospitals. The pauper buildings were pulled down and advertisements referred to the house as being 'recently rebuilt' and 'none but private patients admitted'.[34] An advert of 1859 mentions 'detached dwellings' for 'first class patients and their private attendants', whilst 'experienced male and female attendants' means they can take 'a limited number of idiotic children and adults', and to attempt their education'.[35]

A charming 'anonymous' pamphlet, *'Our holiday in Laverstock Park asylum'* was published in 1860. Clearly promotional, it was produced when the institution

Grave of William Finch (1776-1848), Laverstock churchyard, photograph by Joe Newman

Thatched cottages within the hospital grounds WSA 3433/1/38

was facing criticism. Dr Bushnan, the proprietor, invited 50 (Southampton) medical men to view his 'House' and their visit was described. The patients were compared to 'happy school boys at play' with bowls on billiard smooth lawns and a well stocked library. The ladies had their own 'elegantly furnished sitting rooms' and flower gardens. There were outings to the Cathedral and Stonehenge, fly fishing 'in the neighbouring streams' and both diet and treatment were described in glowing terms, 'a model of the very best type of asylum for the insane'.[36]

Later the house fell into the hands of a 'non-medical proprietor who regards it as a money speculation only'. The renewal of the licence for just three months led to improvements. By 1867 Joseph Haynes of The Avenue was the owner while Dr S L Haynes and Dr Henry Manning were listed as the joint medical superintendants, and by the 1870s reports had improved.

During this decade Julia Wood, aged 60, was placed in the asylum by her nephew. She became a benefactor to an obscure 'Children of God' religious sect, the New Forest Shakers, and was certified insane after offering £2000 to build them a lodge in the New Forest. Wood's nephew wrote out a lunacy order and went with police officers and doctors from Laverstock to the Shaker camp. Julia resisted arrest but was taken to the asylum where she was said to be suffering from 'religious hallucinations'. Her entry in the Register states that she was admitted in February, 1875 and finally discharged in December, 1881 'not improved'. She spoke highly of her treatment under Dr Manning, the principal, but considered it 'ignominious' that she should be so confined.[37]

Laverstock House Mental Hospital 1930s (photograph, private collection)

By 1901, still under Dr Manning, there were just 48 patients, normally with 'no occupation' and 15 servants including five mental nurses, all female and young. Details of admissions for 1904 include full medical details and reports of the patients, some violent or suicidal.[38] The register shows no obvious links with the First World War and records are not available after 1918 because of the 100 year closure on medical records under the Data Protection Act.

Despite the obvious propaganda, and a handful of contradictory reports, there is much to be proud of in Laverstock's mental health record. The Finch family, moving from non-medical to medically qualified proprietors, believed in preventative treatment in a quiet, rural environment. The emphasis on rehabilitation and minimal restraint ensured that Laverstock was among the most progressive of the early 19th century asylums while the careful selection of attendants and their supervision proved an important precedent to the modern profession of mental nursing.

Personal memories of Laverstock House

In the 20th century, the mental hospital appears to have been accepted in the village. Throughout the 1940s and 1950s, where possible, patients were allowed out unattended and were well known and liked in the village. The gardens and grounds were immaculate, and the hospital was virtually self-sufficient in vegetables.

Children were sent to buy 'lunatic dripping' at 5½d a pound, from Mrs Maggs, the cook.

The majority of the patients were either wealthy or had wealthy relatives and most were middle aged or elderly'.

I knew some of the people who were patients. One lady came to our whist drives. We often saw patients out with their nurses or attendants . . . but always polite when we met them, but of course, we all knew that there were some very bad cases.'

The village then, [in 1940s] was very small to what it has become now. There were quite a few Irish families where the parents worked at Laverstock House'.

The late Ernest Norton, who came to the village when he was seven in 1910 recalled, 'Half way up Duck Lane, there was a pump station which used to make the electricity and pump the water for Laverstock Park . . . The patients used to go to St Andrew's Church . . . and then there was a Rev – and he was a resident up there and he often used to read the lesson. He used to come to our house and take our dog out for walks. They were all private patients . . . Some of the patients were very bad. The kitchen staff were all locals . . . The House was a nice looking place. There was a pagoda in the gardens where the patients could go to sit and relax. That's when they were alright of course . . . The whole of the island belonged to the asylum.'

I must say that the grounds and out houses at Laverstock Park were kept beautifully. After Dr Hill (the last medical superintendant) died in 1953, the ownership passed to his wife . . . In 1955 the whole lot, House, grounds and all were put up for sale. We were quite distressed at the time'.[39]

The late Dr John Norris was the last visiting doctor from about 1948-1955,

Entrance to Laverstock House on left, just beyond Ivy Cottage; looking up road, (currently The Avenue) 1913. The wall of the stables to the Hall is on right (post card private collection).

calling every day and writing certificates for the patients. The institution went bankrupt in 1955, the hospital was demolished and 42 houses were built in the grounds. Dr Norris confirmed that the staff was mainly Irish RC nurses who lived in Laverstock, the head male nurse was a Scot, while the matron was an Irish Protestant! In the 1950s padded cells still existed, then called 'seclusion' and there were fenced areas where patients could go outside but not be able to escape. At its closure all the patients were dispersed, some to the Old Manor which had been taken over by the NHS in 1954.[40]

The three doctors' houses

Other houses were associated with Laverstock Asylum, notably the accommodation provided for the medical staff. Of the three doctors' houses, only The White Cottage (Kerrycroy) is still standing.

The White House

This was a large house on Riverside Road, near the junction with The Avenue (current road). Described by a former resident, as a big, three storey house, 'square and plain', Gordon Hoskins remembers that 'the house abutted right on to the road, indeed the steps leading down to the road from the front door jutted out into the roadway, there being no footpath'.[41]

Documentation is difficult for The White House because of the changing name and frequent movement of the asylum medical officers. Known as

The White House, on Riverside Road (the medical superintendent's house), now demolished, photograph 1890s, WSA 3433/1/38

Postcard of Laverstock, from Riverside Road showing The White House with The White Cottage beyond c1906. Private collection

The Cottage for much of the 19th century, it is hard to imagine a dwelling less resembling a cottage.[42] It dates from c1840; on the tithe map of 1842 the landowner of the site was William Finch, the asylum owner, with John W Finch Noyes as occupier. This is confirmed on an 1844 plan showing the house with its private garden in a corner site of the asylum grounds. On the night of the 1851 census four young Finch Noyes children under nine with their governess were in residence while their parents, John and Ellen and the rest of their offspring lived at Belle Vue House in Salisbury, previously the Finch family home.

By 1855 The Hall and the White House were both 'occupied' by John Finch Noyes. The Hall was sold but The White House was retained by the asylum to rent out. Photographs from the late Jean Morrison (died 2006) indicate the difficulty of matching residents with their houses. She was the great-granddaughter of Joseph and Mary Haynes (see below) and appears to have lived in all three staff houses describing each as 'her house'. Dr Benson, medical superintendant 1925-1938 also resided here as well as in the White Cottage. The final resident and the last medical superintendant at the 'Home for nervous and mental disorders', Dr Horace Hill, lived in The White House from 1939 until his death in 1953 when the ownership passed to his wife. In 1955, the house, grounds and whole estate, were put up for sale with the land sold for building.

The Avenue – The Haynes' house, within Laverstock Park. They were the first occupants in 1867. A pretty thatched cottage, but surprisingly large, WSA 3433/1/38

The Avenue

The second large staff house within the grounds was The Avenue, with no direct road frontage and almost hidden from view within the asylum grounds. It had not been built in 1844 when its site was partly occupied by the 'wash-house and laundry' (see 113). The house appears to be a rebuilding of one occupied by a Mr Windsor in 1820; it was unusual, a pretty thatched cottage but surprisingly large with an 'arts and crafts style' feel. It was first mentioned in 1867, occupied by the owner of Laverstock House, Joseph Haynes, solicitor and his wife, Mary. His eldest daughter Ellen married Henry Manning (1835-1910), forty years medical superintendant at the asylum. The Haynes' occupation continued until the 1930s with Joseph's granddaughter Miss Clara Haynes living there in 1901, replaced ten years later by her aunt, Jane Adela Haynes aged

Mary Haynes, wife of Joseph Haynes, the owner of Laverstock House. Portrait given to the current owner by Mary's great-granddaughter, Jean Morrison, by kind permission Steven Hobbs

58, single with private means, cared for by three servants. The sale of The Avenue in 1933 following her death gives an indication of the size of this 'pretty thatched cottage'. Held over three days by Woolley and Wallis, the house plus contents came under the hammer, with its seven bedrooms plus two maids' rooms, library and drawing room, and also an 'important jewellery sale' with diamonds, pearls and rubies.[43]

The White Cottage

Finally, next door to The White House, and still standing, is the attractive White Cottage, currently (2019) 'Kerrycroy'. This was also a doctor's house and Henry Manning, the long serving medical superintendant was resident here in 1901. It is older than its larger neighbours and extended in the 19th century. Essentially a cob house, probably dating to the mid-18th century, the front two rooms were the original thatched cottage with a stairwell in the

The White Cottage (the doctor's house), now 'Kerrycroy', on Riverside Road, photograph 1890s, WSA 3433/1/38

corner. It was in the asylum 'triangle' with a back entrance to the institution beside the house, with a gate leading through to The Avenue.

In 1841 it was owned by William Finch with the occupant shown as Sarah Read, 65 years old, of independent means. It is marked as 'cottage' on the 1844 asylum map.

The White Cottage, like The White House, came under the ownership of the Finch Noyes family. A document of 1885 between John G Finch Noyes

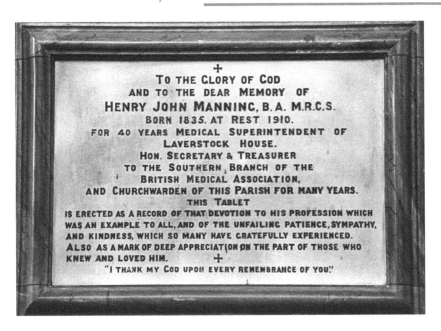

Plaque to Henry Manning, St Andrew's Church, Laverstock, photograph Roy Bexon

and his brother Augustus conveyed the property equally between their two sisters Mary Agnes and Louisa. All four were born in Laverstock, children of John W Finch Noyes. On Louisa's death in 1929 Dr John Benson (from The White House) and his brother, Colonel Charles Benson bought the property. A further agreement of 1937 stated that Dr Benson was to assist Dr Hill in carrying on the business of 'successfully' running Laverstock House.[44]

The last resident doctor Neil Mackinnon, physician and surgeon, lived here in the early 1950s.

Other staff houses within the Asylum grounds

Ivy Cottage

This cottage or lodge was at the entrance to the drive of Laverstock Asylum, which can be seen in the photograph just beyond Ivy Cottage. The house name changed over time but in 1911 Arthur Roffe, aged 40 lived there.[45] He and his wife both worked within the asylum and were still there in 1939 when he was described as 'male nurse (mental) retired'. By this time locals referred to it simply as 'Granny Roffe's Cottage'. It belonged to the mental hospital and was demolished after the institution closed in 1955. The houses in Laverstock Park

Ivy cottage (the lodge): 'I have had a walk past this cottage . . . it is a lovely little spot. There are a few thatched cottages about this place' (postcard March 1914) private collection

were built in the 1960s and early 1970s, the east side was built first, followed by a long delay before the completion of Laverstock Park West as the main road was cut through the gardens of the estate.[46]

The cottage could date from the early 18th century with improvements made in the 1820s–1830s.[47]

Appleby, Duck Lane, lies within Laverstock Park and unlike the other houses on the estate, was completely converted in about 1965 from a period property with old roof tiles and smaller windows. It possibly provided staff (nurses') accommodation and may previously have been used as a barn.

Nearby the section of ashlar, flint, brick and clunch (chalky limestone) wall in Duck Lane marks part of the original boundary. It dates from the late 17th century so predates the asylum.

Looking up the current road, The Avenue, towards Ivy cottage with The Hall grounds on right, photograph private collection

Appleby, Duck Lane; note the original wall nearby of ashlar, flint brick and clunch, photograph by Joe Newman

1   The madness of George III brought a growing awareness of mental health treatment.

2   Smith, Gertrude, 1982, *The Old Manor Hospital,* prologue and Parrett, 15 both have 'after 1754' for its founding; VCH *Wilts* 5, 329 suggests the 1760s. Andrews' and Dury's 1773 map shows the house as the property of Thomas Cooper Esq.

3   *SJ* 3 December 1770; *SJ* 1 July 1771. Salisbury was an early centre for the prevention of smallpox through inoculation.

4   *SJ* 20 March 1775, 19 June 1780, 13 Aug 1781. The assumption that William Finch founded the asylum has proved to be incorrect and Charles Curtoys is now recognised as being the founder. Thanks to Jenny Hayes for information.

5   *SJ* 8 February 1779

6   *SJ* 9 August 1784

7   *SJ* 31 December 1798

8   *SJ* 7 January 1799

9   *SJ* 01 October 1810

10   WSA A1/560/9

11   WSA A1/563 medical certificates 1834-5

12   *The Pheasant Inn* lioness, www.iolfree.ie/~dorsetbigcats/marcushistory.htm, accessed 2013; Beattie, William, 1855, *Life and letters of Thomas Campbell,* vol 2, Harper and Brothers. Reprinted 2012, 140-146

13   *The Times* 26 May 1838 6

14   Legacies of British Slave-ownership, https://www.ucl.ac.uk/lbs/person/vi: accessed September 2018

15   Thomas Campbell, (1777-1844), poet, Carnall, Geoffrey, ODNB

16   Beatie, William, 145-6

17 John Hillier, worked at the asylum for Dr Finch from 1815-1848. He died shortly after Finch and is buried in the local churchyard. *SJ* 22 January 1848 4

18 Beatie, William , 147, 154, 162-3

19 WSA 1861/1; Minutes of evidence 1815 Select Commission, 22

20 *SJ* 12 September 1814

21 WSA A1/560/9

22 WSA A1/560/9

23 WSA A1/562/6; the general layout of the grounds remained essentially unchanged until 1950s except for the addition of another doctor's house, 'The Avenue'.

24 Full names are occasionally given on gravestones eg Capt Alexander Kennedy RN, 1864.

25 WSA A1/561, 1829 Report

26 WSA 499/27

27 WSA 1020/108

28 *SJ* 12 September 1814

29 Beatie, William, 144

30 WSA A1/564

31 *SJ* 9 July 1832

32 In 1841 Laverstock and Fisherton asylums were of comparable size but the latter by 1881 had 672 patients.

33 *SJ* 22 January 1848

34 *SJ* 21 July 1855

35 *Dorset Chronicle*, 1 Dec 1859. Several references suggest an attempt to appoint specialist nurses for the asylum.

36 Anon, 1860. *Our holiday at Laverstock Park Asylum;* article 'Medical Merrymaking', *Hampshire Advertiser*, 11 Aug, 1860 4

37 Hoare, P, 2005, *England's Lost Eden. Adventures in Victorian Utopia*; WSA A1/560/9

38 WSA A1/563 certificates of admission

39 Much of this information from former village residents comes from interviews in 1985 undertaken by Gill Newman as part of a university project.

40 Information kindly supplied by Dr John Norris to the author in June 2008.

41 Information from the late Jean Morrison. Hoskins, Gordon, 1992, *When the larks sang, Cameos of life in Laverstock 1937-1940*, self published. All that can be seen today are the pillars of the house wall fronting on to Riverside Road where the bungalows are (RN)

42 To avoid confusion I have used the term 'White House' here. In 1841 the house was called 'The Cottage'. As late as 1925 it is still shown on the OS map as 'The Cottage' but Kelly's directories refer to 'The White House' from 1901.

43 WSA 2699/32. It has been impossible to discover what happened to The Avenue after the sale. It might well have been incorporated into the asylum buildings, lasting until their demolition.

44 Abstract title to freehold premises known as 'The White Cottage, Salisbury' 1955. Private ownership

45 Known at different times as Ferne Cottage (1911), Yew Tree Cottage and Ivy Cottage

46 Information from the late Vera Drake's memoirs, 1995

47 Advice on dating from Pamela Slocombe, Wiltshire Buildings Record

The Green, The Parsonage and Living Farm

Jenny Hayes

The Green, as it is today, was created as late as 1971. Before then, the area was the centre of the village, with farms and cottages clustered near the little Church of St Andrew. Until the 19th century the Laverstock road from Salisbury wound its way past the Mill and Manor farm on the left until the beginning of what is now The Green. Here on the left was a farmhouse (1), outbuildings and two cottages (2&3) surrounding a farmyard. A short distance from these was another cottage (4) on the corner of the lane leading straight down to the front of the Parsonage (6). Another cottage (5) was half way down this lane and opposite was the Parsonage Barn (7), a large L-shaped building forming a square farmyard with the back of the Parsonage. The church path turned right at the top of the Parsonage Lane, behind the barn, to the old church.

Bordering the church path was a cottage, currently (2019) Elmcott (8) tucked into the corner where the main road ran past a field known as the Church Croft (9). The road divided at this point, left to Ford along the current Church Road and right to Milford, now Duck Lane. The small triangle created by these roads was later known as the Square or the Clump, with a few trees growing there, the forerunner of 'The Green.' Along this road, opposite the Clump was a cottage now The Thatch (10), Rustic Cottage on its left (11) and a pair of cottages on the right, the site of the present Lynwood Cottages (12). Opposite Elmcott and the Church Croft were the grounds of Laverstock House (13).

Towards the end of the 18th century more building took place; a wheelwright and carpenter's shop (16) was built on the Church Croft fronting the road and next to Elmcott, another cottage, Merivale(15) was built. Opposite, a village school was established in 1835 on land from the kitchen gardens of Laverstock House.

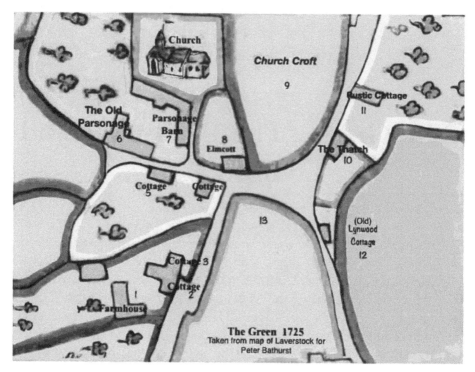

1725 Map of the village centre, taken from a map drawn for Peter Bathurst, by Jenny Hayes

The Parsonage now known as The Ancient Rectory (6)

The Parsonage, church and nearby buildings were destroyed by fire in 1410. The Parsonage was rebuilt in a large L-shape, the entrance of which faced south, towards the Cathedral.

Following the Dissolution of the Chantries in 1547, the wealth and income of the Cathedral and Diocese rapidly declined. The behaviour of many clergy of all ranks became disorderly, with gross mismanagement of rents and leases of the remaining church properties, by the Vicars Choral. In 1615 the Archbishop of Canterbury intervened, stipulating that leases for one, two or three lives should only be granted when the old ones had expired, and charged an appropriate rent.

When the lease for Laverstock Parsonage expired in 1642 it was renewed for three lives and the rent raised from £15 to £85 yearly. By 1648 the Vicars Choral, managers of the properties, was abolished and the following year most of the lands of the Dean and Chapter were sold. However, Laverstock Parsonage and Glebe remained leased from the church as a farm, the rent providing the support for a curate provided by the Cathedral.[1]

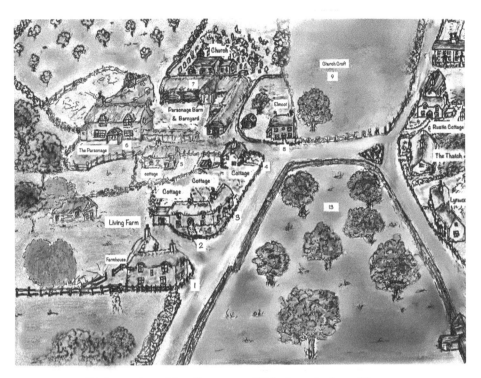

Bird's-eye view of the village centre 1725, drawn by Jenny Hayes.

The terms of the Lambeth Parliamentary Parish Survey from 1649 stipulated:

> A rent of £44 at the four usual feasts by even portions.[2]
> Ten quarters of good sweet and well winnowed wheat,
> Ten quarters of such barley by the measure of the ancient bushel,
> Yearly a good large collar of Brawn and a couple of Capons, at the Feast of St Thomas the Apostle to be delivered to the Canons hall of the Cathedral.
> The Lessee is to find a sufficient Bull and Boar for the use of the Parishioners and to dwell upon the premises and to manure the Glebe lands in his own keeping,
> The Tithe of the Parsonage of Laverstock of all sorts of grains growing within the parish, Hay, Wool, lamb and a tenth of the yearly profit of all pasture grounds and all private tithes....

The Parsonage was described as 'consisting of a hall, parlour, kitchen, wash house, buttery, malt house, and dairy room: three chambers above stairs and four lofts, a barn well-timbered of eight bays, a pigeon house, orchard and courtyard.[3]

Richard Williams, yeoman, was the first of three to hold the lease of the Parsonage farm and Glebe of 21 acres in 1649. His mother Joan left farm accessories and stock in her will in 1605, so it is possible that the family had already been farming this land. Richard died in 1671 and was followed by his son Thomas who died in 1680. His young son Simon succeeded him when he came of age in 1688, with his mother Mary continuing the lease in the intervening years.

When Simon died in 1730, Nicholas Maton held the lease until 1750. Then John Baker, a clothier from Salisbury, rented the property from the Church Commissioners, for three lives. The Baker family continued until 1862 on the death of the third holder, Edward Baker. Henry Cooper, a solicitor from Salisbury took up the lease until 1869, when the glebe lands were sold.[4]

Andrew Hibberd was the tenant farmer in 1792 until he died in 1825. Possibly it was then that the Parsonage was converted into three dwellings, as the 1841 census shows three families living there. It remained as three cottages until the 1960s when one was demolished. The two remaining were then converted in 1994 into a single dwelling and extended. The cottages were variously named 'The Yard' or Barnyard cottages, Rose cottages, Meadow cottages and currently The Ancient Rectory.

The ground floor is of brick in irregular bond, the oldest form of brick bonding, with a base plinth. The upper story is of brick of the second half of 19th century, in Flemish garden wall bond, with some evidence of 16th century roof structures.[5]

Numbers 2&3 Meadow Cottages after 1970, part of the old Parsonage.

Glebe lands

Surveys giving details of lands and property in the parish owned by the church were taken over the years, called glebe terriers.[6]

In 1616 the glebe terrier for Laverstock shows that the church held; 'A dwelling house with barnes, stables, backsides, outhouses, orchard & garden' and 21 acres dispersed in Laverstock and Ford.[7] By 1841 the glebe lands had diminished, consisting of the church and churchyard, the Parsonage Barn and barnyard, three tenements (the old Parsonage) the orchard below the churchyard, a field and bank by the river, at the north of the village now Bishops Mead, and land in Ford.

The remainder partly made up the farm known as the Living Farm, having been part of the 'living' of the clergy in the 16th century.

The Parsonage Barn now Meadow View House (7)

The Parsonage Barn followed the same history as the Parsonage. The brickwork is part English bond and part irregular bond, used until the late 17th century. The Church Commissioners held it with the church until 1865.

From 1795 the glebe lands with the barn were sublet to farmers Richard and John Cooe who also owned and leased other properties in the area. When the brothers died in the 1840s, their lease was taken over by Henry Cooper. He also bought the freehold of the 'Living Farm', following Edward Baker's death including land up to St Thomas's bridge and the fields under the Downs.

In 1857 the Barn was used temporarily as the church, whilst the new church was being built (see 176-7). However it was much too cold, so services were held at the school nearby.

The Fire

In September 1865, at the end of the harvest, fire broke out at the Parsonage Barn. Children, playing with matches, set fire to straw in a skilling (lean-to) adjoining the thatched barn. Fire took hold and rapidly spread to the surrounding thatched walls of the barnyard, reaching the end cottage of the old Parsonage, also thatched. Several ricks in the yard caught fire and sparks floated over to the adjoining paddock of Henry Cooper's 'Living Farm.' The farm house and two neighbouring cottages were reduced to ruins. The devastation also led to the loss of six hayricks, two barns, a granary and the year's harvest of 160 acres. The fire brigade from Salisbury summoned by 'mounted messenger' was unable to halt the fire, but was able to prevent it reaching the adjacent Manor Farm. The flames could be seen for miles around and many people came to see its extent the following day.[8]

Meadow View, part of the old Parsonage Barn c1970.

Henry Cooper built a new farmhouse on the northern end of the village on the road towards Ford in 1866, called 'New Farm', which he sold in 1868.[9] After the fire in 1865 The Church Commissioners sold the Parsonage Barn to Francis Attwood of the Close and Henry Rigden, land agent of Salisbury. The barn was then converted into a house. The L-shape was demolished, retaining the old back wall. This was incorporated into the house and two storeys built above with brickwork of Flemish bond. A washhouse/outhouse was built onto the western side, which by 1939 had been converted into a separate dwelling of two storeys.

Following the fire, the first occupants of the Parsonage Barn, now called Meadow View were George Tryhorn, a builder and his family until 1871. They were followed by Charles Cooper, also a builder and his wife Emma, who stayed for the rest of their lives, with Emma dying in 1922 and Charles in 1930.

The Rigden family continued to own the property until 1939, when they sold it to Emily Pickford. After her death in 1945, Rev Stanley Baker, then Vicar of Laverstock, purchased it. He died in 1950 and it has continued in private ownerships since then.

Adjacent to Meadow View was the path leading to the old Church of St Andrew. When the new church was built in 1858 on the Church Croft, the

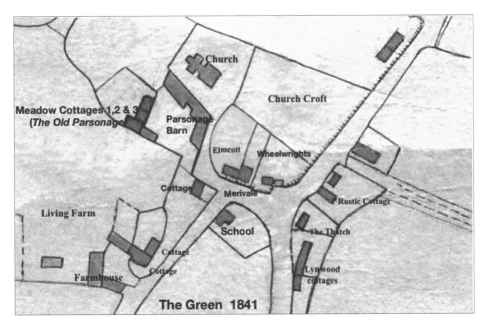

Tithe map of village centre in 1841, drawn by Jenny Hayes.

Bird's-eye view of Laverstock village centre 1841, drawn by Jenny Hayes.

original path fell into disuse and by 1966 was incorporated into the garden of Meadow View House.

Mews Cottage

This bungalow was built as a laundry in the late 1860s and used by Maria Cooper from Meadow View, next door. She bought the freehold from Henry Rigden in 1907 and it was converted into a single story dwelling. The cottage continued in private hands after Emma's death in 1922.

The Living Farm, thatched Farmhouse destroyed by the fire of 1865 (1)

The ownership of this freehold property had followed the history of the Parsonage since 1644, previously being part of the living of the Lay Vicar for Laverstock. Henry Cooper bought the freehold of the farm in 1862. His bailiff, Samuel Gray from East Grimstead, was living in the farmhouse at the time of the 1865 fire. The house was so severely damaged it was uninhabitable and subsequently demolished. Samuel had previously experienced two separate fires whilst a farmer and publican at East Grimstead. A year after the Laverstock fire and still the bailiff, he suffered a fourth fire, this time from gas leaking into their house from St Edmund Church Street, causing extensive damage from the explosion.[10]

Farm Cottages (2 and 3) now the site of Meadow Croft

At the entrance to the farmyard and opposite the farmhouse were two thatched, semi-detached cottages. In 1841 carpenter William Goddard and his wife Jane lived in the first cottage and farmworker Charles Whitlock with his wife Elizabeth in the second. These two cottages were also severely damaged by the fire and subsequently demolished. Meadow Croft was built on this site in the 1930s, a rendered, brick built detached house, with a tiled roof.

Cottage, later the Village Stores (4)

On the corner of the lane leading down to the Parsonage, there was a further cottage. This survived the fire but had been replaced by 1910 with a large old wooden hut. This later became a small village shop and Post Office. Mabel Jerred, wife of Ernest, was registered as the postmistress in 1927 followed by Henry Baldwin from 1929 and Mr J Hampton in 1935.[11] By 1937 Percy and Vera Drake had moved there. They bought an old army hut; half became the village stores and Post Office and the other half was living accommodation. The shop and Post Office were enlarged and substantially improved in 1955 (see 212-13). They continued to trade until 1965, later moving across the road into

Elmcott, Merivale, and four cottages in the early 20th century, (photograph, private collection)

Elmcott. The wooden Bungalow 'Woodville' was replaced by a new bungalow 'Kismet' in 1971 and a 'Wavy Line' Food Store with a Post Office which later became a Machine and Tool shop until 2016.

Elmcott (8)

Elmcott was built as early as the 17th century; a cottage on this site is visible on the map of 1725. The front brickwork of Elmcott is English garden wall bond from the late 18th century, now rendered but the back wall is of irregular bond of a much earlier origin.

By 1841 the cottage was owned by John Roe, a cooper, maltster, and cider merchant of Winchester Street, Salisbury and occupied by John and Emma Mussell, both born in Laverstock. They married in 1820 and rented Elmcott, a two-bedroomed cottage, for £16 10s annually, until 1849 when it was sold by John Roe's son.[12]

In 1853 John's sister Elizabeth Mussell, previously the schoolmistress, was registered as the first Postmistress for Laverstock.[13] Elmcott then became the Post Office (on left). By 1861 the Postmaster was Charles Uphill, who was the son of Robert living close by, in Meadow Cottages. Charles remained in this position until 1901, when his granddaughter Elizabeth was sub postmistress. She married postman James Baker and they were still living at Elmcott in 1911. The Post Office later moved across the road to the Village Stores. Deliveries were reliable and frequent. In 1903 letters received from Salisbury by cart twice daily were despatched at 11.45am and 7.50pm with a Sunday delivery as well.[14] Elmcott remained as a small two-bedroomed cottage until 2012 when it was renovated, and an extension added at the side and rear.

Merivale (15)

Merivale, adjoining Elmcott, does not appear on the 1812 map, but had been built by John Roe by 1828. Like Elmcott it was sold by Roe's son in 1849. The rent was identical to Elmcott's, suggesting that they were of similar size. The brickwork on the ground floor is irregular on the east side and Flemish bond at the front (see brick bonds); there is a blocked first floor window with the date and initials 'J.R. 1828'.

Widow Mary Ghast and her daughter were living at Merivale in 1841 and were of independent means. By 1856 Merivale had become the schoolhouse for the schoolmaster or mistress of the elementary school across the road. In December 1855 the Rev Townsend placed an advertisement in *The Salisbury Journal*:

> Wanted immediately, an experienced Master for a mixed National School, required to play the organ and a wife to teach needlework and take charge of the infants. They must be communicants and of sound church views[15]

The first schoolmaster to live there was William Prewitt from Alderbury, with his sister Sophia, the schoolmistress. By 1871 the schoolmistress was Mary Ann Lodder followed by 27-year-old Katherine Shergold from Downton. In 1881 she was living at Merivale with her parents; her mother Elizabeth was a milliner of bonnets. Katherine became Headmistress in 1886 and oversaw the move to the new school two years later. She remained in Merrivale until her death in 1929.

Merivale appears to have been extended with two attic rooms early in the 20th century followed by a further extension in 2005 and a new roof in 2016.[16]

The Wheelwright, Carpenters and Joiners (16)

The wheelwright's premises consisted of a cottage and a workshop built at the beginning of the 19th century. It encompassed the corner of the church croft, where the road branched around to the left, on the edge of the field where the church now stands. The cottage and workshop, which had been the property of the Manor until 1835, was owned in 1841 by Richard and John Cooe.

George Read had run the wheelwright's shop since 1787, having worked previously at Breamore and Winterbourne Earls. After George died in 1803, his wife Ann continued the business with their eldest son John who ran it until he died in 1824. His widow Sarah remained with her daughter Matilda and son-in-law William Maton, also a carpenter. They had married in 1823 and possibly it was at this time that their cottage was built on the Church Croft. So the business continued in the family for another generation.[17] Matilda and William ran the business from 1835 and by 1851 they were employing five men. At his death in 1866, Matilda sold the business to William Holloway.

Following the sale, four cottages were built on the site; the last cottage remained the carpenter's house with land going back behind the other three cottages. There was an entrance onto Church Road and a workshop by the entrance. In 1881 William Saunders of Winterbourne Dauntsey bought the business. In 1901 Robert Kellow and his wife Frances ran it as a builders and undertakers until Robert died in 1913.[18] John and Lilian Adlam ran the carpenter's shop from 1920 to 1924, when they left the small corner property and built new premises in Church Road. In 2011 Latch cottage was built on the site of the workshop.

Rustic Cottages 2-4 Church Road (11)

Opposite the carpenter's shop was Rustic Cottage, which appears on the 1725 map. It was originally thatched although now has a slate roof. The cottage was owned by the Manor until 1835 and by 1841 was owned by Richard and

The Square, Laverstock, showing the thatched Rustic Cottage, early 20th century, (photograph, private collection)

John Cooe. George and Susanna Read lived there; he was the youngest son of John and Sarah Read and brother in law to William Maton. He too was a carpenter working for the family business. When Susanna died in 1859, he remarried and moved away after the business was sold in 1866. By 1900 it was also known as Royal Cottage and divided into two dwellings.

The building is of brick with English bond on the ground floor and Flemish bond on the first.[19]

The Thatch (10)

Built as a two-roomed cottage in the late 1600s and visible on the 1725 map, the original cottage was one and a half storeys, with a central hearth and a well outside at the back. Further extensions were added over the years to the north side and rear, incorporating the well (which can still be seen), into the house.

In 1841 George Benger, widower, was living in The Thatch, a tailor with three children, his wife having died the previous year. Stephen England, a farmworker lived at The Thatch from 1851 until he died in 1893. In the extension adjoining The Thatch was a little shop. Mrs Mary Targett is recorded as being a small shopkeeper here in 1891 and it was a tobacconist's in 1907 run by Jane, Stephen England's daughter -in-law.

The 20th century history of The Thatch was dominated by the occupancy of one family, the Nortons. By 1911 Edward Norton and Sarah had come back to live in the village where Sarah had been born, daughter of George and Lucy

The Thatch in 1909, (photograph, private collection)

Tryhorn of Meadow Cottages. Edward was a whitesmith by trade but recorded as a shopkeeper running the little shop as a tobacconist and sweetshop until 1919. His wife Sarah continued the shop with her daughter Dora Norton, who ran it after her mother died until 1936 when it ceased trading. Sarah, ('Granny Norton'), like many women in Laverstock in the early 20th century, took in laundry at the rear of the cottage.

West View

West View was built attached to the south side of The Thatch early in the 20th century and was also occupied by various members of the Norton family. In 1911 Edward Norton's son Albert, a postman, was living there. He moved back to The Thatch in the 1930s after his mother Sarah died. Albert's son

*'Granny Norton' busy with the laundry,
(photograph, private collection)*

Leslie was living in West View in 1939. The other son Ernest (Ernie) was known locally as 'Mr Laverstock'. Living in The Thatch in 1985 he regaled visitors with tales of the old village especially the asylum (see 118).

Lynwood Cottages (12)

There were cottages on the site of the present Lynwood Cottages visible on the 1725 map & part of the Manor properties until 1835 when they were purchased by Richard and John Cooe.[20]

The present cottages were built after 1880; the brickwork is of stretcher bond used from the 1880s onwards.

Elementary School, The Bishop Burgess School (14)

The present site of the Green was part of the Manor grounds, later the kitchen gardens of Laverstock House Asylum. In 1832 William Finch, the proprietor, leased this land to be the site of the village school. When the new school was built on Church Road in 1888, the old building was used as a Sunday school and Reading Room.

The Square, Lynwood Cottages & White Cottages, (photograph, private collection)

The Sunday School and Reading Room (14)

Many reading rooms were in old school buildings, as was the case in Laverstock. The old school closed in 1888 and six years later, a committee was formed to consider using it as a reading room. Approval was obtained from the Archdeacon, who was glad to hear 'that it would be used to such good account'. Reading rooms in villages started in the mid-19th century; until then, any literary self-education had been mostly in urban areas. The reading room movement in Wiltshire was an alternative to the public house and a place of development for education. In Laverstock, as in many villages, the Vicar took the lead to form a committee, often with support from local landowners.

Rules included no smoking and removal of hats. Larger reading rooms were open for long periods but in Laverstock, it was open on Mondays, Wednesdays and Fridays from 7pm-10pm. The national minimum membership age was 16 in 1887, although Laverstock brought the age down to 13, possibly to increase numbers or to influence boys at an early age. Here there was an entrance fee of 6d and subscriptions of one shilling every three months.[21]

In 1929 Mr J R Benson of Laverstock House bought the property, and it continued to be used as a reading room and for village functions. By the Second World War, it was being used as a social club until 1950, when it moved to a new site on the meadows in Church Road, now the Laverstock Sports and Social Club.

On the death of the owner Dr Hill of Laverstock House, the old building was sold and subsequently demolished.

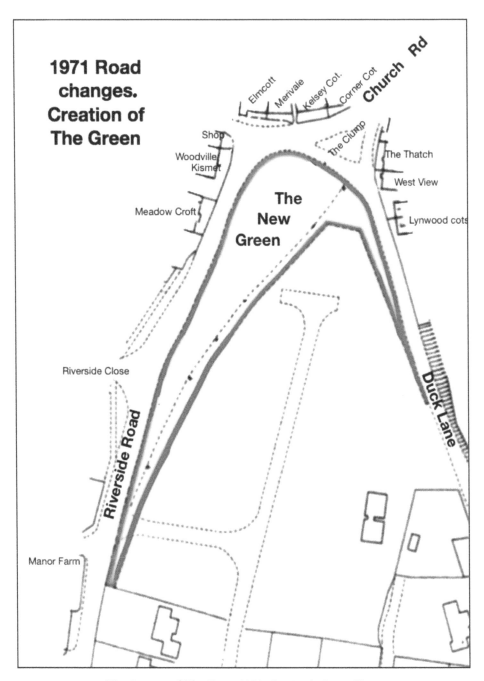

The Creation of The Green 1971, drawing by Jenny Hayes

White Cottages

Behind the old school was the schoolyard, bordered by the remaining kitchen gardens of Laverstock House. Two small cottages were built on this yard after the school moved to Church Road, numbers one and two White Cottages. They were demolished in the 1960s. Many of the occupiers either worked on the land or at the asylum, a large employer.

The New Green

In 1971 a new road was built, producing a different and larger village green, bypassing the existing old road. This road cut through the old kitchen gardens

Brick bonds found in the houses around The Green

A 'stretcher' is a brick laid just showing its side face, a 'header' is a brick laid showing its end face.

Irregular Bond or Flying bond, early random brickwork often used in rustic buildings, before 16th century

English Bond alternate rows of headers and stretchers. used until late 17th century

Flemish bond alternate header and stretcher in one row. Used in the 17th century, largely replacing English Bond by the early 18th

English garden wall bond three rows of stretchers to one row of headers in solid walls widely used from late 18th century onwards

Flemish garden wall bond or sussex bond, three stretchers to one header in one row used in solid walls with facing on both sides.

Stretcher bond continuous stretchers used from the end of 19th century suitable for cavity walls

Refs: Architects Journal, Heritage dictionary, Brick walls Mandy Barrow, and others.

Brick bonds found in the houses around the Green, drawing by Jenny Hayes

of Laverstock House from the Clump or Square at the junction of the old road towards the junction of Riverside Close.[22] The old lower road remains enclosing a much larger Green as the centre of the village.

1   Surveys were ordered by Cromwell's Commonwealth from 1646 -1651 to evaluate lands belonging to the church and parochial surveys of the minister's living, its size, and his character. This decided his salary, and whether the size of the parish could to be served efficiently by one man. The possessions not sold were granted to Trustees in 1649, and the revenues supported the maintenance of the ministry as in the case of Laverstock. NA COMM/12A Lambeth Palace Library

2   Lady Day, Midsummer, Michaelmas, and Christmas.

3   Bodington E J, 1919, 'Church Survey of Wilts 1649-50', *WANHM* 40 403

4   *SJ* 8 Nov 1862 4

5   National Monument record for Laverstock, Wiltshire (NMR), 1971

6   Glebe terriers are surveys of the lands, property, tithes and offerings with which benefices are endowed. Hobbs, Steven 2003, *Wiltshire Glebe Terriers 1588-1827*, Wiltshire Record Society Vol 56

7   WSA Glebe Terriers Laverstock D1/24/129

8   *SJ* 23 Sept 1865 8

9   *SJ* 28 Mar 1868 4

10 *SJ* Jan 1866

11 Parrett, 1999, 57

12 *SJ* 14 Apr 1849

13 British Postal service Appointments Books 1737-1969 through subscription website Ancestry.co.uk

14 Parrett, Sylvia, 57

15 *SJ* 22 Dec 1849 2

16 The 1911 census records 4 rooms. TNA RG 14/12089 f52

17 Wiltshire, Church of England, BMDs through subscription website Ancestry.co.uk

18 It is Frances Kellow who is listed in Brown's directory of 1912 as builder and undertaker.

19 NMR 1971

20 1841 Tithe map of Laverstock through subscription website Genealogist.co.uk

21 Slocombe, Ivor, 2012, *Wiltshire Village Reading Rooms*, Hobnob Press

22 HM Land Registry

The Lost Houses of Laverstock and their Occupants

Ruth Newman

Laverstock in the early 20th century was a small rural community with two farms, and cottages clustered round the Green. But while in 1891 over half the houses had fewer than five rooms this was still a village of large properties. As recently as the 1950s residents referred to 'The Hill, The Hall and The House'. Laverstock House warrants its own chapter but the other 'lost houses' of Laverstock influenced village life.

The Hill

The entrance to The Hill was from the Lodge House, built in 1899 opposite St Andrew's Church; a long driveway led uphill to the mansion.[1] The site was named 'Beacon Hill' on 18th century maps and there was already a cottage and garden there by 1787.[2] Its construction appears to date from 1805 when a 'new brick and slated Dwelling House . . . commanding beautiful and extensive views' was advertised for sale.[3]

By 1820 the land was owned by Lord Holland (the nephew of prominent politician Charles James Fox) but the house depicted was almost certainly enlarged later. It was demolished in the early 1960s and is now occupied by the housing estate beyond Woodland Way.

The first occupants identifiable from the 1841 census were Mrs Maria Maund (née Cooe) [1791-1842], living there with children William and Maria, both 20, and Mary aged 15, employing four live-in servants.[4] Ten years later William Maund, now married to Lucy, was the head of the household with five children under six and the necessary nursemaids, cook, footman and housemaid.

Described as 'a handsome mansion with a fine view', it was set in four acres of ground. When the Maunds were in residence it was listed as one of the main

1. The Hill, 'a handsome mansion with a fine view', 1923 (by kind permission Dave Cooper)

dwellings in the county with two drawing rooms, library, and eleven bedrooms. Extensive outbuildings included a servants' hall, brewhouse, and stables. In 1852 a sale was held, in situ, of the house's contents. Lasting four days it reflected the opulence of a wealthy Victorian family with an eclectic range of luxury items: a bust of Napoleon, a library of 500 volumes, a set of Raphael cartoons and a Dresden porcelain tea and coffee service, 'a very costly present from the late King of Prussia'. The 'newly erected greenhouses, 80 foot in length, with hot water apparatus', represented the latest in modern horticulture inspired by the heated greenhouses at Kew and Joseph Paxton's Crystal Palace of 1851.[5]

Despite the 1852 sale of contents the Maunds continued to own The Hill. In 1856 William leased the property to James Abbott for four years, with precise details about maintenance of both house and estate. An extraordinary clause gave Abbott permission to establish 'a public institution' to be called the "New English University". No additional details were given.[6]

Two months later the *Salisbury Journal* in its literary section referred to Abbott as the 'Managing Director of the "Retreat," at Laverstock'.[7] Nothing further emerged until July/August 1858 with various announcements in London and some Wiltshire newspapers.

INSOLVENT DEBTORS' COURT
James Abbott – A College for Idiots
    The insolvent, a "B.A.," described as a canvasser, had attempted to establish a college for idiots of the higher classes.
    It appeared that the insolvent had advertised for a superintendant of his college,

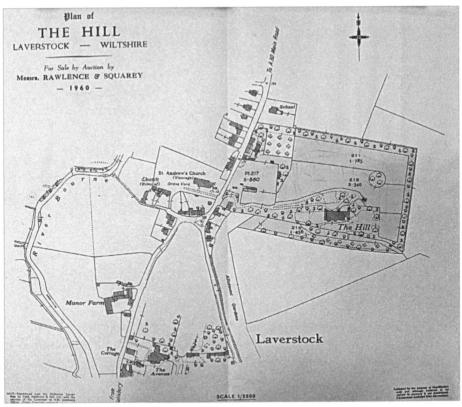

Plan from sale particulars of the Hill 1960 showing the site of the house, WSA 1126/77

Laverstock, near Salisbury, which was for idiots of the higher classes, and also a college which was to rival Oxford and Cambridge. He failed in his project, and hence the insolvency.

He was given 'a judgement of six months' not least for defrauding one of his benefactors of £300.[8]

Several questions arise: What was 'a college for idiots of the higher classes'? Was there any link with Laverstock House Asylum? Was this an institution to offer higher education to mentally disturbed people with family money? Regrettably no answers have currently emerged.

Meanwhile the Maunds returned to Laverstock at the time of Abbott's trial to attend the consecration of the new Laverstock Church in July 1858 and they were again resident at The Hill in 1861. With her husband away, Lucy Maund was described as a 'gentleman's wife' and with considerable domestic help cared for seven young children between one year and thirteen. The family moved to Portswood, near Southampton in the 1860s and the house was unoccupied in 1871.

One of the most notorious residents of Laverstock was Lord Edward Thynne (1807-1884), sixth son of the 2nd Marquis of Bath. He lived at The Hill from 1872, intermittently, until 1884.[9] In the 1881 census he was described as a widower of 74, 'the younger son of a peer', living at The Hill with his 14 year old daughter, along with her governess and five servants.

To set the scene, he was described by a contemporary as a 'hoary old reprobate', and he was known as a compulsive gambler, duellist and womaniser. Despite these 'passions' he sat as an anti reform MP from 1831-2 for the rotten borough of Weobley, Herefordshire,[10] later returning as an arch-conservative member for Frome. His gaming activities led to enormous debts, twice cleared by his father, but eventually he was barred from Longleat House, cut off from the family fortune and imprisoned briefly. He was twice married, the second time in 1853 to Cecilia Gore who died in 1879.

Lord Thynne was attacked on 24 May 1881 when travelling in a pony carriage from his home in Laverstock to Salisbury with his daughter's governess. Approaching the iron bridge (Whitebridge) over the River Bourne three men appeared and one, later identified as the Marquis Townshend, began to strike him with a horse whip. Initially it was believed that the attackers had escaped from the asylum but Dr Manning denied this. The three men were arrested and a charge of assault was brought by Thynne. The ensuing court case led to a wealth of 'tabloid' revelations.[11] Reported widely in the national press, local journalists had a field day in this 'fracas between noblemen'.[12]

First, in the initial hearings and later at the Quarter Sessions at Warminster, revelations came to the fore about an incident nine years earlier, that whilst still married, Thynne had 'eloped' to France in 1872 with Lord Townshend's young wife Clementina (40 years younger than Thynne). In salacious detail the reporters relayed the evidence as Thynne was ruthlessly cross-examined. Townshend's barrister pursued the questioning at the Quarter Sessions:

> 'Then, I believe, it was in 1872 you were kind enough to take his wife away from him?' – 'It was' (laughter) . . .
> 'Before you took this lady away did you write her several letters asking her to go?' – 'I don't recollect whether I did or not' . . .
> 'You can't recollect! Did your wife unfortunately find one of them – do you remember that?' –'Yes'.

And so the inquisition continued with Thynne's affairs coming under increasing scrutiny.[13]

In the event, despite popular opinion, the three defendants were found guilty, and given substantial fines. Edward Thynne won his case but public scorn meant that he lost every ounce of self-respect, and he retreated to The

Harcourt Coates' 'ministering angel' memorial, St Andrew's churchyard, photograph Roy Bexon

Hill where he died intestate in February 1884 aged 77.[14]

His obituary in the *Salisbury Times* was low key. No mention was made of his former notoriety, the report portraying him as 'the quiet country gentleman cultivating choice flowers . . . he seemed to have departed from his old world'.[15] He was buried unceremoniously at Fisherton Anger Cemetery (Devizes Road), alongside his second wife. Having squandered the family fortune, his only daughter Mary left just £25 when she died in 1906.

The Hill was rapidly advertised for sale, first the house with its 'park like pleasure gardens of nearly 11 acres' followed by the furniture and 'effects' including horses and carriages.[16] By April 1884 The Hill had been purchased for £4,300.

Later residents included, in the early 20th century, Mr Harcourt Coates, Medical Officer of Health for the city and senior surgeon at Salisbury Infirmary where he practised for 21 years. He died in June, 1907, aged 54, 'one of Salisbury's best known citizens' and his funeral at St Andrew's Church Laverstock saw a 'very large gathering'.[17] His widow, Maud Emily Coates, known locally as a fine soprano, continued to live at The Hill until at least 1911. Her husband had been a pioneer of early motoring in Salisbury and she became the proud owner of a 1908 green 20hp Beeston Humber, the only registered car in the village at the time.[18] Harcourt Coates' striking 'ministering angel' memorial in the churchyard fronting the road bears witness to his years at Salisbury Infirmary.

The last owner of The Hill was Major Harold Byles (1876-1959) living there from 1925 until his death. He came from a wealthy background and never married.[19]

Major Byles 1900 (by kind permission Dave Cooper)

IN the Picturesque Village of Laverstock, about 1 mile from the Cathedral City of Salisbury, 1½ hours by Rail from London and Exeter, and half an-hour by Rail or Motor from Bulford Camp and Larkhill Aviation Ground.

SALISBURY.

Particulars, Plan and Conditions of Sale

With Views of the

OLD-FASHIONED COUNTRY RESIDENCE

"The Hill," Laverstock

Including the HOUSE, TWO LODGES, STABLING, VINERY, FRUIT HOUSES, ELECTRIC LIGHT SUPPLY PLANT, and nearly

11 ACRES

of luxuriously Wooded Grounds, Old-World Gardens, spacious Lawns, on a healthy eminence on a level with

The Laverstock Downs, which

MESSRS.

WATERS & RAWLENCE

Are instructed by Mrs. Harcourt Coates to Sell by Auction at

Their Rooms, Canal, Salisbury,

ON TUESDAY, SEPTEMBER 17th, 1912,

At 3 o'clock in the afternoon precisely.

Illustrated Particulars and Conditions of Sale may be obtained of the AUCTIONEERS, Canal, Salisbury; or of

Messrs. *FLADGATE & CO.,*

2, Craig's Court, Charing Cross, London, S.W.

Sale of the Hill 1912, WSA 776/110

All family members died without issue and Harold Byles was probably able to buy the property in August 1923 from inherited money. He himself was an army officer serving in a volunteer capacity with home garrison duties during the Boer War, and in the First World War as a temporary major in the Leicestershire Regiment. He later transferred to the Western Front with the West Yorkshire Regiment for the rest of the war.[20]

Major Byles and Mr Taylor with Bobby at fete 1953 (by kind permission Dave Cooper)

In Laverstock he was known for his genial eccentricity; he did not own a car, walked everywhere, held weekly tennis parties, spent much of his time shooting on the Downs and was very attached to his dogs. Villagers enjoyed local fêtes held in The Hill grounds in the 1950s.

A charming anecdote perhaps reflects his idiosyncratic personality: *In the 1930s he agreed to rent out Hill Cottage* [originally the chauffeur's lodge] *for 15 shillings a week but this was thought to be too expensive so then he agreed to only charge 10 shillings on condition that no electricity was used.* (The Hill made its own electricity by a generator). *Later* [he agreed to its use] *but only for one day a*

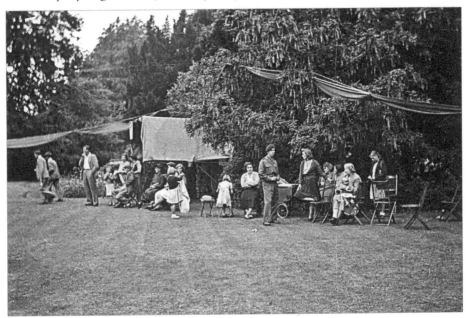

Fete in the Hill grounds 1950 (by kind permission Dave Cooper)

The Hall early 20th century; the mansion with columned entrance and grand staircase was one of the principal houses of Laverstock (photograph private collection)

month'. He then sent down another message that they *'might just as well use it all the time as it only deteriorates'.*[21]

The Hill was demolished following Major Byles' death; his estate was sold for housing, beginning with Dalewood Rise (nine houses built by 1966) with the whole estate covering 12 acres.[22]

The Hall

The Hall dates from the second half of the 18th century and was finally demolished in the 1950s.

A long, wooded curving drive led from a lodge where the current Mayfair Road joins the Salisbury to Laverstock Road. This then ran alongside the road and river for part of its length through substantial 'ornamental grounds'. The total area of the estate in April 1926 was given as 46 acres. The mansion with columned entrance and grand staircase also had a separate service entrance from The Avenue.[23]

The first reference to the probable location of The Hall dates to 1752 when Peter Bathurst sold a 'House and Marshland' to Thomas Cooper and this is confirmed by the Andrews' and Dury's map of 1773.[24] By 1820 the enclosure award shows Sir James Burrough (1749-1837) as the owner of the land, his will referring to 'his house in Laverstock'. On his death, The Hall passed to his daughter Ann who became a major landholder in the village. From 1841-

1855 the history of the house is complicated because of its attachment both to the asylum and to the doctors' houses within the estate. Residents appear to move from one house to another or even to inhabit several. In 1841 the house was leased by Dr William Finch (1776-1848), the asylum owner, but the tenants were Emma (Finch) Noyes (25) and sister Ann (20) plus five others of independent means together with six servants. On adjoining land was The Cottage (The White House)[25] (see 119) and this was occupied by their brother John W Finch Noyes (1814-1884).[26]

There is a fine 1844 map with a plan of The Hall, after extensive alterations, described as the 'residence of Mr Finch'.[27] This shows the site in its spacious

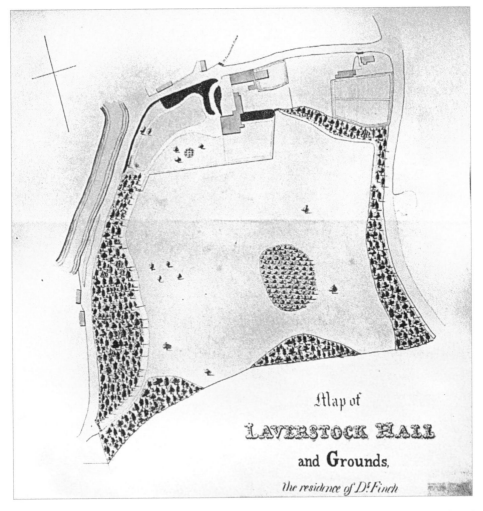

1844 map of The Hall showing the site in its spacious grounds alongside the River Bourne. (WSA A1/562/6)

grounds alongside the River Bourne. The detailed plan reveals a large house with servants' quarters, butler's pantry, library, water closet, as well as the main living rooms, with seven bedrooms on the first floor.

In 1842 Emma Noyes married Dr John Dale Hewson who became the superintendant at the asylum following the death of William Finch in 1848. Hewson remained resident physician until the mid-1850s, in partnership with John Finch Noyes - his brother in law and the non medical proprietor. He later, with Emma and their young children, moved to Cotton Hill lunatic asylum, Stafford, where Emma became the matron.

The Hall and The White House were each advertised for sale in early 1855, both 'occupied' by John Finch Noyes. He sold The Hall, 'a genteel family residence', probably privately, but The White House was withdrawn and retained by the asylum for future use for their doctors. The sales included a 'really choice cellar of about 80 dozen of old wines of the best vintages' mainly 'laid down by the late Dr Finch'.[28] Becoming a landowner John F Noyes moved his family to Titchfield and later Alverstoke, Hampshire, where he died. Although his wife Ellen came from a wealthy family and her marriage settlement enabled their very large family to live comfortably, investment in mental health had obviously paid well.[29]

Thomas Pain (1822-1885), brewer and son of Salisbury brewer and maltster George Pain of Castle Street, moved to The Hall with his young wife Georgiana in about 1856. He was twice mayor of Salisbury, the second time in 1856-57 whilst living in Laverstock. Very involved in city life he was probably responsible for inviting the 'Swedish Nightingale', Jenny Lind-Goldsmidt to sing at the Assembly Rooms (currently Waterstones) in February 1856 following which she donated £25 to the building of the new St Andrew's Church.

In Laverstock, as churchwarden and wealthy resident, he was one of the driving forces behind the new church which was completed in record time between 1857 and 1858. Following the consecration service, visitors were 'entertained with a splendid cold collation' in the grounds of The Hall where Thomas Pain 'extended his hospitality with a most liberal hand'. He also gave part of Cockey Down to be used as a rifle range.

Georgiana died in January 1861, aged just 34, and The Hall was sold the following April with all the lavish effects of a mid-Victorian mansion. Thomas Pain remarried and became an auctioneer; by 1880 he was living in a neo-Gothic mansion, Audley's House just outside Basingstoke.[30] He died in 1885, a philanthropic Conservative, actively involved in both Salisbury and Laverstock affairs, 'devoting himself heart and soul to everything he undertook'.[31]

By September 1862 The Hall became the home of sisters Grace and Caroline Everard both generous benefactors to the community, bequests ranging from the Lancashire Relief Fund to support for the new Salisbury Museum and St Andrew's School. After the death of Grace in 1876, Caroline remained in The Hall with a lady companion and five female servants. When she died aged 98 in 1907 the *Salisbury Journal* wrote of 'Laverstock Lady's Fortune' (£111,607 11s 7d). With no dependents her bequests were considerable; locally she left £500 to the Infirmary and £200 to St Andrew's Church while the £1500 to the National Lifeboat Institution was to fund a new boat, the 'Caroline' stationed near her birth place in Norfolk. Sales of extensive furniture and effects from The Hall followed including five carriages and an invalid chair on bicycle wheels.[32] A choral funeral took place in St Andrew's Church and a large memorial to the two sisters can be seen in the churchyard. The house changed hands several times in the early 20th century. A 1926 sale advertisement shows The Hall in its extensive grounds, including the mill house, carriage drive and pleasure grounds, tennis lawns, bordered by river providing 'a mile of excellent fishing', plus electric light and central heating.

Colonel Walter Barrett lived there from 1929 until about 1932 when the estate was sold to William Forder and Sons, builders, who commenced the development of the Greenwood Avenue estate later in the decade. The southern part began in 1936; building came to a standstill in 1939 with the area north of Mayfair Road not developed until 20-30 years later.[33] The early houses were mainly pebbledash, with the purpose built Buddens bakery selling fresh bread from 1936-89. The Forders apparently kept cement in the derelict former Hall in the early 1950s while some of the streets were named after family members eg granddaughters Vanessa and Rosemary. There was apparently a landing strip for light aircraft prior to the development of Melvin Close before the Second World War.[34]

The Barracks, and thatched cottages in Duck Lane

The houses known as the Barracks in Laverstock have always intrigued people. Why were they known as 'the Barracks'? When were they built and demolished? Who lived in them?

The date of their construction has variously been given as 1815, or conversely as late as 1878-9. Perhaps, because they were built for the village poor, little documentary evidence has survived, but a set of deeds has recently come to light which includes the site of the Barracks. This means that it is possible to date the houses more accurately than ever before and hence look at their place in the social history of the village.[35]

'Eleven cottages with black-smith's shop' was how they were described in a 1907 sale, built on the site of the current (2019) children's play area, behind the former thatched cottages in Duck Lane.[36] By 1881 they were known as 'the Barracks'; there was no military connection, but photographs show a terrace of distinctive white plastered tenements; in Alderbury the term referred to 'a building of plain or dreary appearance'.[37]

Detail showing site covered by the deeds of the Barracks and thatched cottages (plot 34): Ordnance Survey 25 inch England and Wales 1881

Using the deeds, the first reference to the site, which includes both the Barracks and four thatched cottages in front dates to 1765 when Thomas Cooper (1693-1773) leased to William Smart (yeoman) a cottage and little garden.

More substantive evidence for the Barracks site is provided in 1827 when William Windsor (carrier) sold a piece of land for £50 to Mr George Mitchell,

Thatched cottages, Duck Lane, with the Barracks behind, about 1910 (post card private collection)

shoemaker from Britford. Reference is made to the 1820 enclosure award and from that time the site is always known as 'plot 34' of about 40 perches at Lower Dean.[38] It was 'bounded on the south by a private road,[39] on the west by cottage gardens, and on the north and east by Wadham Wyndham's land.

The cottage and garden in front had meanwhile been sold and by 1828 an indenture refers to 'two cottages lately erected' on part of William Smart's original garden of 1765.

One of the most interesting documents, dating from 1841, is the will of George Mitchell, owner of the Barracks site. It has always been assumed that the Barracks were built *en bloc,* but this proves otherwise. Between 1827, when he bought the 'freehold estate', and his death in 1841, he built 'six tenements there'. Complicated arrangements were laid down about their future ownership; son George, and daughter Elizabeth Young (and husband Reuben) were to receive the rents of four houses and the rents of the other two were to go to his wife Ann and daughter. 'The well and other conveniences shall be made use of by all the parties'.

The 1841 tithe map displays both the six Barracks tenements built by George Mitchell and the three thatched cottages both on the original site (plot 34). According to the 1841 census the majority of the occupiers were agricultural labourers with notoriously low wages.

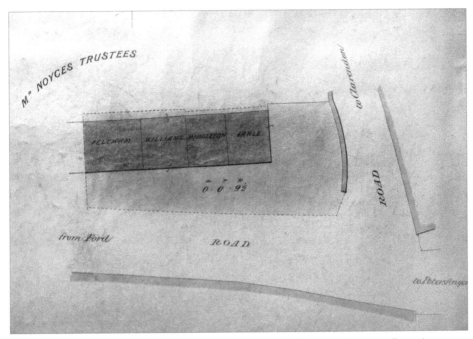

1860 from indenture with plan – conveyance of freehold cottages (private collection)
(From left to right; Feltham, Williams, Middleton, Earle)

The ownership of the Barracks site remained within the family during the next two decades, passing first to George Mitchell's son and then to his son-in-law Reuben Young, master baker of Great Wishford. The six tenements were numbered and tenants named eg numbers 5 and 6 were rented by Widow Phillimore (aged 62) and Louisa England (aged 24) laundress. By 1861 the houses were known as 'Young's Buildings'.[40]

A contemporary plan (1860) also shows the four thatched cottages and their occupiers on a small site (see previous page).[41] Described as producing a rental of '£18 a year and upwards . . . [and] always respectably tenanted', they were sold for £205.[42] An interesting legal declaration from Elizabeth Middleton (retired laundress) in January 1860 summarised the history of the four cottages. She was a single woman, 68 years old, and had lived in her 'current house' for the past 35 years. She wrote about the building additions and cited that 'the property now consists of four cottages . . . and a small garden'. One wonders how Elizabeth felt when she 'signed' this complicated legal document with her mark.[43]

But we do now know that by 1860 there were four thatched cottages separate from the six tenements built by George Mitchell on the site to which the deeds apply.

Reuben Young appears to have added three more tenements on the Barracks site in the early 1860s, and with his wife Elizabeth, sold the property of nine cottages to William Read of New Sarum. Again the houses and the occupiers were clearly stated and the 1871 census mentions Barracks Lane for the first time. One resident, William Noyce, a carpenter, was living with his wife and eight children in one of the tiny dwellings.

The continuity in names and inter-marriage between those in both the Barracks dwellings and the thatched cottages is striking and creates the sense of a small isolated community, not a village just one mile from Salisbury. In 1871, Aaron Middleton, a fellmonger labourer,[44] was still living in his grandmother's cottage and there are other similar examples.

In 1882 the Barracks were sold to a well known figure, Mr Charles Woodrow of Salisbury, Corn Merchant. By the late 1880s (now 11 tenements) they once again returned to George Mitchell's family. The purchaser was George Mitchell Young, baker of Great Wishford, the grandson of Reuben Young and great grandson of the original builder. The site was still called 'plot 34' and the Barracks were referred to directly. The 11 freehold cottages and blacksmith's shop were sold for £400 in 1901.

The 1901 census shows a move away from agricultural labourers in the Barracks. Occupations included a brushmaker and family with four sons, one working as a coal hawker; a maltster's labourer, woodman, carpenter, a bricklayer with an errand boy son of 13, a laundryman and an agricultural labourer. None of the wives, some with young families, was in paid employment. There is evidence too of greater mobility; residents had travelled from further afield within Wiltshire and neighbouring counties, while the bricklayer and family came from London and the carpenter's three year old son William was born in Argentina.[45] By this time the Duck Lane allotments offered a haven where residents could grow their vegetables or simply escape the overcrowding of the tiny houses.[46]

A glimpse of the housing conditions was given by the Medical Officer in the *Salisbury Times* in 1904 when he reported a case of overcrowding in an insanitary house at the Barracks; 'four adults and three children living in a house with three rooms'. He stated that there were 'nine houses together at Laverstock more or less in the same condition', the problem being that 'if they closed the house there was nowhere for its inhabitants to go' [but at present] 'it was a danger to the inhabitants and to the general community'. The council decided to write to the owner![47]

There were also infrequent accounts in the local papers about the Barracks' residents. An amusing case in 1901 referred to 'over zealous news boys' who loaded their trucks at the station with copies of the *Salisbury Times* and then raced each other down Fisherton Street using the pavement rather than the road. This was regarded as dangerous to pedestrians who were 'cheeked' by the boys when reprimanded. An offender caught by the police was Alfred Aylott, of No 8 the Barracks, aged 13, born in Notting Hill and son of the bricklayer. The defendant was fined five shillings.[48] Were they regarded as outsiders by the locals of Laverstock?

Perhaps as a result of the bad publicity, the Barracks were once again put up for auction in 1907 when they were sold for £350 to the Rev Oldfield (from Sedgehill Rectory and later owner of Burrough's Hill).[49]

By 1911 the houses were renamed Downside Cottages in an attempt perhaps to change their image, but the term 'the Barracks' remained in general use. The early 20th century saw continued mobility. No residents from 1901 were still living there in 1911, although several surnames suggest a family link eg Rattues and Pearceys.

Mrs Pearcey in front of her home at the Barracks, c 1920 (photograph Salisbury Journal , from a descendant)

Thatched cottages with residents in Duck lane, 1920s. The well was for communal use (photo private collection)

As a generalisation, in 1911, the inhabitants were aged from the mid 20s to 40s with young children, often at school. The houses contained between two and four rooms but the overcrowding did not appear to affect the infant mortality rate. Almost without exception the residents were described as 'workers' – farm labourers, waggoner, shepherds. Only Frederick Damen (31), cattle drover, was described as working on his 'own account' while Charles Pearcey, (from Number 11) was a plate layer working for the London & South Western Railway. In the two/three roomed thatched cottages with no back doors lived Phoebe Jerred aged 63, widow, described as a nurse (domestic) with her son and daughter, all born in Laverstock; Frederick Dyer, groom and coachman and family; next door was Joseph Love an asylum attendant. By the 1920s the Barracks and the thatched cottages were described as 'two rows of very small cottages, with no drainage' or basic facilities. Many had wells which were shared.

The history of the Barracks and thatched cottages is sketchy from the 1920s. Local papers carried a dramatic account of a chimney fire in 1928 which destroyed 'two ancient timbered cottages, with thatched roofs, at Laverstock'. No lives were lost; the sleeping baby was rescued by its mother's 'rescue dash' but as a result 'two families are homeless'.[50]

By 1937 the twelve Council Houses in Duck Lane had been built and it is probable that they replaced the Barracks at this time.[51] The tiny thatched cottages lingered on; they were still there in the late 1940s and possibly the early 1950s with no back gardens or indoor lavatories.[52] Kelly's directories suggest

Watercolour by Edwin Young, Cottages near the Duck Lane Laverstock, road leading to village, EY224. The Barracks can just be glimpsed behind the cottages, (courtesy of the Trustees of the Edwin Young Collection)

that between 1953 and 1959 the residents moved into the Council Houses, both in Laverstock and the newly built ones in Ford. By 1959 Edwin Young's 'picturesque' thatched cottages had been replaced by houses more fitting to the second half of the 20th century.[53]

1   The current lodge was built in 1899 but replaced an earlier lodge causing the entrance driveway to be moved. The stone pillars marking the former entrance can still be seen.
2   WSA 776/421 deeds relating to the Hill
3   *SJ* 14 Oct 1805. Information kindly supplied by Jenny Hayes.
4   John and Richard Cooe (her brothers) were wealthy local farmers and provided generously in their wills for their sister and family.
5   *SJ* 21 June 1851, 3 April 1852; sale catalogue, Salisbury Reference Library, LAV 014753206
6   WSA, 906/W/169
7   *SJ* 30 Aug 1856
8   *Bell's Weekly Messenger*, 7 August 1858. James Abbott served his sentence in Surrey Gaol.
9   A deed of 1871 granted Thynne the lease of The Hill for 21 years. WSA776/421
10 Weobley was disfranchised by the 1832 Reform Act.
11 *ST* 28 May 1881, 4 June 1881
12 *Wiltshire Times* 2 July 1881
13 *Wiltshire Times* 4 June 1881
14 Chandler, John, *The Day Returns, Excursions in Wiltshire's History*, 1998, Ex libris Press, 202-5
15 *ST,* 9 Feb 1884
16 *ST* 23 Feb, 29 March, 2 April 1884
17 *ST* 21 June 1907 5
18 Kelly's directory of Wiltshire, Laverstock, 1911. www.historicaldirectories.org/; accessed 24 Feb 2017, Hicks, Ian, 2006, *Early Motoring Vehicle Registration in Wiltshire 1903-1914,* Wiltshire Record Society, Vol 54, AM–1275
19 His grandfather, Sir John Byles, was a judge, his father and brothers, barristers, and Harefield House, Uxbridge was the family seat.
20 Information on Byles' army career kindly supplied by John Loades from London Gazettes and Medal Index Card.
21 Quoted in Parrett, 1999, 62-3
22 Thanks to Dave Cooper for personal memories of living at The Hill as a child. His mother was housekeeper and later Byles' personal assistant.
23 In this instance, the current road called The Avenue, not the house.
24 Messuage and lands in the Marsh conveyed by Peter Bathurst of Clarendon Park . . . to Thomas Cooper of Salisbury. 1752, Somerset Heritage Centre. The will of Thomas Cooper of New Sarum 1693-1773 mentions his 'estates' in Laverstock.
25 To avoid confusion, the name 'White House' has been used in this section.
26 There is a complicated relationship between the Finch Noyes and the Finch families. Why did John (Finch) Noyes add Finch to his name? John Noyes' father was Robert Noyes (paper maker) from Bulford. But Robert Noyes' sister, Mary Noyes married Dr William Finch (1776-1848) the asylum owner. Robert Noyes appears to have adopted the name 'Finch' and the family kept the name. Robert's children were baptised in Laverstock and all included 'Finch' in their name.
27 WSA A1/562/6 The Hall, across the road from the main entrance to the asylum was owned by first William Finch and later John Finch Noyes and so is included in the

asylum plans.

28 *SJ* 10 Feb, 17 Feb, 10 March, 17 March, 7 April 1855

29 WSA 1134/2/1 marriage settlement J W F Noyes

30 Currently a luxury hotel

31 Hampshire Chronicle, obituary, 5 Sept 1885

32 *ST*, 4 Oct, 25 Oct, 1 Nov 1907

33 The 1936 map shows the first 15 houses.

34 Information given to the author, courtesy of Gordon Hoskins.

35 Especial thanks to Christopher and Eileen Kirkup for the loan and use of their site deeds which made this investigation possible.

36 *Western Chronicle* 26 July 1907. The 'weekly rentals together amounted to £70 per annum, the landlord paying the rates'.

37 Alderbury & Whaddon Local History Research Group, 2011 '*More of the mosaic of Alderbury and Whaddon*', 18

38 A perch is an old form of measurement equal to a rod. As a unit of measurement a square perch is 30.25 square yards or 25.29 square metres. 40 square perches would be just over 1000 square metres or four (large) 10 rod allotments!

39 This is shown on the enclosure map, and currently the track going up to the Downs beside the Duck Inn.

40 Presumably named after Reuben and Elizabeth Young

41 By 1861 William Lee (blacksmith) had replaced Feltham, but Samuel Williams brushmaker, wife and two children, Aaron Middleton (40) labourer plus mother Elizabeth (69) and Mary Earle, widow, (57), laundress +2 nieces, correspond with the named plan.

42 *SJ* 19 Nov 1859

43 7 Jan 1860 Kirkup deeds (private collection)

44 Dealer in hides and skins

45 William Stout, born Argentina, fought in WWI and died in captivity, aged 20, in April 1918 and is buried in Germany. He is listed on the war memorial in St Andrew's Church.

46 The allotments are shown on the 1901 25" map extending round the rear of the Barracks.

47 *ST* 29 Jan 1904

48 *ST* 22 March 1901

49 *Western Chronicle* 26 July 1907

50 *Wilts and Trowbridge Advertiser* 21 July 1928

51 They are still shown on the 1936/7 25" map but Gordon Hoskins confirms that when he came to Laverstock in 1937 only the foundations of the Barracks remained.

52 Gordon Hoskins has suggested a row of communal privies in Duck Lane.

53 Edwin Young's (1831-1913) delightful watercolours of Laverstock are held in the Young Gallery of Salisbury Library. Despite their idealistic view of village life they remain an important source for local history.

People and Places

Laverstock in the News:
two deaths in the village
Bryan Evans

'Death at the late prize fight' September 1842

Described as one of 'the most melancholy and disgraceful occurrences that has happened in this neighbourhood for a long period',[1] the fight was reported nationally from Dublin to London. It was premeditated, unusually brutal for the age and condemned widely.

In September 1842 two teenagers, James Lenton and Joseph Coombs, met for a 'pitched battle', in a field near St Thomas's Bridge in Laverstock parish. They were cousins, both shoemakers and neighbours in Bedwin Street, Salisbury. There had been bad feeling between them for some time, and they agreed on a 'trial of prowess' for a prize of 5s with wagers laid. About 200 came to watch and 'egg them on', and the fight, with at least 23 rounds, lasted for an hour before Lenton fell senseless to the ground. Witnesses disagreed on whether or not he fell and hit his head or was struck by a blow.

Lenton was lifted on to a hurdle and seen first by the house-surgeon at the Asylum, who declared that he could do nothing for the man. He was then taken to Salisbury Infirmary, where he died only ten minutes after arrival. A *post mortem* showed that there had been a rupture of a blood vessel on the brain, and this was the cause of death. The inquest jury brought in a verdict of 'manslaughter' and Coombs was arrested.[2]

At the Wiltshire Assizes in Salisbury Guildhall, in March 1843, it was argued that Lenton had been the aggressor, and that he was taller and stronger than the younger Coombs who produced a good character reference. The verdict hinged on whether or not Lenton had fallen rather than been punched to death. In the event the jury acquitted Coombs.[3]

A suspected murder in Laverstock, 1845

Early in March 1845, George Woolford arrived in Salisbury with his two daughters. He was a travelling showman bringing with him a drum, bugle, donkey and a white pig, the latter being exhibited as his 'learned pig'. The animal had been taught to respond to commands in such a way that it appeared to answer questions on arithmetic or spelling by picking up cards in its mouth. Woolford was joined by his wife, Elizabeth, and his younger son. Relations between husband and wife were not good; Elizabeth seemed in low spirits and George unsympathetic.

On the evening of Palm Sunday (16 March) Woolford went to the Post Office to send some letters. About ten minutes later Mrs Woolford also went out. When Woolford returned he was cross that his daughters had let their mother venture out alone. He searched for her, and asked at the city lodging-houses.

A mother and daughter, returning to the city from Laverstock, saw a woman coming down Laverstock Hollow and later met a man by the gravel pits at the top of Milford Hill. The daughter recognised the man as Woolford, the travelling showman. Two other young women also saw the pair, and one said she had overheard the man muttering 'I be d---d if I don't'.

Woolford remained in Salisbury, staying initially at 'The White Lion' in Ivy Street.[4] Eventually, on Wednesday 9 April, Henry Thomas, a local drowner, found the body of a woman six inches under water, about 200 yards downstream from Whitebridge.[5] At the subsequent inquest Henry Thomas stated that there were some holes in the river-bed about five or six feet deep, where someone might drown. Sarah Rose, servant at 'The White Lion' testified that she had heard Woolford say 'it was time the old woman was out of the way.' William Mitchell, who lived in Gigant Street, saw Woolford on the night in question, and testified that the latter's clothes were neither disordered, nor wet. The surgeons at Salisbury Infirmary stated that there were no bruises on the body, and that they were sure the marks of discoloration were the result of decomposition, not of violence. They agreed that the considerable quantity of water in the stomach was most likely the result of struggling in deep water, and not of someone having been held down in shallow water.

After conferring for over two hours, the inquest jury returned a verdict of 'Wilful Murder' against George Woolford, and he was committed for trial at the Assizes. The trial took place on 14 August at the Crown Court, Devizes, where Mr Justice Erle told the jury that if they thought the prisoner guilty of committing murder it was their duty to return a verdict accordingly. But if they felt there was any reasonable doubt, then the law stated that the accused should have the benefit of that doubt. The jury retired for just 15 minutes, then returned a verdict of *Not guilty*.

Certainly there would seem to have been doubts. Woolford had apparently made some veiled threats, but the testimony of William Mitchell about the man's clothes, and the medical evidence, did not seem to point to murder. Woolford made no attempt to leave Salisbury, but stayed, making enquiries and telling people he was sure his wife had done away with herself. [6]

Prominent Victorians from
Laverstock Detached
John Loades

Until 1884, the Laverstock and Ford parish included a southern portion that was 'detached' from the rest of the parish by a narrow strip of Milford the width of one field. The detached area was triangular, with the Avon on its west and the old Southampton Road towards Alderbury forming its eastern side. It extended north to Petersfinger as far as the present Salisbury - Southampton railway line.

Predominantly agricultural, many of its fields were water meadows, dependent on the Avon for seasonal drowning activities. In addition, there were a handful of households along the western side of old Southampton Road that fell within the parish. Two islands within the Avon were also included. From 19th century tithe and census records, the activities in this detached section included at various stages a malthouse, two dairy farms, a tollhouse and a chemical manure manufacturer. There were also two significant properties occupied by notable personalities of the time.

John Staples (1780-1870), whose father was from Salisbury and his wife from nearby Great Durnford, retired from a prosperous career in the City of London to **Belmont**, his home on the old Southampton Road within Laverstock Detached, living there from at least the 1830s until his death. He was recorded in census returns as a wine merchant and a gentleman of independent means. His son, **Sir John Staples** (1815-1888) was privately tutored by Henry Hatcher[7] in Salisbury and was recorded as resident at Belmont in the 1861 census. He was prominent in the City of London, becoming an Alderman and serving as Sheriff of London in 1877 and then Lord Mayor of London in

St Marie's Grange: sketch drawing of the home Augustus Pugin built in Laverstock. From Ferrey, Benjamin, 1861, Recollections of A. N. Welby Pugin, Edward Stanford.

1885-6, while retaining his family connections with Laverstock. At the time of Sir John's death, his brother Thomas lived at Belmont and is recorded as proving his will, valued at over £103,000. Remarkably, Sir John's sister, Mary Anne (1824-1901), became Lady Mayoress of London through her marriage to Sir John Whittaker Ellis who served as Lord Mayor 1881-2.[8] Mary Ann was recorded at Belmont in the 1851 census. The house still stands on the road to Alderbury.

Augustus Welby Northmore Pugin (1812-1852) built a home, **St Marie's Grange**, within Laverstock Detached on the old Southampton Road at its junction to Shute End and just before the parish's boundary with Alderbury. Pugin became a national figure renowned as the architect who influenced the Victorian Gothic Revival and remembered for the decorative interior detail in the House of Lords, and for the design of its clock tower housing Big Ben. He moved to the Salisbury area with his second wife, Louisa and during 1835 he purchased from the elder John Staples a half acre plot of land[9] at a site that provided 'a magnificent view of the cathedral and city with the river Avon winding through the beautiful valley'.[10] Pugin built St Marie's Grange to his own design in the Gothic Revival style. The red-brick house with turrets and spiral staircase was considered eccentric but not very practical as 'he had not yet learned the art of combining a picturesque exterior with the ordinary comforts of an English home'.[11] By 1837, his wife was ill and did 'not appear to be pleased with the residence'[12] and as demand for his services in London and other regions was increasing, the family relocated to the capital. The Grange was retained until 1841 when it was bought back by John Staples for £500.[13] Since the cost of building alone had been upward of £2,000, Pugin suffered a significant financial loss on the property. During his period in the locality, he converted to Roman Catholicism and wrote his seminal book on architecture, *Contrasts*, which helped establish his reputation.[14] His lasting contribution to Salisbury was to design, in 1847, the Roman Catholic church of St Osmund. St Marie's Grange residence is still extant, although considerably altered to improve practicality.

Burrough's Hill and Sir James Burrough
Ruth Newman

The majority of the large houses of Laverstock have long gone, but Burrough's Hill still stands remote from the village and at 90m (300ft) above sea level offers total seclusion. Described in the 1977 sale document as 'an exceptionally well appointed mid-19th century house in an outstanding setting commanding panoramic views across the city', there is very little evidence for its early history. It did not exist in 1841 but had been completed 30 years later and is shown on maps from 1881.[15]

The Burrough family members were leading figures in Laverstock in the 18th and 19th centuries and several are buried in St Andrew's churchyard. These include John Burrough (died 1735), leaving large estates in Laverstock to his children, including the Rev John Burrough, the father of Sir James.[16] Thomas Burrough is mentioned in the 1772 poll book as one of only two eligible voters in Laverstock in a poll of Wiltshire freeholders, and Catherine

Burrough's Hill dating from c1860s with panoramic views of the city

(died 1813) has a memorial in the church porch.

Sir James Burrough (1749-1837) was born in Abbotts Ann. He later had homes in Bedford Square while his will also refers to 'his house at Laverstock'.[17]

He became one of the principal landowners of the village as shown on the enclosure map. In 1820 he almost certainly lived in The Hall and owned the hill above and to its east, hence the name Burrough's Hill.

He was Deputy Recorder for Salisbury and a successful lawyer, knighted when he became a judge in 1816. He had a reputation for being 'down to earth' and able to explain legal terms in simple language to a jury. This 'no nonsense' approach is seen in a far more serious light in Burrough's handling of crimes against property. He was an arch-conservative acquiring a national reputation as a 'hanging judge'; there are numerous examples from the Old Bailey records. One infamous case was passing the death sentence on two young poachers found guilty in 1822 of wounding the gamekeepers on local lands at Tidworth and on the Broadlands estate of Lord Palmerston. William Cobbett, the tireless traveller and radical reformer, waged a fierce public campaign against the judge. When Cobbett journeyed south along the Avon in August 1826, he climbed up the 'accursed hill' of Old Sarum,[18] and then rode over 'to Laverstoke (sic) where "Jemmy Burrough", the judge lives'.[19] There is no evidence that Burrough's hard line views changed, but he retired in 1830 and it was generally felt that he had stayed too long at the bar being 'wholly incompetent'. He continued to enjoy Salisbury society, attending the races, local concerts, contributing generously to the education of poor local children, eventually dying in 1837, aged 88, at his London home.[20] His only surviving daughter Ann erected a plaque to him in St Andrew's Church, a 'handsome Gothic monument' by Osmond, with a glowing eulogy in his memory.[21] By his will, all his 'lands, tenements, mills . . . situate at Laverstock and Ford' were left to his daughter, Ann 'during her natural life' as well as £5000 and as many of 'my English and French books as she may choose'. Following his death, Ann became a major landowner, owning not only the Hall and grounds but also the mill and the Burrough's Hill site above the present Potters Way.[22]

The 1860s sale of the mill (see 91) also mentions 'a small plot of land commanding one of the most beautiful prospects in the neighbourhood', referring to the Burrough's Hill site. By 1871 'Mr Dew's house on the Hill' had been constructed and ten years later Charles Dew, solicitor was resident, aged 46, unmarried, with three staff. The house was built of flint, part tile hung with stone mullioned windows under a tile roof and the exterior has changed little.

The owner by 1885 was Robert Stokes (senior), described in 1891 as a widower of 80 and retired tea dealer, living there with two middle-aged servants. His oldest son, Robert (born 1847), a wealthy grocer with a large family and staff, moved into Burrough's Hill following his father's death. Kelly's directory of Wiltshire (1898 and 1907) describes him as 'tea dealer, coffee roaster and Italian Warehouse, Silver Street, Salisbury'. In 1911 we find him as a 'retired grocer' in a new villa, aptly named 'Laverstock' in Boscombe, near Bournemouth. His son, another Robert Stokes, was by 1911 living in Manor Road, with his sister, and running the family business. Many of us still remember 'Stokes' fine grocery store which served its loyal customers until the 1970s. Signage remains visible on the rear of the warehouse in New Canal.

Canon George Biscoe Oldfield (1840-1932) was the next resident at Burrough's Hill with wife Edith and four servants. Born in Calcutta, he was a canon of Salisbury Cathedral

Sir James Burrough (1749-1837) acquired a reputation as a 'hanging judge'. Portrait by Sir Thomas Goff Lupton, after Thomas Phillips 1827, © the National Portrait Gallery, D32451

and became actively involved in village activities. Edith stayed in the house until her death aged 86 in July 1936.[23]

From 1937, Francis Robert Way (1888-1969) lived at Burroughs Hill with wife Emily and family. He was a partner in the firm of building contractors, Wort and Way Ltd, part owner of Woodrows, and also ran auctioneering and estate agent enterprises. His fleet of Wolseleys was well known in the village. Not long after moving in, the family lost their elder son Alan in Belgium during the opening battles of the Second World War. The house was sold in 1977 when Ray McEnhill (died 2004), millionaire businessman, chairman and benefactor of Salisbury City Football Club bought Burrough's Hill from the Ways and the family still owns the property.

The Duck Inn
Ruth Newman

There was no public house in Laverstock in the mid 19th century but beer was sold in the village by members of the numerous Rattue family. In both 1851 and 1861 David Rattue, living near the Green, was listed as a brewer although there appeared to be no formal brewing or sale of beer. By 1871 Henry Rattue (David's brother) was the publican, with his 20 year old daughter Emily working as a barmaid probably on the current site. He was still there

The Duck Inn – 1920s, much altered but recognisable

Mr and Mrs Macklin retire from the Duck Inn, 1965,
© The Salisbury Museum / The Salisbury Journal

ten years later while nearby John William England was employed as a drayman at the brewery. Another David Rattue (Henry's son) was listed as 'beer retailer' in Kelly's directories of 1889 and 1898. At the turn of the century the building on The Duck Inn site was called a beer house and Laverstock's village pub was developing with Mrs Louisa Smallbone (54) as the licensee and beer retailer, one of several influential women in Laverstock at the beginning of the 20th century.

The present building was first erected in 1906 following an invitation for tenders for rebuilding The Duck Inn for Messrs. Gibbs, Mew & Co (implying that the name 'The Duck' was already in use).[24] Annual dinners in November from 1906 of the Slate Club were reported in the local papers with Frederick Hallett, the new 'beer house keeper' as host with his wife as assistant, and 'about 40 sitting down to a splendid spread'. After the toasts 'the evening was spent in songs and mirth' with selections on the gramophone and songs sung by local residents of Laverstock (including well known names from the Barracks and thatched cottages).[25]

In the Kelly's directories from 1915–1927, Hedley Charles Chase is recorded as the sole beer retailer in Laverstock. Staying even longer, Cecil Macklin (1896–1977), a wheelwright by trade, became the landlord to the Gibbs Mew pub in 1933, assisted by Olive his wife, finally retiring in 1965.

Gordon Hoskins described the inn he remembered from the late 1930s. 'The beer was pumped from a cellar at the back of the building and was always cool because the cellar was built into the hillside . . . The Duck was a typical village ale house'. Macklin's licence did not include the sale of spirits, but 'he could stay open until 10.30pm while Salisbury pubs closed at 10pm, so late drinkers could and did make their way to the Duck' to enjoy an extra few minutes drinking.[26] By tradition the building still retains an 'egg' inserted into a side wall, which 'must never be removed'.

The current extensions to the Duck were made in the late 1960s.

Today it is a popular local pub with a friendly atmosphere, Hop Back beers and live music.

1   *SJ* 26 Sept 1842, 4

2   London *Times*, 22 Sept 1842, 6

3   *SJ* 4 March 1843, 2; 11 March, 4

4   Currently (2019) 'The Cloisters'

5   Drowners were skilled workmen who maintained the water meadow channels.

6   London *Times*, 16 August 1845, 7

7   Henry Hatcher, the Salisbury historian, owned a school at 56 Endless Street from 1824. It is reported that John Staples received tuition from Hatcher as part of his education. Details from a biographical article in *The Graphic*, 1885 on his becoming Lord Mayor.

8   *SJ*, 21 December 1901, Obituary under Alderbury local news

9   Ferrey, Benjamin, 1861, *Recollections of A. N. Welby Pugin*, Edward Stanford, London, 72

10   Santon, Phoebe, 1971, *Pugin*, Thames and Hudson Ltd, 14

11   Eastlake, Charles I., 1872, *A History of the Gothic Revival*, Longmans, Green & Co., London, 148

12   Eastlake, 1872, 149

13   Ferrey, 1861, 96

14   Pugin's research included copying illuminations from ancient manuscripts held in Salisbury Cathedral Library, where he had access as a friend of the librarian, Rev John Greenly, formerly a vicar of Laverstock St Andrew's. Ferrey, 1861, 93

15   Strutt & Parker sale document, 1977, OS 25 inch England and Wales 1881

16   The will of John Burrrough of Laverstock, April 1735

17   The will of Sir James Burrough, 1837. Ann, his only daughter, was the sole executrix.

18   Old Sarum in the 1820s, just before it was disfranchised in 1832, had seven voters and was the most infamous of all the 'rotten boroughs'.

19   Cobbett, William, *Rural Rides* (1830), Penguin Books 1983, 322

20   He was buried in the Temple Church, London.

21   *SJ*, 02 Oct 1837. The monument is currently partly obscured by the church organ.

22   Ref, 1841 tithe award

23   *Western Gazette* 17 July 1936

24   *SJ* 10 March 1906

25   *ST* 30 Nov 1906. A Slate Club is a society whose members contribute small sums weekly or monthly to a fund distributed normally at Christmas. Slate clubs derived their name from the original practice of chalking the names of the members upon a slate. Frederick Hallett served in the Royal Flying Corp in WWI (information from David Waspe).

26   Hoskins, Gordon, 1992

The Church and the Village School

The Church: decline and renewal
Bryan Evans

We have seen (chapter 6) that the life of Laverstock church was at a low ebb at the beginning of the 18th century. The time was characterised as one of 'general neglect'. Then, towards the end of the century, a reforming bishop was appointed to Salisbury.

Bishop Barrington's 1783 visitation

Shute Barrington was Bishop of Salisbury, 1782-91. He was keen to get to know his diocese and he sent out a list of fairly standard questions ahead of what was to be both a visitation and a confirmation tour. How were things in Laverstock? In their Presentments of that year 1783 the churchwardens declared 'all things well'. The answers to Bishop Barrington's questions given by the curate, Rev Richard Trickey, present a less comfortable picture.

First, the Bishop wanted to know if there were two services on a Sunday, as required by the canons of 1604, and if not, why not? Rev Richard Trickey answered that divine service was performed only once on a Sunday, the reason being 'custom & the narrowness of he stipend.' Laverstock was not alone. Only 93 of the 232 parishes making returns met this standard.[1] Moreover, the Lord's Supper was administered only at 'the three grand festivals' of Easter, Whitsuntide and Christmas. There were usually about 15 communicants, but the previous Easter there had been only eight.

The Bishop was concerned about pluralism, and in answer to his question Rev Trickey acknowledged that besides Laverstock he served Winterbourne Earls and Winterbourne Dauntsey.[2]

Bishop Barrington, a staunch evangelical Anglican, wanted to know if there were any 'Papists' in the Parish or Dissenters. Rev Trickey answered that there were no Papists and but one family of Presbyterians, of 'mean Rank.' He believed that there were no persons who wholly disregarded religion. Did the parishioners send their children and servants for catechetical instruction (teaching in the basics of the Christian faith)? Rev Trickey said that they did not, even though notice of the same had been given.

Did the church have a Register Book of Births and Burials, and how far back did it go? Rev Trickey answered that the registers went back to 9 May 1567.[3] The Parish also had a Register Book, duly kept according to the Directions of Parliament against clandestine Marriages.

Old St Andrew's Church, painted by John Buckler, 1804 © Wiltshire Museum, Devizes

Education was another concern and Rev Trickey had to acknowledge that there was no public or charity school in the parish. Absenteeism was a further worry and the clergyman acknowledged that he did not live in the parish, but in Salisbury Close, one mile away. (He may well have had cathedral duties as a Vicar Choral.) And it seems that the practice of serving a rural parish from a base in a neighbouring town was not uncommon.

Lastly, what was done with the money given at the Offertory each week? Sadly, Rev Trickey had to answer, 'There is none given.'

Dissent in Laverstock

Under the Toleration Act of 1689, dissenters could register with the authorities – either the bishop of the diocese or the local justices of the peace – and so gain immunity from prosecution under earlier (and still unrepealed) statutes against dissent. This system remained in force until 1852, when the work of registering was handed over to the Registrar General.

Records of the certificates issued to dissenting meeting houses give us some information about dissent in Laverstock, Milford and Ford. In 1797 the house of Elizabeth Rattey in Laverstock was registered as a Methodist meeting place. The paperwork bore the marks of Elizabeth Rattey, George Rattey, John Cundick, Elizabeth Cundick, and the signatures of Francis Hall, James Oder, John Parsons, George Hacker, and George Higton. The home of Harriet Phillimore was registered in 1852.[4]

A number of certificates were issued for dwellings in 'Milford in Laverstock'. In 1796 the house of Thomas Pottle, Independent, of Milford in Laverstock was registered. The paperwork bore the signatures of Thomas Pottle, George Offer, Elizabeth Pine, Sarah Geffery, Jane Lamberd, Jane Decket, William Sainsbury, William Butl(e)r. In 1823 a field in Milford in Laverstock called the Horse Pits, of six acres, was registered by William Sanger of Church Street, Salisbury, gentleman, Independent Methodist. (The field was probably used for open air meetings of the Camp Methodists or Primitive Methodists.) In 1829 a building in the occupation of Sarah Holloway was registered in Milford in Laverstock. The paperwork was signed by Sarah Holloway, John Cubitt, Henry Bowman, and George Barrett.[5]

According to Returns submitted in the 1851 Religious Census (see below) a congregation described as 'Independent', was meeting in a private house in Laverstock. On census day 28 attended an evening service. Average attendance over the previous year was stated to be 12 in the afternoon and 30 in the evening. Ford seems to have been more noteworthy as a home of nonconformists.

The 1851 Religious Census

Three factors lay behind the Religious Census of 1851: the rapid growth in the population and its shift from rural areas to the new industrial towns; the neglect and decay of many church buildings (the outcome of pluralism); the fears of the government that the Established Church was losing ground to the Nonconformists.

Altogether there were strong reasons to seek some hard figures on the state of the nation's religious health. Thus in the 1851 census year two censuses were held on Sunday 30 March. One was the general census, and the other sought details on church accommodation and attendance. The imaginative answers to the census questions given by the Laverstock curate of the time, Rev Lewis Tomlinson, perhaps tell us more about the man than the church. On the eve of the events of 1857/8 (see below), when the seating capacity of the church was stated to be 156, and when the population of Laverstock was 553, including 121 in the Asylum, Rev Tomlinson stated that the church could hold 250, and that 300 attended the Sunday service on census day. The form asked for numbers at the morning, afternoon, and evening services, and Rev Tomlinson wrote 'Services alternate'. This seems to imply that there was only one service held each Sunday, so that the figure of 300 was not achieved by filling the church twice, with different congregations at two different services.

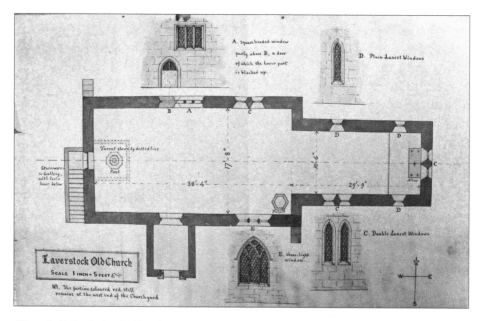

Plan of old St Andrew's Church – a copy made in 1890, and signed 'J R Jerram'. (The length of the chancel should read 23 feet, 9 inches – as in Colt Hoare.) © WSA 1324/49

The events of 1857/8

By the 1850s St Andrew's church was in a poor state. The architect, Thomas Henry Wyatt, was asked for his assessment, and he declared that the church was 'very damp and ruinous', and the walls and roof 'wholly insecure'. The churchyard soil was in some places three feet, six inches higher than the inside floor level as, over the centuries, more and more people had been buried in the same ground. The church could seat only 156 adults and children, and it was thought wholly impossible to enlarge the church without very extensive restoration work. For the funding bodies of the time (the Incorporated Church Building Society in London, and the Salisbury Diocesan Building Association) the preservation of ancient churches was not the priority, but seating, and value for money. If 'taking down' was cheaper, then funds for restoration were refused.[6]

At a Vestry meeting in February 1856, Rev C H Townsend of Laverstock told members that further burials 'cannot take place without disturbing the remains of the Dead which must be distressing to all right thinking people'.[7] In April application for funding was made to the Incorporated Church Building Society. Subscriptions towards the cost of a new church (referred to as 'Exertions'!) came to £850.[8]

One of the frustrations of this tale is the hint of problems to be overcome, without any details as to what these problems were. Bishop William Kerr Hamilton commented, in a letter, that the Rev Townsend had had 'every kind of difficulty to overcome.' The *Salisbury Journal*'s account of the consecration service for the new church noted the bishop's remark that 'but for the energy and determination of a particular parishioner the connection between the old and the new churchyard could never have been retained.'[9] What was the nature of these obstacles? Was it village reluctance at the thought of losing its ancient church? Or was it simply a lack of money?

Bishop Walter Kerr Hamilton laid the foundation stone of the new church on 11 July 1857. The next day, Sunday 12th, divine service was held in the old parish church for the last time.[10] Rev Charles Townsend wrote to Bishop Hamilton, 17 July, asking him to license the use of a barn for divine service, which barn was made available by Henry Cooper. The licence was granted the following day. Rev Townsend wrote again, 8 January 1858, saying that 'the barn is found so pervious to cold as to endanger the health of those resorting thereto in the Winter Months.' He therefore asked for a licence to hold divine service, and administer holy communion, in the National School Room, then on The Green.

The new church, built in 'Early Decorated' style, was the work of Thomas Henry Wyatt, best known for his Italianate church at Wilton. The final cost was £2,353,[11] and at the time of its consecration on 8 July 1858 there remained a heavy debt to be cleared.[12]

Yet much had been achieved in a few short years. Could the church build on this, and give spiritual leadership through the many changes in the village in the later nineteenth century?

The Village School
Sharon Evans

Much of this article was originally published in Sarum Chronicle 17

The school was started in 1835 when Bishop Thomas Burgess purchased land from William Finch in the area now known as 'The Green' and formerly part of the grounds of Laverstock Asylum. There appears to be no educational provision for poor children in the village before 1835. It was reported in the late 18th century that there were no Charity or Sunday Schools in Laverstock. It is possible that a small Dame School may have existed but in reality most village children simply received no education. The Burgess School was one of the earlier ones in the Salisbury district perhaps reflecting both the urgent need for a local school and the growing national pressure in the 1830s for a system of elementary education.[13] Its founding also reinforced the belief that such schooling must be given within a religious framework and this was true for the Church of England National School of Laverstock.

Old school. Newspaper cutting 1940s. Unknown occasion.
Private collection courtesy of Ruth Newman.

The Bishop financed the building of the school, which consisted of just a small classroom, and porch. He also made an endowment of £600 to meet ongoing costs directing that the school was to serve the poor children of Milford and Laverstock parishes. Pupil numbers were regulated by managers (school governors) who were to give preference to those from the larger parish of Milford if capacity fell short. They also appointed the teacher, oversaw provision of books, expenditure, and the delivery of a very basic teaching syllabus, the three Rs as a minimum. Appointment of the Cathedral Dean and the Archdeacon of Sarum as Trustees ensured ongoing accountability to the Church of England,[14] and regular Diocesan inspections were conducted.[15] Fees were charged ('school pence')[16] and the school qualified for government grants, as long as a minimum number of sessions were held (at least 400 were required with a full day counting as two sessions), and teaching and premises satisfied government inspectors.[17]

List of donors, new school. WCC Primary School rebuilding 1887/8,
WSA F8/600/169/1/26/1

By 1887, demand for places had far outstripped the capacity of the school building, which could not be enlarged, so alternative premises were urgently needed.[18] The new building, completed in 1888, cost £762 19s 11d and was built by H J Kite of Wilton Road. Local individuals provided £754 of this sum, the major donor being Miss Caroline Everard, of the Hall, Laverstock, who gave £400.[19]

The new school had two classrooms, and it was designed to accommodate 85 pupils. It still stands, incorporated into the present school, and the date 1888

'New' school, unknown date. Courtesy of Mrs K Walker, Headteacher, St. Andrew's School

is clearly visible above the front window. This building was extended in 1964, and again since.

The original building on the Green was eventually sold in 1929, having been used after the school moved, for community activities – social club, reading room, and Sunday school.[20]

The school has been known by various different names over the years. Initially, it was 'Bishop Burgess' Day School'.[21] It is now consistently known as 'St Andrew's Church of England Aided Primary School, Laverstock'.[22] The adoption of 'St Andrew's' reflects the long standing, close links between the school and the parish church.

School funding exercised the Trustees and managers repeatedly. In 1900, a meeting of ratepayers was called as the balance of school funds had fallen to £2. Subscriptions were collected from those present, and the chairman, Rev H C Bush, was to follow up non-attenders. A subsequent application for government funding 'to meet current expenses' indicates that ratepayers provided £34 11s in 1900 and similar amounts in the following two years. The London and South Western Railway had raised their contribution from three to five guineas in 1902.[23]

In 1902, government policy required the Local Education Authority (LEA) to hold responsibility for the school. When the school leaving age rose to 15 years in 1949, Laverstock School was designated for infants and juniors only, and older pupils went to secondary schools in Salisbury.[24]

Log Books

Most of the information about day to day activities is taken from the school log books which cover the periods 1864-1915, 1915-1933, and 1933-1976. A more recent one kept at the school has fewer entries, and none since 2001.[25] Headteachers made entries covering subjects including syllabus, inspection reports, staffing and disciplinary matters, school closures and outings affecting school routine, and attendance figures. Minutes from managers' meetings and school inspection reports (Diocesan and Government) give extra information.[26]

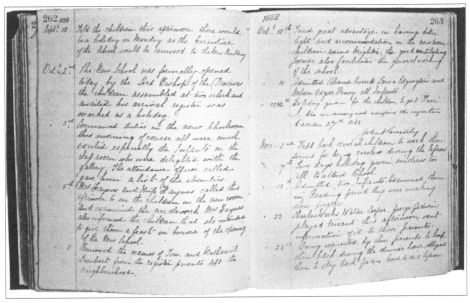

September 1888 extract from the school log book of 1864-1915. Log book, WSA F8/500/169/1/1

Attendance and illness

Comments on attendance are frequent. Poor attendance was often attributed in the log book to bad weather – a very significant factor for children who walked long distances to school – sometimes from Ford, or over the downs from the Clarendon estate. There were notable occasions when the school had to be closed because of heavy snow, making travel difficult, but also blocking toilet entrances, piling up in the porch, and even entering the classroom (1947). In January 1963, a snow drift, higher than the school entrance, blocked the road, and in March had frozen solidly enough to prevent workmen clearing it. The toilet system was also frozen. Such conditions caused the school to be closed completely for a week in 1947, and for three weeks in January 1963. Even when pupils came to school, weather conditions could affect work. The earliest log records that children were too cold in October/November 1870 to sit still, and had to be marched around the room. Many children were not adequately shod for walking to school in bad weather, and were sometimes absent with chilblains, or arrived with very wet feet. This was enough of an issue for the managers to provide funds in 1923 for the provision of footwear for use in school 'for necessitous cases'. The Salisbury Michaelmas fair was notorious among local schools for leading to truancy and St Andrew's was no exception; in 1905 25 children were absent without leave.

Serious infectious disease was very much part of life until the availability of vaccines and antibiotics, and affected school attendance frequently and seriously. There were nine outbreaks of measles between 1864 and 1935, and a smallpox scare in 1864. In 1892, more than half the infants were ill with whooping cough. Scarlet fever figures frequently in the record between 1881 and 1945 – often affecting several children in the same family. Diphtheria is reported four times in the early 20th century with the school medical officer advising on quarantine measures. St Andrew's pupils received diphtheria immunisation in 1941, a year before it was nationally available for all schoolchildren. Influenza struck pupils in the 1930s, and chickenpox left only 13 children fit to attend school in 1939. In 1904 the headmistress herself contracted mumps, and in 1915 was away for three months with whooping cough.

School attendance was not compulsory at first, but in 1875 the log reports the activity of a 'Relieving Officer' whose role was to ensure the attendance of children of very poor households whose school fees were paid, or subsidised, by Parish Relief. Education became compulsory for all children from five to ten years following the Elementary Education Act of 1880. The activities of an Attendance Officer (AO) are then referred to quite often. He warned irregular attendees and their parents, and sometimes issued summonses. Parents were 'called before the Managers' and in one case 'prosecution' followed. In 1908, three children living at Savage's Farm attended irregularly. The AO discovered that their route to school was through very long and often wet grass, which seriously wet their boots. So the land agent, Mr Keevil, was asked to arrange for the grass to be regularly cut 'as in the hire agreement' made with their labourer father. Boys absent from school because of being employed by local farmers, especially in harvest season or beating for shooting parties on local estates, were reported, and farmers, boys and parents were cautioned by the AO. At 13 years of age, boys could be officially allowed to work in agriculture during their last year at school, but in 1920 permission was withheld by managers from Mrs Pearcey's 13 year-old daughter, who wanted to leave school and enter domestic service.

Pupil Numbers

The numbers of children on the school roll fluctuated widely during the period between 1851 and 1956 when numbers were 47 and 36 respectively, the latter very low figure explained by the 1949 transfer of all older pupils to designated secondary schools. There was a peak of 80 in 1889 – possibly reflecting the effect of the 1880 Act. The all-time low of 17 was in 1871, when the government inspector reported that discipline was very bad. The mistress in charge left soon after his report. There were 102 on roll in 1968, which had grown to 157 in 1976, reflecting the expansion of Laverstock's population. More housing development since has resulted in a roll number of 195 in December 2016.[27] The school was extended in 1964, and infants were taught temporarily in the village hall, which at that time was Hill Hall (now no longer in existence), while work was in progress. A further rise in numbers required the use of a mobile class room in 1970, and restriction of the catchment area, with taxis provided by the LEA to take pupils who could therefore not be accommodated in Laverstock, to St Martin's school.[28] Admissions had to be further restricted in 1976 when new applicants living south of The Avenue were told they would have to go to St Martin's school, even if siblings were in St Andrew's. This provoked local fury, but was a short-lived measure, as the crisis had eased by the start of the new school year in September.

Teaching staff and facilities

In the early years it seems that there was a preference for couples to run the school, with Mr Edwin Lang recorded as master in 1855 and Mrs Jane Lang as mistress.[29] Similarly, in 1859, the master is recorded as Mr William Prewett with his sister Miss Sophia Prewett as the mistress.[30] By 1864 the school was run by one mistress, who was also responsible for teaching in the Sunday School. By 1874 the infants were taught by a paid monitor, while the mistress taught the older pupils. Until 1876 there was a high turnover of mistresses (seven between 1864 and 1876), but then Miss Katherine Shergold began a long career which lasted until 1914.[31] She was assisted by monitors, and later by assistant mistresses. In 1903 her salary was £90 per annum and that of the assistant mistress £45,[32] contrasting with the provision of an annual £10 for the single-handed mistress when the school began in 1835.[33] Since then, the leadership of the school has been very stable, with Miss E M Dale headteacher from 1918-1947 (her salary in 1920 was £208 10s a year), Miss Belfield from 1950-1973, Mr Richardson from 1974-1998, and the present headteacher, Mrs Walker, in post since 1998. Conditions in school were very basic until the mid-1900s. Initially, classroom space was seriously deficient, with all pupils – infants and juniors, taught in the single classroom. This first schoolroom was not lit or heated adequately. The 'new' (1888) school relied on coal fires for heating. In 1917, 'boys were sent out into the lanes to collect loose wood' when coal supply failed. A boiler and radiators were installed in 1928 fuelled by coal, and later, coke. Fuel shortages caused a number of school closures. Gas heating was installed in 1974. Pupils had to collect water from nearby houses for the old school's needs. The new school was provided with a well and pump in the grounds. Mains water was laid on in 1959. The original 'privy' system was replaced in 1914 by earth closets with buckets and dry earth, and a sawdust urinal. In 1915, the headteacher requested separate facilities for staff, and managers suggested the coal store could be used! Toilet closet refuse had to be disposed of outside the school perimeter on to neighbouring farm land, by arrangement. In 1924, 'owing to prevalence of Foot and Mouth Disease' resulting alternative arrangements 'gave extra trouble to the caretaker, and so 5/- was voted as a gratuity from the school funds'[34]. The earth closets were replaced by water closets in 1961. The installation of electric light in 1944 was paid for by 'locally raised funds'.

Curriculum and inspection

When the school was established, 'reading, writing and cyphering' were the compulsory subjects. The teacher in charge had to be certified proficient to teach. Clergy were involved in school life as managers with a lot of influence, and generally engaged actively in teaching. Church services were held for the school community at Lent, Easter, Harvest and Christmas. Not surprisingly, the basic syllabus was added to by religious instruction, including teaching of the catechism, ten commandments and hymns. Writing assignments on Bible characters and Bible stories reinforced the teaching. 'The Daily Life of a Christian Child' is mentioned a number of times, and seems to have been a resource used by both teachers and clergy.

In 1864, together with an impressive list of religious subjects, Miss Hales records having taught the obvious pence and shillings table but also simple proportions, mental arithmetic and even multiplication by factors. Poetry, writing letters, making out bills and a composition on Noah are noted. Needlework was taught, blackboards were used as teaching aids and slates mentioned in 1865. Presumably choice of subjects covered was influenced by the competence of the teacher, age range, number, and boy/girl ratio of pupils, and any teaching support. By 1868, pupils wrote on paper, used copy books by 1870 and ink wells in 1873. In addition to basic subjects, knitting, darning, button holes, and cutting out clothing were taught in the early 1870s. This rather female-orientated list perhaps reflects the mix of children as well as the skill of the mistress, as in 1877, the Diocesan inspector commented strongly on the very marked under-representation of boys in the school. Out of a roll of 33, only seven were boys. By 1879, probably due to the Education Act of 1876, the number of boys on roll had tripled and girl-targeted handiwork was reduced to simple 'needlework'. [35] Tonic sol fah is listed in the subjects covered at that time.

The first definite evidence of assistance for the mistress is in a Diocesan inspector's report of 1874. He names a paid monitor, or pupil teacher, and describes her work with the younger children as 'painstaking, accurate, animated, and simple.' On that occasion, he in fact rated her performance more highly than that of the mistress working with the older pupils. Again, the ability, interests and knowledge of monitors would have influenced the subjects they were able to teach. During the early headship of Miss Shergold in the ten years leading up to the move to the new school (1888), monitor-teaching of 'object lessons' covered a variety of subjects including the furniture of a house, the bee, leather and blacksmith's shop. Over this period, providing appropriate teaching for the different age groups sharing the same classroom became increasingly challenging, and the variety and possibly the quality, of lessons declined. Amazingly, given the limited space available, Miss Shergold had two monitors in 1886, when there were four classes. Increasingly urgent comments about this unsatisfactory situation, particularly the lack of separate classroom accommodation for infants, were made by inspectors, and when the new school (but still with only two classrooms) was finally in use, in 1888, there is a clear note of relief in the log book entries.

As government took an increasing responsibility for education, school inspections became more important and the log books record visits, and digests of the Inspectors' reports. Annual visits were made in the 1890s and then less frequently. The 1890s HMI visits are the main source of information about the syllabus taught then, particularly the three Rs, but go further to mention grammar, spelling, composition, mental arithmetic among other subjects. Needlework, singing, and drawing lessons for boys were remarked on. The latter became an important and popular part of boys' school work from 1891 to at least 1897. Miss Harris, a drawing teacher, taught them twice weekly in 1891-2. Drawing exams were held annually and in 1897 a drawing report from a Science and Art group assessing work as 'Good', entitled the school to a special grant. In 1901, the children were very interested in some 'geographical readers', and map drawing was done with enthusiasm. For girls, in 1914, sock making was added to the options taught while in 1916, seven boys were taken to a pruning demonstration locally, and grafting instruction was given by the County Instructor, Mr M Sharpe.

Although from the 1880s, reference to teaching of religious subjects becomes less prominent, regular Diocesan inspections were made, and their comments recorded in the log. These were detailed and show strong approval of the religious content of the curriculum, and how it was being taught.

Open days for parents in the 1920s gave opportunity for showing pupils' work, as well as dances, songs and recitation. Regular visits to the Salisbury museum for lectures on historical topics are noted, and 'juniors made Plasticine models to illustrate a Bible story'. In the 1930s, eight girls attended cookery lessons in Salisbury. Upper group pupils studied more specialised subjects including geography, history, local nature study and folk dancing. The log records 'further attention needed to speech training'. Road manners, taught by a visiting police sergeant, kindness to animals by the RSPCA, handicrafts by a 'travelling teacher', and swimming for older pupils are noted in the 1940s, when also the top class went to the Southern Railway sportsground for a games session. Organised games were not part of the school syllabus before this; children played their own games such as bat and ball in the playground during break times. By the 1970s, lessons reflected the changing times: football, netball, French, science, mathematics and woodwork were taught by visiting teams of staff and students from local secondary schools.

Wartime

The log books give no indication that the school routine was greatly affected by either of the two world wars. No note was made of outbreak or end of the First World War, but mention is made of a few national war efforts (collection of eggs, and money to fund 'smokes for soldiers'). Children also 'gathered five cwt horse chestnuts for munitions purposes' for the home production of acetone used in making cordite for shells. Payment of 7s 6d per cwt of chestnuts was made.[36]

The Second World War outbreak is only mentioned in explaining the reason for the delayed start of the school autumn term in 1939. During the war, schoolchildren were given instruction about use of the gas masks provided, and air raid procedures were organised. A former pupil remembers 'lots' of air raid warnings and how pupils were allocated in small groups to different nearby dwellings, to which they would run. He and a couple of others 'had to go to Mrs Anderson's house, and huddle under the stairs'. He is not convinced it would have afforded safety.[37] Evacuees were enrolled as pupils in 1939 (eight children), and 17 boys from Lyndhurst school in Portsmouth joined in 1940, with a seconded teacher. This strained facilities, inflating the number of children on roll by 50%.

Discipline

Discipline must have been challenging in all the years when the age range of pupils was very wide, including at times, under-fives up to seniors, some of whom were mature enough to be recruited to give teaching assistance. Most of the comments in the log books about punishment record and explain reasons for canings given. These were used largely, but not entirely, for boys. In 1928, Jimmy Lake was caned with two others for disobedience and inattention. 'J.L. smiled on the way back to his seat, so was given an extra stroke'. Some boys' names appear repeatedly. It is clear that some headteachers used caning far more often than others, and Miss Ethel Dale (1918-1947), was accused by parents on several occasions of cruelty, but after official investigation, complaints were not upheld and her pay was not compromised. She was a stern disciplinarian, but a head boy from the 1940s describes her as 'Fair. If she gave you a rocket, you knew you deserved it'. He recalls witnessing an incident in the playground, intervening and fighting one of the Portsmouth evacuees ('Jimmy Corps, who was a bully'). Miss Dale's comment afterwards was 'Well done. He deserved that'.[38]

The School in the community

In the early 1900s, the work of the school was generously supported by a number of local benefactors who gave rewards to acknowledge good work, effort, and attendance. They also organised visits to places of interest, and provided entertainment and feasts for the school children. In 1913 Mrs Manning (wife of the medical superintendent of the asylum) provided a strawberry feast, when each child was 'regaled with a half-pound of strawberries and caster sugar'.

The log books reveal some of the realities and difficulties of rural life. For instance, there were families who moved around in response to the availability of work, resulting in severely interrupted and patchy education of their children. Between 1908 and 1914 a number of children left school at 'Michaelmas changing of hands' when hiring of manual labour traditionally took place, and required their families to move home.

Education for one child with severe deafness was not possible in Laverstock in 1909, but was required by law. The child had to go to a school in Exeter, causing family consternation.

School milk was first provided in 1935, on payment of a half penny per bottle. Special occasions were noted in the log books: In 1910, an airship passed over the playground, and children were allowed to go out and watch. Empire Day was first reportedly observed in the school in 1909, when a half day holiday was given, and children sang songs in the playground. Between then and 1938 Empire Day observance, often with patriotic songs and an address by a prominent local person, is recorded on eight occasions.

Holidays were given for royal events such as the Coronation on 21 June 1911 and the 1947 wedding of Princess Elizabeth and Prince Philip. No doubt the children also welcomed the closure of the school for its use as a polling station for the general elections of 1929, 1931, 1935, 1945, and for the EU referendum in 1975.

As motorised transport became more common on the road outside the school, which had no pavement, the school authorities tried unsuccessfully in the mid-1960s to recruit a school crossing warden. The headmistress reported that parents parking their vehicles outside the school were causing a hazard by blocking the view of the road for safe crossing. On a happier note, in 1973 the school acquired a television from Radio Rentals and in 1975 parents lent a colour TV to enable the children to watch the investiture of Dr Donald Coggan as the new Archbishop of Canterbury.

The log books have afforded a varied, sometimes amusing and colourful picture of both this school, and the rural community and way of life which has been its setting.

The school has grown further between 1976 and 2018 as the population of Laverstock has increased, requiring the addition of new classrooms. The syllabus reflects national changes and trends, with digital technology being widely and competently used by the pupils. Children still produce impressive art creations, and sport, music, and drama play a large part alongside the basic three Rs. The school takes advantage of the opportunity to widen pupils' interests and understanding by visits to various outside places of interest. St Andrew's has a good reputation in the local community.

1   Ransome, Mary (ed), 1972, *Wiltshire Returns to the Bishop's Visitation Queries 1783*, WRS 27, 5

2   Many Wiltshire clergy were pluralists at this time, some out of economic need – there seem to have been many poor livings in the county. Ransome, 1972, 14

3   Today, sadly, the earliest surviving registers go back no earlier than 1726.

4   Chandler, J H, (ed), 1985, *Wiltshire Dissenters' Meeting House Certificates and Registrations 1689-1852*, WRS 40, entry numbers 465, 1777

5   Chandler, 1985, entry numbers 475A, 1044, 1259

6   Wright, Trevor, 2007, 'The Last Days of St Clement's Church, Fisherton Anger, *Sarum Chronicle* 7, 7. Only a few years earlier St Clement's, Fisherton Anger had been pulled down. It, too, was a small medieval church, in poor repair, and with an overcrowded burial ground. (St Paul's, on another site nearby, replaced the old church)

7   WSA 1324/33, *Laverstock and Ford, Minutes of Parish Meetings, 1846*, Entry for 14 February 1856

8   One of those who 'exerted' herself was Jenny Lind-Goldschmidt, the 'Swedish nightingale', probably the most famous soprano of the 19th century. While fulfilling a concert engagement in Salisbury she heard of the dilapidated state of Laverstock church, and gave £25 towards the project. *SJ*, 16 February 1856, 3

9   *SJ*, 10 July 1858. The unnamed parishioner was most likely Thomas Pain of Laverstock Hall, churchwarden at St Andrew's and twice mayor of Salisbury.

10   *SJ*, 18 July 1857

11   Laverstock Church Rate Book 1857-8 WSA 1324/24

12   *SJ*, 10 July 1858

13   Government grants became available to schools from 1833 which may have influenced the construction of the Laverstock school.

14   Diocese of Salisbury Land for National School 1832-93, WSA D/632/2/10

15   WCC Primary school Diocesan inspection book 1874-89, WSA F8/600/169/1/12/1

16   School building applications 1833-81, TNA ED 103/47/19

17   Laverstock CE School Log book from 1864-1915, WSA F8/500/169/1/1

18   WCC lease of land for school 1887, WSA F8/600/169/1/1/1; D/632/2/10

19   WSA D/632/2/10

20   WCC Draft deeds and papers 1887-1947, WSA F8/600/169/1/1/2

21   WSA D/632/2/10

22   General Education Committee Cuttings books 1905-39, 1940-62, WSA F8/230/2/1,3 Managers' minutes 1903-1972, WSA F8/600/169/1/3/1,2 Log books WSA F8/500/169/1/1,2; Correspondence WSA F8/600/169/1/26/2

23   WCC Primary school correspondence 1901-1928, WSA F8/600/169/1/26/2 Log book, WSA F8/500/169/1/1

24   WCC HMI reports 1920-93, WSA F8/300/176; Log books WSA F8/500/169/1/3 Log book 1976-2001, held at school

25   Log books WSA F8/500/169/1/1,2; Log book 1976-2001

26   Managers' Minutes WSA F8/600/169/1/3/1,2; Inspection book WSA F8/600/169/1/12/1; HMI reports WSA F8/300/176

27   Information from St Andrew's School office

28   HMI reports, WSA F8/300/176

29   Post Office Directory of Wiltshire, 1855, 69

30   Post Office Directory of Wiltshire, 1859, 440

31   Katherine Shergold lived in the schoolteacher's house, Merivale, on the Green

32   Managers' minutes WSA F8/600/169/1/3/1,2

33   Bishop Burgess Educational Foundation 1880-1931 TNA ED49/8205

34   Managers' minutes WSA F8/600/169/1/3/1,2

35   Gillard, D (2011), *Education in England: a brief history*

36   Importing acetone from across the Atlantic was now unreliable, and although it could be made from maize or rice, these were needed for food. www.historyextra.com/conker

37   Annetts, P, 3 January 2017 Personal communication

38   Annetts, 2017

Into the Modern Age

The Church from the mid-Victorian period to the present day

Bryan Evans

We have seen (chapter 13) how a medieval church, run-down and too small for a growing population, was replaced with a completely new building. Rev Townsend took the lead in this project, and he was strongly backed by his bishop, and key figures in the village.

Rev Charles Townsend left the parish in 1861, and he was followed by Rev John Prosser Greenly (1861-1885). Greenly's father, Rev Andrew John Greenly had served the parish briefly, about 1812-1813. Before that he was a naval chaplain, and served on board HMS *Revenge* at the battle of Trafalgar in 1805. Tragedy overtook the family in 1855 when four daughters of the younger Greenly – Mary, Edith, Ellen and Rachel – all died from scarlet fever within one month of each other. The eldest of the four was only eight years old. The Greenly family are commemorated in the windows in the north wall of the chancel.[1]

Rev Greenly was followed by Rev Herbert Cromwell Bush (1889-1900), who was very proud of his lineal descent from Oliver Cromwell. After him came Rev Arthur Aldworth. Both these clergymen lost a son in the First World War. James Cromwell Bush served with the Royal Flying Corps and was shot down and killed in 1917. Douglas Aldworth, a Second Lieutenant with the Royal Berkshire Regiment, died just before the end of the War (see 200-1).

St Andrew's was still very much a village church in the 1920s and 30s. Thus, at the Annual Meeting in April 1930 it was decided that a notice should be fixed on the gates of the new portion of the Churchyard asking that the gates be kept shut, because cows had been straying where they ought not. Numbers attending Sunday services were often in single figures, rising to 65-80 for Easter communion. Weekly offerings (generally 5s-9s in the early years of the century, £1-£2 by 1947) went towards the Altar Fund, the Chancel Lamp, the Choir

Fund, and charities such as the Infirmary, Waifs and Strays, the Coal Club, and the 'House for Fallen Girls'.

Canon Stanley Baker (1938-1950) was one of the most active, and colourful, clergy to serve Laverstock. Among his students at the Teacher Training College in the Close he had a name as 'a rather eccentric and lovable character'. He once tried to climb to the last row of pinnacles at the base of the Cathedral Spire 'where he stuck firmly and could only be freed with much intake of breath and pushing and pulling.'[2] At the Cathedral he held the record (kept by the choristers) for the longest delivery of the Friday litany, driving choristers (who otherwise loved him) and clergy to distraction. As late as 1949 there was a request by a retiring St Andrew's churchwarden, at the Annual Church Meeting, that the church services might be shortened, as their length was a deterrent to attendance.

Canon Baker's years at St Andrew's saw electric lighting installed (1938), then a carved oak chancel screen added, and medieval glass from Salisbury Cathedral inserted into the west window (see below). In 1943 a painted reredos (the screen covering the wall behind the communion table) depicting the supper at Emmaus was placed in the sanctuary. Canon Baker was also asked to open a Mission on the edge of the parish. This was the former Methodist Chapel at Ford, which was re-named St Christopher's. This small building was, in effect, a Chapel-of-Ease for the Ford end of the parish.

Dr Baker also took a lot of interest in the village school, where he gave lessons in singing, Scripture and local history. During the Second World War he visited the Balloon Unit, and the Searchlight team, and held brief services for them. Post-war changes at St Andrew's saw the church at last made a benefice (1955).[3] In 1973, under Pastoral Measure arrangements the Riverbourne Estate and the Petersfinger Farm area were transferred to the parish of Sarum St Martin, and Ford to the parish of Winterbourne (St Christopher's Chapel at Ford closed in 1980).

Church attendances rose steadily from 1976, and numbers on the electoral roll of church members reached a peak of 217 in 1990. At the 1984 Annual Parochial Church Meeting Rev George Bull reported that about 100 people were taking communion each week, and for family services the church was often completely full. Tentative discussions began about providing more seating, with an extra floor, perhaps, or even a new all-purpose building. None of these plans was followed up in the end, and after 1990 numbers began to fall again. In fact in the early 1990s it became clear that when Rev George Bull retired Laverstock would not be given another parish priest for itself alone, but would have to join with a neighbouring parish. It linked up, first, with Sarum St Martin (1995-2011) then with St Mark's, Salisbury from 2012 to the present.

The present church: a few points of interest

The oldest memorial in the church is a brass removed from the old church. It reads: *Off yor charite p^y (pray) for the soul of Antony Ernley esquier and Margarett his wyfe, which Antony decessid the 17 day of November An.Dm. MCCCCCXXX (1530), on who^s soule Ih'u have m'cy* (that is, 'Jesu have mercy'). The William Erneley (*sic*) who was instituted as curate in 1514 was Antony's younger brother.

Memorial brass for Antony and Margaret Ernley, 1530

left: Silver chalice inscribed 'Benjamin Freemantle Will Hartford Churchwardens of Laverstock 1697'; right, detail of the base of the chalice, inscribed with the initials of Rowland West, a goldsmith and silversmith who was living in St Thomas's Churchyard, Salisbury in 1698.
© *Peter Marsh*

On the north wall of the nave (but now half-hidden by the organ) is a memorial to Sir James Burrough (1749-1837), who, as a judge of the Court of Common Pleas gained a name as a 'hanging judge' (see 167-9).

Also on the north wall of the nave is the only post-1858 memorial in the church (other than the war memorial). It honours Henry John Manning, who died in 1910, aged 74. He was medical superintendent at Laverstock House Asylum for forty years, and a churchwarden.

The church owns a silver chalice dated 1697 inscribed with the names of the churchwardens. It bears the initials RW which must be Rowland West, a silversmith and goldsmith. (see photos) The Laverstock chalice was probably the final communion cup made by Salisbury silversmiths.[4]

A 1553 inventory of church goods lists two bells at Laverstock.[5] By the early 1800s there was only one, cast by James Wells of Aldbourne, Wiltshire in 1817.[6] In 1857-58 two new bells were cast from this older one. At the April 1945 Annual Parochial Church Meeting it was reported that the bells had been repaired, including putting right the damage done by a wartime barrage balloon. The bells were recast in 1959-60, and made slightly smaller. (The diameter of the larger bell was only one inch less than the turret space, and it had been rubbing against the stonework.) Following the parting of a bell rope in 2014, the bells were taken down again and treated to a much needed refurbishment.

Canon Stanley Baker and the medieval stained glass in the west window

On the stonework beneath the west window there is this inscription: 'The XIIIth century glass in this church for 500 years formed a part of Salisbury Cathedral. It was thrown away about 1790, recovered 1933, and was placed here 1939.' Behind these plain words lies an amazing story of dogged searching.

Bishop Shute Barrington had enlisted the fashionable architect, James Wyatt, to carry out restoration work at the Cathedral, and to make it lighter. Medieval stained glass was replaced with clear glass, and the old glass was 'shot into the town-ditch', or used to level the ground near the Chapter House.[7] This was not deliberate philistinism on Wyatt's part, but rather the outcome of one of his failings. He would often take more interest in the next job than the one in hand, and so did not always exercise proper supervision.[8]

It was in 1924 that Dr Baker began his search.[9] The key question concerned the exact location of 'the town-ditch' where the old glass was thrown. Over the next few years Dr Baker scoured the ground around the Chapter House, then dug up gardens (with the owners' willing consent) along the route of the former city ramparts and ditch. He bought a house near St Martin's church, so that he could dig up its garden, too. (It ran down to the line of a former deep water channel.) He also explored a ditch at East Harnham, with the help of a water diviner who reckoned he could find glass. But they drew blank. Then came a breakthrough in April, 1932, when glass was found at the west end of De Vaux Place, near the Harnham Gate.[10] Later, more glass was found in the former glazier's workshop over the Trinity Chapel of the Cathedral, and more again in 1935 when a great deal of 'rubbish' was cleared from the triforium (the arcade leading into the space above the aisle roof). Dr Baker sieved out a lot of medieval glass from this material.

However, Salisbury Cathedral did not want the glass back, fearing it would darken the interior. Instead Dr Baker gave twenty-four panels of the glass to Winchester Cathedral, twenty panels to St Andrew's Church, and some glass for the east window of Boyton church, near Warminster.

The fine 14th and 15th century woodwork of the chancel screen was found by Dr Baker when, searching for glass, he followed a false trail to Shrewsbury. The complex tracery of the oak that Canon Baker gave to St Andrew's is perhaps of Welsh origin.[11] The screen did not quite fill the space, and a local joiner, John C Adlam, with guidance from the architect JH Jacob, carved a matching piece to fill the gap.[12]

Excavations in the old churchyard, 1969 and 2008-9

Some exploration of the old churchyard was undertaken in August 1969, and the searchers stumbled on the Bathurst family vault, with its five 18th century lead coffins. Then in 2008-9, on the 150th anniversary of the present church, professional archaeologist Alex Langlands led a small team of volunteers in a search for traces of the walls of the medieval church. For their general guidance the team had Buckler's watercolour of the church, and a plan of old St Andrew's found in Sir Richard Colt Hoare's *The Modern History of South Wiltshire*.[13] They also had the one piece of surviving masonry, a buttress and short section of wall that had been part of the south-east corner of the nave.[14]

In an archaeology week in 2008 three test pits were dug. The work was afterwards written up in an article by Alex Langlands in the journal of the Wiltshire Archaeological and Natural History Society.[15] The test pit in the presumed area of the chancel revealed some fragments of church foundations, and small fragments of glazed floor tiles and of painted wall-plaster gave slight hints of the internal decoration of the medieval church.

Another test pit was meant to throw light on the junction of the north wall of the chancel with the north-east corner of the nave. It soon became clear

Buttress and short section of wall of the medieval church. Drawing by Jenny Hayes

that the unevenness of the ground here was the outcome of earlier digging, probably in 1969. No medieval wall foundations were uncovered. A third test pit was opened in the hope of finding the north wall of the nave. The pit had to be sunk some way before a few flint nodules bonded with clay were found, giving some indication of the medieval wall.

In the follow-up dig in July 2009 the three pits were re-opened and extended, and a fourth pit was dug at the western end of the site. With the first pit the hope was now to find the chancel floor. A few inches below ground level the tombstone of 'Nathanael Marshall, Gentleman' (died 1698) was uncovered again (it had been located in 1969). This memorial is mentioned in Colt Hoare's account of the old church as having been in the chancel. The dislodging of a stone on the floor of the pit opened up a view into the Bathurst vault to the north of the chancel. The location of the vault had been forgotten since the 1969 dig. The vault was recorded but not explored, for this was not the purpose of the project. The hole was filled and re-sealed at the end of the week.

Five lead 18th century coffins of members of the Bathurst family of Clarendon Park were discovered in the brick lined family vault.

At the nave/chancel junction quite extensive sections of medieval wall foundations were uncovered. The new western pit revealed compacted earth flooring, then nothing beyond it but soil, tree roots and broken roof tiles. Alex Langlands was confident that this was the west end of the medieval church, and that the Victorian workmen had, as elsewhere on the site, very thoroughly robbed out the wall foundations.

In tidying up the floor of the nave/chancel junction pit, at the end of the week, Alex realised that he was uncovering an articulated skeleton. After some careful work the arms, backbone, hip bones and tops of the leg bones could be seen (the rest of the legs were buried in the side of the trench). There was no skull. On the basis of pelvis size it was believed that this was probably the skeleton of a man. The burial was thought to be below the level of the medieval wall foundations, and it was aligned east-west, so possibly a Christian burial. This man may not have been the only one laid here. Alex noted a brown stain at the western end of the trench, and he thought that this probably marked another burial.

In April 2010 the projected lines of the walls of the medieval church were marked in flints. Regarding the east wall of the chancel the evidence from the test pit in area A was held to indicate that the chancel did not stretch as far east as Colt Hoare suggested. It was therefore marked as being about 16ft 9ins long. However, since the dig, attention has been drawn to an architect's drawing of the old church, made in 1890, which confirms Colt Hoare's plan.[16]

Conclusion

In many ways Laverstock seems like a backwater, on the fringe of greater events in Salisbury or Clarendon. Yet it has shared in the upheavals of Reformation, Civil War, and World Wars. Through many twists and turns the church has sought to make the Christian gospel known, and it endures, still here at the heart of the village community.

War and Peace: 1900 to 1945
John Loades

Early 1900s

At the dawn of the twentieth century, Laverstock and Ford remained a predominantly rural and agricultural community, with the asylum at Laverstock House providing a significant additional employment opportunity. The other large houses at Laverstock Hill, Laverstock Hall and Burroughs Hill were occupied by local worthies, providing employment to domestic staff. Farming was spread between the Manor Farm, New Farm, Ford Farm and the mills at Laverstock, Ford and by Milford medieval bridge.

Whilst village life would have been relatively tranquil, Britain was engaged in a distant colonial war in South Africa against Boer republicans. The British

The Laverstock rifle range
Ken Smith

The rifle range, marked on Ordnance Survey maps up until the 1930s, was on the slopes below Cockey Down. Large scale maps indicate that it consisted of two narrow sets of targets and butts, 100 yds apart with one at the base of Cockey Down and the 2nd higher up the slope. Southwards of the targets, seven separate firing point markers are also indicated at 100 yd intervals, with the 300 and the 400 yd firing points sharing the same position, by aiming at the lower and higher targets respectively.

It is likely that it was first laid out following a grant of a strip of land by Thomas Pain, of The Hall in Laverstock and twice Mayor of Salisbury, to allow rifle practice for the Wiltshire Rifle Volunteers, following its formation in 1860. At this time, the government of Prime Minister Palmerston anticipated attack from Napoleon III's France. Forts, such as Fort Nelson at Portsmouth and Hurst Castle were strengthened in expectation of a descent upon the south coast by the French navy.

Crises in the Empire, such as the great insurrection in India in 1857-58, required large numbers of British troops to be sent overseas from time to time. As a result, it was feared that this might leave the country defenceless and open to invasion. To provide a Home Defence force, fit, local men were recruited, including the Wiltshire Rifle Volunteers.

First World War cartoon from the Salisbury Volunteer Magazine, Vol 5, October 1917. © The Salisbury Museum

A book on the Corps, published in late Victorian times, describes the Laverstock range in rather unflattering terms: 'The rifle range of the Salisbury Corps was at some distance from the city on the London road and was a particularly difficult range at which a good score could be made. The ground undulated somewhat and each range was subject to varying currents of wind; a knowledge of these and their vagaries was a necessary ingredient in the formation of a steadily good shot at Salisbury rifle ranges'.[17]

Examination of the range today shows brick butts for targets at the base of the hill though these are now difficult to see as they are overgrown with shrubbery. Sometimes bullets are washed by rain from molehills and these identify the weapons fired. Shot includes rounds from Enfield rifled-muskets, Martini-Henry breech-loaders and mark VII Lee-Enfield rifles. These latter were used by British forces in both World Wars and probably reflect use of the range by the Wiltshire Volunteers during the Great War and possibly by Home Guard detachments during the Second World War.

We can only wonder what the good people of Laverstock must have thought when the Volunteers and others were blazing away and gunshots echoed from the hills.

Army's manpower resources were stretched by this commitment, resulting in local militia reservists being encouraged to volunteer for service overseas. Laverstock had become a location of military training with the presence of a rifle range on Cockey Down. This military activity in the parish may have stimulated some young local men to volunteer for service, although no record has yet emerged of Laverstock and Ford men serving in the Boer War. In addition, the accessibility of an expanding media ensured that the general public were well informed about events in South Africa.

Queen Victoria died in January 1901, an event that was observed by national mourning and remembrance. Laverstock village had celebrated the Queen's Diamond Jubilee only four years earlier and her death would have caused sadness. [18] From the census conducted in April 1911, it was recorded that the civil parish then consisted of 108 households with a population just over 500 persons, including 36 patients at the asylum. The table indicates the different occupation categories recorded in that census, and how these were spread across localities within the parish.

1911 Census, Laverstock and Ford: Principal Occupations by Locality

	Asylum	Bishopsdown	Ford	Laverstock	Petersfinger	Total
Agriculture	0	18	21	31	4	74
Domestic	6	7	8	41	3	65
Patient	36	0	0	0	0	36
Laundry	0	0	0	19	0	19
Nurse	15	0	0	2	0	17
Self employed	0	2	2	11	1	16
Railway	0	3	1	4	0	8
Construction	0	0	0	7	0	7
Private Means	0	1	0	6	0	7
Gen Labourer	0	0	0	6	0	6
Clerk/Industry	0	0	0	4	2	6
Education	0	1	0	4	0	5
Retired	0	1	1	2	0	4
Postal Services	0	0	0	3	0	3
Apprentice	0	0	0	2	0	2
Doctor	1	0	0	0	0	1
Scholar	0	15	13	53	1	82
Unspecified	0	21	28	91	7	147
Total:	**58**	**69**	**74**	**286**	**18**	**505**

The First World War

The relative tranquillity following the end of the Boer War in 1902 was to be disrupted with the declaration of war against Germany in August 1914. In common with every village and hamlet in Britain, Laverstock and Ford parish was to bear the scars from the next four years of relentless war. The brass tablet war memorial inside Saint Andrew's Church originally commemorated the names of twelve men of the parish who lost their lives while serving. The 1911 census shows there would have been approximately 100 men in the village of fighting age, most of whom would have volunteered or been conscripted into military service.[19] To lose twelve of this group is a one in eight fatality rate, which seems high but is not untypical, as the national mortality rate during the conflict was 11.5%.[20] Several of the fatalities were infantrymen on the Western Front at Flanders and the Somme, while three lost their lives in Middle East campaigns in Iraq and Palestine. War memorials were erected locally throughout the country in the years following the Armistice but were not always a complete record of the casualties. There is evidence of several other men with links to Laverstock or Ford who also lost their lives and who are commemorated elsewhere.

For instance, one war fatality from Ford who is not listed on the plaque in the Church is 29 year old Vester Viney, recorded as dying on 13 November 1918. His grave is in Kassel, Germany where he was a prisoner of war. Vester was born in Ford and baptised in St Andrew's Church on 17 October 1890. The Census of 1891 shows his father William was employed on the railway as a labourer, living with his wife and eight children at Broken Cross Cottage in Ford. The family was still living there ten years later with two of Vester's brothers now also working as 'navvies' on the railway. By 1911, the rest of the family had moved a couple of miles upstream to Hurdcott, with Vester enlisted in the Army and being recorded as a private with the 1st Battalion Wiltshire Regiment, stationed in South Africa. Three years later, it seems he was still in the battalion when it deployed to Flanders in the first weeks of war. Many of the battalion were captured during the rapid German advance through Belgium, including Vester. His Red Cross records confirm that he was among the earliest prisoners of war, captured during the Battle of Mons in August 1914 and he remained in captivity throughout the war.[21] Tragically, he died two days after the Armistice and never returned home.

Among those villagers who are commemorated on the war memorial tablet is Richard Salisbury. He died of wounds in a field hospital in Belgium in December 1917, serving as a private in a Mechanical Transport Company. In 1911, aged 18, he had been living with his parents in Burroughs Hill Lodge and was employed as a chauffeur. His father William was coachman to Canon Oldfield of Burroughs Hill, while Richard undertook similar duties with the more innovative mechanised vehicles, a skill that he then took with him into military duties.

An older casualty at 34 was Charles Victor Hensler who served in the Royal Navy and died of pneumonia at Royal Naval Hospital Haslar, Gosport in November 1917, leaving his widow Alice in Laverstock. Charles's burial took place in St Andrew's churchyard, conducted by the vicar, Reverend Arthur Aldworth. During the following year, the vicar and parish would suffer further loss. In April 1918 news was received of the death in action in Flanders of the peacetime churchwarden, George Fulton. He had been commissioned as an officer in the Wiltshire Regiment and rose rapidly to the rank of Lieutenant-Colonel, given command of a Battalion of the Warwickshire Regiment in Belgium. He was recognised for his exceptional efforts, being awarded a Distinguished Service Order (DSO) and mentioned in despatches from the front on three occasions, before losing his life during the German spring offensive of 1918.

Further tragedy was to follow for the vicar in October 1918 when he was notified of the loss of his son, Second Lieutenant Douglas Aldworth, aged

Rev. A. E. Aldworth.

Rev. Arthur Aldworth, Vicar of Laverstock St Andrew from 1901 to 1929. From Wiltshire and Dorset at the Opening of the XX Century: Contemporary Biographies edited by W T Pike, 1906, p111

19. Sadly, he drowned in the Irish Sea when the ferry *RMS Leinster* was torpedoed by a German submarine shortly after departing from Kingtown port, near Dublin. Douglas had recently been commissioned as a junior officer and joined his battalion of the Royal Berkshire Regiment in Ireland. It seems that he never experienced action in the trenches as he died while under orders to proceed to the Front, just a month before the war ended.

Shortly after fighting had finally ceased, Reverend Aldworth was again conducting a funeral service at St Andrew's in November, for 38 year old parishioner Alice Way. She had died from influenza and her gravestone records that her husband, Arthur, a private in the Wiltshire Regiment, had died in Germany in April that same year. The death certificate indicates that Alice was a victim of the 'Spanish flu' global epidemic which spread rapidly during 1918 and persisted into 1919. In Britain, it peaked in the late autumn of 1918 and was unusual in the high level of fatalities among the 20-45 age group. Alice was an example of this trend, dying at the peak of the outbreak at an age that was low risk in previous influenza epidemics. The local newspapers reported much illness in the city in October 1918, including many deaths.[22] The Laverstock and Ford community was undoubtedly affected as there are records that many schools were closed during the peak infection period, including the Laverstock village school. Apart from the death of Alice Way, there is no evidence from church burial records of any significant surge in parish deaths, so it seems that the village escaped the worst of the epidemic.

The vicar was actively involved in arranging for the Laverstock Memorial Brass Tablet to be erected in St Andrew's Church. He submitted the necessary Petition for a Faculty to the diocesan authority, including a draft design of the tablet, in March 1919.[23] It was noted that the tablet was a gift from Mr Hamilton Fulton of the Close, whose son George had lost his life as described above. The tablet was duly installed and unveiled on Sunday 23 November

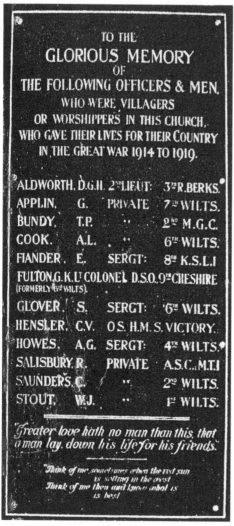

TO THE
GLORIOUS MEMORY
OF
THE FOLLOWING OFFICERS & MEN,
WHO WERE VILLAGERS
OR WORSHIPPERS IN THIS CHURCH,
WHO GAVE THEIR LIVES FOR THEIR COUNTRY
IN THE GREAT WAR 1914 TO 1919.

ALDWORTH, D.G.H. 2ᴺᴰLIEUT: 3ᴿᴰR.BERKS.
APPLIN. G. PRIVATE 7ᵀᴴ WILTS.
BUNDY, T.P. ,, 2ᴺᴰ M.G.C.
COOK. A.L. ,, 6ᵀᴴ WILTS.
FIANDER. E. SERGT: 8ᵀᴴ K.S.L.I
FULTON,G.K.Lᵗ COLONEL D.S.O.9ᵀᴴCHESHIRE
(FORMERLY 6ᵀᴴ WILTS).
GLOVER. S. SERGT: 6ᵀᴴ WILTS.
HENSLER. C.V. O.S. H.M.S. VICTORY.
HOWES. A.G. SERGT: 4ᵀᴴ WILTS.
SALISBURY. R. PRIVATE A.S.C.,M.T.I
SAUNDERS. C. ,, 2ᴺᴰ WILTS.
STOUT. W.J. ,, 1ˢᵗ WILTS.

*'Greater love hath no man than this, that
a man lay down his life for his friends.'*

*"Think of me sometimes when the red sun
is setting in the west
Think of me then and know what is
is best*

*Laverstock Great War Memorial Plaque, St
Andrew's Church, unveiled on Sunday 18
November 1919.
Picture by author with Roy Bexon*

1919 by the Archdeacon of Salisbury and commemorates 'those villagers or worshippers in the Parish Church who gave their lives for their country'.[24] In addition, Reverend Aldworth donated to the Church a Processional Cross with the figure of our Lord and an inscription to the memory of his son Douglas.[25] The Cross continues to be used regularly in the Church.

As well as its manpower contribution, Laverstock and Ford witnessed a variety of military activities linked to the war. Salisbury Plain was a focal point both for training troops and for temporary garrisoning before deployment to the front, with Salisbury being a hub for troop movement. Military camps were established in the vicinity, with one resident recalling troops being billeted in a barn on a farm in Ford.[26]

The War Office requisitioned Ford Farm during 1917 for use as a Royal Flying Corps airbase. Briefly referred to as Ford Farm Airbase, it was subsequently renamed Old Sarum. This facility expanded rapidly, with the erection of aircraft hangars, maintenance buildings, a wireless mast and barrack accommodation. Both German prisoners of war and Chinese labourers were employed in this construction programme.[27] By April 1918, the airfield became a flight training base for operational crews. Parish residents, particularly at Ford, would have seen and heard these early military aircraft above the downs.

Between the Wars

During the 1920s and 1930s, Laverstock began to transform from a small rural village into a larger community. The asylum remained the largest single enterprise within the parish with agriculture continuing as an important activity, together with other home-based businesses, including laundries and a light engineering business with scrap yard along Church Road.

Mary Poulton grew up in the village during this period, while her father ran a carpentry and undertaking business. She recalls:

> We had a good village cricket team. Arch Cable, who was my father's carpenter, and his brother Albert, who was the painter, were our leading batsmen. We also had one of the inmates of Laverstock House *(asylum)* in the team. He had been a county player, and more often than not scored 50 or so for us. My Mother was the scorer. We played on a pitch on a flat area of the Downs at the back of Burroughs Hill, and our tea was provided by the cook and kitchen staff from the big house, and organised by Amy Cable who was Arch's wife.

The rural nature of village life during the 1920s is also recalled:

> The farm, to me, was also a centre of interest. The children in that area, including my brother and I, took our jugs every afternoon and went to collect our milk, straight from the afternoon milking. While waiting, we played games in the road, which was quite safe as there was no traffic of any kind.
>
> There were two laundries, one next to the Church, and the other was further up Church Road at the other end. The washing was all done by hand, and the washing was collected and returned by means of a horse and covered van each week, and an old bicycle or two.

View of Laverstock Clump in the 1930s.
Private collection

Utility services, now taken for granted, reached Laverstock gradually:

> When first we came in 1921 there was no piped water, no gas or electricity and no sewage. In fact, when my Father built our new house, he built a new well, 24ft deep, and lined half-way by brickwork. We used a hand pump as did everybody else, with the exception perhaps of Laverstock House. The toilet in each house consisted of a bucket, which was emptied once a week by the man of the house. We all had oil lamps and candles for lighting and the gas company did not run their pipes to Laverstock until about 1926 and the electricity did not arrive for some years after that. So far as I can remember, we still used our hand-pumps until after the war, while the sewage pipes were only put in after I was married which was in 1933.'

Major Byles had turned one of his stables into a Village Hall, which he gave to the village so we had one or two concerts there run by our own pack of Girl Guides and the Sunday School was also held there.[28]

The Hoskins family moved to Laverstock during 1937 into a new build house in Church Road opposite the Primary School. One of the Hoskins' sons was Gordon who was about seventeen at the time and later recorded his Laverstock memories from the years before he went into military service in 1940.

There was no roundabout on the A30 *(London Road)* at St Thomas's Bridge. To get to Ford or Winterbourne from Laverstock, one turned right on the A30 for a few yards before turning left on to the Winterbourne Road. With no roundabout to interrupt the traffic flow, St Thomas's Bridge was a notorious accident black spot; despite numerous warning signs many drivers descending Three Mile Hill did not reduce their speed and, failing to negotiate the bend, ended up in the river. Repairs to the parapet were a source of regular employment.'

After entering Church Road from the A30, the first building on the right about a hundred yards down was the Police House, wherein lived PC Brown. There was a noticeboard erected in his hedge covered with many notices setting out the regulations governing cattle movement, fishing rights, game laws and all the rural matters under his jurisdiction. On occasions it was his duty to see that customers left the Duck Inn premises by the expiration of drinking-up time … Whenever he felt called upon to make the required visit, he never found any evidence of the law being flouted. In general, PC Brown lived at peace with the villagers; he pedalled his large bicycle sedately throughout … his territory and was universally liked and respected.

Mr Bert Cook was the roadman employed by the Council to keep the village clean, and he was responsible for all the roads from the White Bridge to St Thomas's Bridge. He lived in West Harnham and travelled to Laverstock on his bicycle. His tools were a riphook, a billhook, a shovel and a broom. These he left in the hedge where he finished work for the day. When he arrived, he stuck … a piece of red flag tied to a stick, in the bank and set to work. There were more bends in the road, more banks and more hedges than there are today and with no footpaths, many more ditches. Starting from the White Bridge he worked steadily along the left hand side of the road until he reached St Thomas's Bridge, then he worked back along the other side. He took advantage of the wet weather to turn his attention to the ditches because he could then check the flow of the water and ensure the outlets to the neighbouring fields were clear. By the time he had attended to the main road, Duck Lane and the Avenue, and worked his way back to the White Bridge, it was time to begin all over again.

With no mains water supply, there was, likewise, no mains sewage disposal. Progress was being made from the basic earth closet to flush lavatory and the builder of houses in Church Road devised a simple but effective, if somewhat disagreeable, method of solving the disposal problem. Not for him the luxury of a septic tank – he dug a large hole at the bottom of each garden and piped the effluent into it. He constructed a slab over the hole into which he let an inspection cover and installed a simple lift pump. Beneath the outlet of the pump he fitted a gutter made from a piece of corrugated iron which passed through the fence into the adjoining field on which grew nothing but rough grass and stinging nettles. When occasion demanded, and this was often, the procedure was to light a strong cigarette and pump steadily for anything up to an hour. Being in a similar situation, the neighbours were tolerant of the resultant nuisance but, if the wind was in the right direction, passing strangers taken unawares could be heard making succinct comments.

Salisbury Gaslight and Coke Company had extended its services to most of Laverstock but not so the Salisbury Electric Light Company. There was no mains electricity in old Laverstock and most homes had a wireless set operated by batteries. Listening to the wireless was a much more expensive pastime than it is today: the original cost of the set was about two weeks' wages, the cost of the dry battery would have bought you twenty five pints of beer, and of recharging the wet battery ten cigarettes. In addition to this it was necessary to buy a licence to listen to the wireless.[29]

A national survey was conducted of the civil population in 1939 as part of the preparations for war. These records have been partially released and indicate that Laverstock and Ford had about 250 households with a population approaching 1,000, representing a doubling of both figures since 1911. Expansion included some ribbon development along the west side of Church Road and council housing near the Duck Inn, but was largely the result of the sale of Laverstock Hall and grounds to building contractors Forder & Sons. They progressively built residential properties in the rectangle from near the Mill on Riverside Road, and bounded by The Avenue and by Duck Lane. One of these properties on Beechcroft Road was established as a bakery by the Budden family, which functioned from this site into the 1970s. About half of this housing development was completed before war interrupted construction until after hostilities ceased. One resident from this area recalls that the new houses were being advertised in the Salisbury cinemas to encourage interest and title deeds indicate that the original price of a new house was in the region of £500.

The Second World War

Vera Drake, whose husband Percy ran the Post Office shop, recalled some of the events during World War Two:

> War was declared in 1939. The Food Office was formed in Salisbury. We were told that in case of emergency or should Laverstock be cut off from the city, Laverstock should have its own supply of food. Gas masks were issued at the Village Hall. Ration books were issued and villagers were required to register with a specific shop. Most people registered with the Post Office shop on the Clump *(vicinity of the present day Green)*.
>
> Evacuees arrived from Cosham *(near Portsmouth)*, young boys between 8-11.

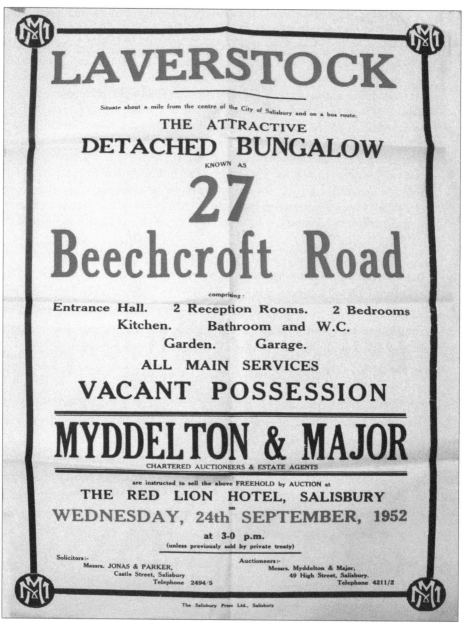

Estate Agent Notice for sale of Bungalow in Beechcroft Road in 1952.
WSA 776/113

Volunteers went round finding homes for them. I took in 2 brothers. They were good lads. They went to St Andrew's School and joined the Sunday School and the church choir. The Home Guard was formed, also the Fire Service. They went out evenings for fire drill and practice.

Most things were on ration, and lots of other items were on the Points System.

On Wednesday mornings, there was a queue outside the Post Office shop reaching down to Meadow Croft, waiting for Brent's from Winchester to bring sausages and pies.

There was an army searchlight platoon stationed in the field which is now Riverside Close. One particular Tuesday afternoon the enemy planes were overhead, the sirens were screaming and the searchlights in action. Then suddenly we heard – bang, bang, bang. A stick of bombs had dropped over the downs. Luckily, no-one was hurt. During the war the old school opposite the Post Office shop was made into a men's club, so it was very busy in the evenings. Sometimes a group of Australians visited the club.[30]

Although the timing and location of the invasion of the continent was top-secret, most people realised it was coming. The night before the landings, streams of aircraft carrying paratroopers and towing gliders must have disturbed many Laverstock residents.

In the early hours of D-Day, it was a marvellous sight. The sky was full of planes roaring overhead, which lasted quite a long time. We knew then that something important was happening.

Sylvia Parrett records that there were two barrage balloons set up in the village. One was in Latham's field by the bus stop and the other was tethered in the field past the Duck Inn by Gypsy Lane. From September 1942, a church service was held at Laverstock House at 10am with a Balloon Unit service at 10.40am. Other Balloon Unit services were taken and through the winter of that year they alternated with a Searchlight service at 10am. A searchlight was placed on the road past the Duck Inn coming to Milford between Savages Farm and Rangers farm. One day a bomb fell near the searchlight.[31] Documents also show the presence of air defences in neighbouring Clarendon Park, with three searchlights positioned just to the east of Laverstock Down, in the vicinity of Ranger's Cottages.[32] In addition, there was a dummy airfield and control bunker just north east of Cockey Down, erected to deceive enemy air observation and targeting. This was probably located there to lure enemy bombers away from the nearby Old Sarum airfield. Anderson shelters are also recorded alongside many of the houses. Similarly, Laverstock would have air raid shelters in residential areas for refuge during enemy bombing raids. One resident of Greenwood Avenue recalls a shelter in the back garden that was shared with the neighbour. Another resident recalls that the Local Defence Volunteers (later renamed Home Guard) established an observation post in a shepherd's hut on top of Laverstock Down, with six on duty every night. It is likely that this was during the period from May 1940 through to the autumn of 1941, when there was considered to be a strong possibility of a German invasion along the southern coast of Britain.

In Ford, Old Sarum Airbase remained an RAF establishment during the inter-war years, throughout the Second World War and continued into the 1970s. The buildings and facilities were expanded in the second half of the 1930s as the country re-armed in response to the growing threat from Nazi Germany.[33] During the war years, the base was in continuous use by a variety of air force units, with one of the principal activities being the training of army pilots in the role of Air Observation Posts, the airborne eyes of the artillery to help identify and adjust fire onto enemy targets. The airbase was then used as a concentration point in the build-up for D-Day and remained a staging post for several months. Large tented camps were established round the vicinity and thousands of personnel and vehicle transports passed through Old Sarum on the way to Normandy. Once again, the residents of Laverstock and Ford would have been familiar with the frequent sound and sight of military aircraft of various types and sizes flying across the landscape.[34]

As well as the considerable military activity in and around Laverstock and Ford, the village community again made its manpower contribution to the war effort. The 1939 register records that civilians, both men and women, were actively involved through the voluntary services, including the Home Guard, Air Raid Protection, Auxiliary Fire Service, Special Constabulary, St John's Ambulance and British Red Cross First Aiders. Readhead's light engineering and scrap metal business was located where Bishops Mead estate is now situated. Run by Frank Readhead, he converted to war production of shell casings and other munition products. In common with similar operations, his workforce

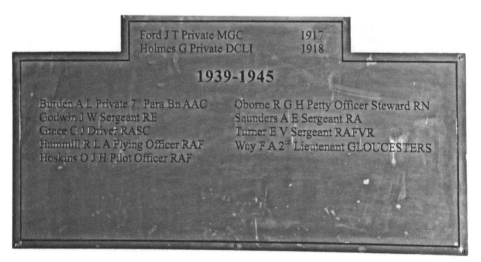

Laverstock WW2 Memorial Plaque, St Andrew's Church, added immediately below the Great War plaque in a rededication on 30 October 2011. The first two names are from WW1. Photograph by Roy Bexon

included local women. Village men of fighting age either volunteered or were considered for conscription, with many signed up for military duties in various capacities and serving across the many theatres of war. Tragically, some never returned and nine war fatalities are commemorated on a supplementary brass tablet inside St Andrew's Church, beneath the First World War memorial.

This casualty number is made up of one sailor, three airmen and five soldiers. The sailor, 38 year-old Reginald Oborne, had been in the Royal Navy since 1921 and was a mess steward aboard the flagship battlecruiser *HMS Hood* and died when it was sunk by the German battleship *Bismark* in May 1941. There were only three survivors from the ship's complement of 1,418. Reginald, his wife and daughter had moved to newly built housing in Greenwood Avenue during the early part of the War.

Also recently moved into Greenwood Avenue was Reginald's cousin, Cecil Grace. He had enlisted in the army as a driver, had been evacuated from Dunkirk in 1940 and was then captured in Greece in 1941. He subsequently died as a prisoner of war in Austria during May 1943.

Among the airmen casualties from Laverstock was 26 year-old Ormonde Hoskins, one of the brothers whose parents had moved to Church Road in 1937. Ormonde became an RAF fighter pilot and died in a tragic accident in Somerset while training in formation flying. He is buried in Laverstock churchyard, alongside other members of the family.

By 1945, the war had reached its concluding stages. Germany capitulated in May, followed by Japan in August. One resident remembers that no party was held in Laverstock at the end of the war, although apparently people collected for one.

Despite the lack of celebrations, the community would have been relieved to reach the end of the second major conflict within a generation. On 19 August 1945 a Thanksgiving Service was held at St Andrew's Church. By the end of the year, servicemen would have started to return and wartime measures would have been reduced. Gradually, a more normal lifestyle was resumed.

Notes:

Background material and population data was derived from census records for Laverstock and Ford, every 10 years from 1841 to 1911 and for 1939; also from St Andrew's Church Registers for Baptism, Marriages and Burials.

Use was made of personal reminiscences reproduced from time to time in the Laverstock and Ford Parish Newsletters, by kind permission of the Editor, as well as oral histories from residents collected by the Laverstock and Ford History Group.

David Waspe kindly shared his unpublished research into Laverstock's War casualties, WW1 and WW2, including material from the Commonwealth War Graves Commission website. [35]

1 The four Greenly girls, and the grandparents, are commemorated in North Walk, Salisbury Cathedral Cloisters.

2 Head, Jenny and Johns, Anne, 2015, quoting Phyllis Gattrell (1929-1931) in *Inspired to teach*, ELSP, 108

3 A benefice is a parish, or group of parishes, under a single stipendiary (paid) minister. Responsibility for the pastoral care of Laverstock was now transferred from the Vicars Choral of the Cathedral to patrons for the St Andrew's living.

4 Deane, Richard, 2015, 'Salisbury Silver', *Sarum Chronicle* 15, 156-7

5 Mackenzie, Rev E C Walcott (annotator), 1870, 'Inventories of Church Goods, and Chantries of Wilts', *WANHM* 12, 369

6 Lukis, Rev W C, 1855, 'Bells of the County of Wilts, with their inscriptions', *WANHM* 2, 208

7 Brown, Sarah, 1999, *Sumptuous and Richly Adorn'd, The decoration of Salisbury Cathedral*, RCHME, HMSO, 97, citing Winston 1865, 106

8 Durman, Richard, 1997, 'James Wyatt and Salisbury Cathedral: The demonising of an architect', *Hatcher Review* 5 (43), 8

9 For a fuller account of Dr Baker's search see 'Stanley Baker and the search for Salisbury's lost Cathedral glass', 2016, *Sarum Chronicle* 16, 42-57

10 *The Times*, 9 January 1934, 7. In his Winchester lecture Dr Baker gave the date as Spring, 1933.

11 RCHME, 1987, *The Churches of South-East Wiltshire*, HMSO, 40

12 *SJ*, 28 November 1958, 15

13 Colt Hoare, 1837, *The Modern History of South Wiltshire*, 5, 108

14 The buttress has been patched up from time to time, so that it is not a wholly medieval remainder.

15 Langlands, Alex, 2009, 'The past on your doorstep: community history and archaeology in Laverstock', *WANHM* 102, 306-14

16 The architect's drawing is now held at the Wiltshire and Swindon History Centre (WSA 1324/49). The stated length of the chancel is 29 feet, nine inches, but this is out of proportion with the outline as drawn, and is clearly a mistake for Colt Hoare's 23 feet, nine inches. (This is in fact the actual space available between the east end of the nave and ground occupied by old tombstones)

17 Gibney, R H, 1888, *The History of the 1st Battalion Wiltshire Volunteers*, W H Allen & Co, London, 74

18 WSA 1199/36, Queen's Diamond Jubilee accounts, Laverstock, 1896

19 In January 1916 the Military Service Act imposed conscription on all single men aged between 18 and 41, with certain exemptions. In May 1916 conscription was extended to married men. www.parliament.uk/about/living-heritage/transformingsociety/private-lives/yourcountry/overview/conscription/, accessed July 2018

20 In the UK about six million men were mobilised of whom just over 700,000 were killed, around 11.5%.www.bbc.com/news/magazine-25776836, accessed July 2018

21 https://grandeguerre.icrc.org/en/File/Search#/3/2/224/0/British%20and%20Commonwealth/Military/Vin, accessed March 2018

22 *SJ* 26 October 1918, 5

23 WSA D1/61/56/17, Proclamation for Faculty, Laverstock Wilts, 10 April 1919

24 *SJ* 29 November 1919, 3

25 Petition for Faculty, Laverstock Wilts, 27 March 1919, WSA D1/61/56/18

26 Coggan, Audrey with Evans, B, 2015, Memories of Wiltshire, the Hunt and Brooks Families of Ford and Salisbury, *Wiltshire Family History Society Journal*, Issue No 137

27 http://www.bbc.co.uk/programmes/p01rp07t, accessed March 2018, BBC and IWM World War One At Home - Wiltshire. Quote from Squadron Leader (Rtd) John Sharpe of the Boscombe Down Aviation Collection.

28 Poulton, Mary, c1990, *Reminiscences of Laverstock from 1923 to 1933,* personal memoirs, by kind permission of Mrs Sylvia Parrett.

29 Hoskins, 1992

30 Drake, 1995

31 Parrett, 1999, 67

32 HER, MWI31654,http://www.wiltshire.gov.uk/ wiltshireandswindonhistoricenvironmentrecord/ wshermap.htm, Bombing decoy at Pitton, accessed March 2018

33 Kelly's Directory 1927 records the airbase Station Commander living near Ford as Wing Commander Trafford Leigh-Mallory who was to subsequently play a prominent role during WWII within RAF Fighter Command.

34 Old Sarum Airbase: http://www.laverstock-ford.co.uk/old-sarum-airfield---a-history. html, accessed January 2018

35 www.cwgc.org/find/find-war-dead/

Years of Expansion

John Loades

Post World War Two into the 21st century

The immediate post-war years were a period of austerity. One Laverstock resident recalls:

'The war at last ended, but not the rationing. The first thing that was taken off ration was sweets. Gradually other items were taken off and at last we were cleared of all rationing *(by 1955).*'[1] Another villager remembers surplus tanks lined up along Church Road for scrapping at Readhead's yard, located at the current Bishops Mead estate.

The growth of housing in the Parish that had started in the 1930s was soon to resume. Forder and Sons were now able to complete building at Mayfair Road northwards to The Avenue while further homes were constructed along Church Road. In the early 1950s, Potters Way was opened up as a residential development, resulting in the uncovering of further archaeological finds associated with the medieval pottery site.

left: Opening of the new Post Office, 1955. Mr Percy Drake in white coat on the left; Mrs Vera Drake in centre with hands folded. Private collection
right: A view of the occasion. © Salisbury Museum / The Salisbury Journal

In 1955, the Post Office shop on the Clump was rebuilt, replacing the old corrugated structure. The Head Postmaster of Salisbury officially opened it by cutting a tape on 3 December, 'a nice bright frosty morning with the children and parents gathered all around.' In the same year, Laverstock House Mental Home closed and its grounds were designated for redevelopment. Over the next dozen years, forty two houses were built on this site.

During 1958, the centenary of St Andrew's Church was celebrated. 'It was a lovely summer's evening, and people gathered at the church gate. There was a procession to the downs, where refreshments and games took place. Mr Drake from the Post Office shop took all the food and necessities in his small van. It was a very enjoyable evening.'

Following the death of Major Byles in 1959, the twelve acre site at Laverstock Hill was sold for development. 'For a long time, there was the continual daily humming of the saws felling all the trees, and the transportation of the trees through the village to their destination. At last, the estate was cleared and building commenced.' This became Woodland Way and its surrounding estate. As a result, three of the major houses of the nineteenth century had been demolished and built over by 1970, with only Burroughs Hill House remaining.

1958 Church Centenary Barbecue. Procession turning from Church Road up Duck Lane, with The Thatch to the right and the Church roofline visible above sheds at centre. © Salisbury Museum / The Salisbury Journal

Bert Latham of Manor Farm sold two parcels of land above Duck Lane to the Council in 1958 and in 1961. These were used for council housing and sheltered accommodation around Park Road, Hill Road and Down View Road.

Major Byles had permitted the Hill House stables on Church Road to be utilised as the Village Hall. After his death and with the housing development, alternative arrangements had to be considered. A new Village Hall was built along Duck Lane in the vicinity of Park Road. A Melvin Close resident recalls: 'When the hall was pulled down to make way for housing, a brick-a-week fund was set up to build a new one, it was sixpence a week, which the people

Opening of the Village Hall, November 1966. ©Salisbury Museum/The Salisbury Journal

Official opening of old people's housing by the Minister of Housing, Richard Crossman, July 1965. © Salisbury Museum / The Salisbury Journal

of Laverstock paid. On our estate all the money was collected by Mrs Williams from Beechcroft Rd, who also delivered the Parish Magazine, in those days we paid a shilling for it.'[2] The new Village Hall was opened in November 1966. It continued to provide a venue for a cross-section of local activities, including Cubs, Brownies, Scouts, Evergreen Club, Women's Institute, Young Wives Club and for local entertainments and functions.

The 1960s also saw the development of the secondary school campus along Church Road below Laverstock Down, where the Manor Farm dairy herd had once grazed. St Edmund's Girls' School moved first, completed on 3 February 1964 at a cost of £218,217.[3] It was followed in 1966 by Highbury Boys' School, renamed in 1995 as Wyvern College, which operates as a technology college for boys. St Joseph's Catholic School also moved onto the site as a school initially for 300 pupils, completed on 7 September 1964 at a cost of £152,900.[4] This educational focal centre, with approximately 1,800 pupils across the three establishments, caused a step change in the volume of people and traffic that moved through the village on a regular basis. It became a priority to improve the thoroughfare through the village centre, resulting in a realignment of the road in the early 1970s.

This road upgrade involved demolition of the old school building that was then being used by the social club. As a consequence, Laverstock and Ford Sports Club was established on the fields between Church Road and the River Bourne, just to the North of St Andrew's Church. An old army hut was moved there to act as the initial clubhouse.

On the death of Bert Latham of Manor Farm in 1965, a secondary school playing field became Elm Close, and the field by the farm house became Riverside Close.

In late January 1969, Laverstock received coverage in the national press, including a half-page article with photograph in *The Times*. The event that prompted this was the mysterious overnight appearance of a chalk carving of a giant Panda, some 17 by 12 metres, on the slopes below Cockey Down. The initials UCNW above the distinctive carving was a clue to its origin and the story soon emerged. The carving had been the work of a team of enthusiastic Rag week undergraduates from the University College of North Wales, Bangor that included one former Bishop Wordsworth student with local knowledge. The effort was aimed at attracting publicity towards fundraising. It nearly misfired as the police became involved and there was the possibility of charges. However, by pure coincidence, it seems that the Principal of the University

Laverstock Panda below Cockey Down, January 1969. WSHC P15397

had connections with the landowner of the field and this resulted in no charges being pressed and instead admiration being expressed for the hard work over a single winter night that produced the Laverstock Panda. The students returned the following year during daylight to maintain the carving. Regrettably, this routine soon slipped and the panda has virtually disappeared from view.[5]

In 1971, some 16 acres of Cockey Down was designated a Site of Special Scientific Interest (SSSI), recognising its rich variety of chalk grassland flowers due to it not being 'improved' by chemical fertilisers together with its long history of grazing that has kept the coarser grasses in check.[6]

Residential developments continued steadily through the 1970s up to the present time. Infilling took place both around Bishops Mead, off Church Road, and around Riverbourne Road, adjacent to Potters Way, and also at the Hampton Park area of Bishopdown Farm. Within Ford, residences were added in the Merrifield Road area while at Old Sarum the business parks expanded, providing for approximately a hundred businesses. This included the airfield, which converted from military to civil use in 1982 and began offering activities such as club flying, flight training and skydiving. Its rare WWI 'Belfast' hangars were designated as Grade II listed buildings in 1989, with one becoming home to the Boscombe Down Aviation Collection in 2012. Nearby the 'Ray Mac' Football Stadium was opened in 1997 as the home of Salisbury City Football Club. This was followed by residential developments at Pilgrims Way above Laverstock Village Hall and at Old Sarum Park. The trend continued with Riverdown Park development north of Bishopdown and with Longhedge to the north of Old Sarum on the A345 Amesbury Road. Certain amenities were provided to support this growth in housing and population. Primary schools were included in the Hampton Park and Old Sarum developments, as were community halls. Landscaped leisure areas have also been incorporated, with country park green space and play areas. By utilising a neglected area between Cow Lane and the railway line, once the site of a nursery operated by Gullicks florists of Salisbury, a Community Farm project was established in 2010.

Laverstock and Ford: Population by "Locality", Census 1841 to 1951											
	1841	1851	1861	1871	1881	1891	1901	1911	1921	1931	1951
Asylum	160	120	96	75	75	58	72	58			
Laverstock	287	299	248	254	260	290	270	286			
Ford	58	82	78	91	68	72	72	74			
Petersfinger	34	51	48	31	0	0	0	18			
Bishopdown	0	0	0	0	0	0	0	69			
Longhedge							10				
Clarendon					46						
Total	539	552	470	451	449	420	424	505	765	823	1,610

In 1884 part of Laverstock and Ford Civil Parish (pop. 41 in 1891) was transferred to Clarendon Park Civil Parish.

In 1904 part of Milford Without Civil Parish (pop. 86 in 1911) was transferred to Laverstock and Ford Civil Parish.

(Author's analysis of Census data.)

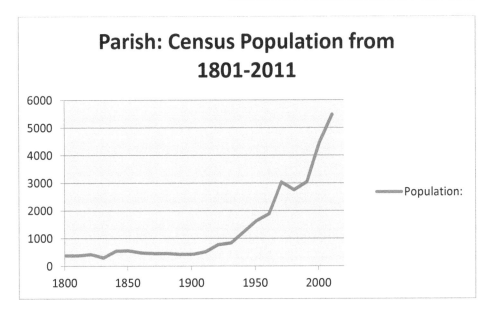

Through the efforts of a dedicated team, mostly volunteers, this has grown steadily to provide accessible educational and recreational activities including agriculture, livestock and conservation.

Over the last hundred year period, the population of Laverstock and Ford has grown from the 765 people recorded in the 1921 Census to about 9,500 people across some 4,000 households.[7]

With the ongoing demand for housing in the Salisbury district, there remains the possibility of expansion within Laverstock and Ford. However, the Parish Council has embarked on the production of a neighbourhood plan which looks at development, environmental and infrastructure needs through to 2036. This aims 'to preserve the character and sustainability of our semi-rural parish'.[8] A high proportion of the parish remains greenfield, with most residents enjoying easy access to open spaces, country parks or downland. This defining attribute of its history will hopefully be preserved in the future.

Notes:
Use is made of personal reminiscences reproduced from time to time in the Laverstock and Ford Parish Newsletters, by kind permission of the Editor, as well as oral histories from residents collected by the Laverstock and Ford History Group.

1 Drake, 1995
2 Sharpe, Renée, 2014, interview by Laverstock and Ford History Group.
3 http://st-edmunds.eu/about-us/103-2/, accessed February 2018
4 https://history.wiltshire.gov.uk/community/getschool.php?id=849, accessed March 2018

View looking east across Laverstock Village and Cockey Down, 1960s. New secondary school building at bottom left with new Woodland Way/ Silverwood Drive housing at centre. WSHC P3177

5   Based on reminiscences published in Laverstock and Ford Parish Newsletters, 2017
6   www.wiltshirewildlife.org/cockey-down-salisbury, accessed July 2018
7   The Parish Clerk kindly provided information on Parish Newsletter circulation, February 2019
8   https://history.wiltshire.gov.uk/community/getschool.php?id=849, accessed June 2018

Community Farm – The Devenish Bradshaw Charitable Trust
Peter and Maggie Bradshaw from Canada visited the Community Farm in April 2019. Peter, who owned land at Longhedge, generously purchased 53 acres of water meadows for the farm, both conserving them for the future and securing an important green belt area between Laverstock and Salisbury, (photograph Joe Newman, 2019)

Appendix 1
Glossary of Medieval terms

Attaint: Acts of attainder used by monarchs to deprive nobles of their lands and sometimes their lives, often reversing attainder in return for promises of loyalty

Bordar: peasant, lower than a villein

Burgage: a plot of land rented from a lord or king

Carucate (see hide)

Demesne: land and property worked for the direct benefit of the owner

Disseize: disposess land or property

Dsp: *decessit sine prole*, died without issue or heir

Enfeoff: giving freehold property or land in exchange for pledged service

Eyre: a circuit court held in medieval England by a judge (a justice in eyre) who rode from county to county

Fee, fief, or feud: land or revenue producing property granted by a lord in return for a vassal's service

Fee tail: an estate of inheritance limited to a particular heir according to provisions in settlements or wills

Geld: Anglo-Saxon land tax continued by the Normans, assessed on a number of hides

Hide or carucate: land tillable by a team of eight oxen in a ploughing season; the amount of land able to support a household, approximately 120 acres or four virgates

Honour: a feudal domain, the total of all lands granted by the king to a nobleman to hold as a fief. Each honour was made up of parcels of land distributed around the entire country to prevent any challenge to the king.

Inquisition post mortem (IPM): an inquiry after the death of a tenant of the crown to establish what lands were held and who his heirs were

Messuage: a property, often a dwelling house

Manor: an hereditary estate whose lord had the right to administer the law within the boundaries of his manor

Quitclaim: renouncing any rights to a property

Sergeanty: A form of land tenure in return for a specific service to a lord, in this case the king

Tenant in chief: tenant of the crown

Toft: the land on which a peasant's house and any outbuilding stood

Verderer: responsible for protection of game habitats and including the vert or green

Virgate: one quarter of a hide, approximately 30 acres

Villein: of higher status than bordar, subject to the Manor court living in village

Appendix 2
Laverstock clergy

John de Netherhaven	1305	Francis Bushell	fl 1649
John de Karleton/Carleton	1329	Christopher –?	fl 1670
Henry de Lodelewe	1339	W Powell	fl 1673
John le Hurne	1349	Samuel Jecocke	1677–1680
Thomas Faukes	–1363	Charles Barnes	1684–1688
Richard Boltford	1363	Benjamin Whitear	c 1698–1720
John Kentyff	–1389	Jos Albert	c 1722–1729
William Dalton	1389–1392	John Talman	c 1729–1731
John Whyton	1392–1393	Thomas Edwards	c 1756–1759
John Douke	1393–1408	Richard Matthews	1759
William Neldere	1408	Richard Trickey	c 1760–c 1796
William Coche/Cothe	1409–1433	P Harrison	1797–1798
Peter Fadur/Fader	1433–1435	John Malham	c 1799–c 1803
William Balne	1435	Charles Henry Hodgson	c 1807–c 1812
John Wilkins	–1438	Andrew John Greenly	fl 1812–1813
Robert Tomson	1438	Edmund Benson	1813–1814
John Colson	–1441	George Lewes Benson	1815–1836
William Spaldyngton	1441–1445	Charles King	1836–1849
John Holy	1445–1446	Lewis Tomlinson	1849–1853
John Batill	1446	William Reynor Cosens	1854–1855
William Batyll	–1459	Charles H Townsend	1855–1861
John Donnyng	1459	John PW Greenly	1861–1889
William Forrester	–1503	Herbert Cromwell Bush	1889–1900
Richard Madock	1503–1514	Arthur Aldworth	1901–1929
William Erneley	1514	Charles AW Pain	1930–1938
John Trayleman/Traelman	1550–1553	Canon Stanley Baker	1938–1950
Robert Rawlyns	–1569	Alan Gilbert Barker	1950–1955
Thomas Ellys	1569	Philip Rigby Rounds	1956–1967
Nicholas Clun(e)	1613	Douglas Arthur Martin	1968–1975
William Smithe	fl 1622	William George Bull	1975–1993
Hugh Williams	c 1624–1637	Keith Robinson	1995–2011
James Clarke	c 1641–1642	James Findlay	2013–2017
Francis Bayley	fl 1649	Andrew Bousfield	2018–

Sources:

Sir Thomas Phillipps, abstracts from the *Institutiones Clericorum in Comitatu Wiltoniae* of the Bishops of Sarum, 1297–1810, published 1825

Clergy of the Church of England Database (CCED)

Bishops' Transcripts from 1622

Protestation Returns for 1641–42

Parish Registers from 1726

Index

Numbers in **bold** indicate page references to illustrations, maps and tables. Laverstock houses and properties are indexed under Houses and Properties; Laverstock streets under Laverstock; Salisbury streets and locations under Salisbury.

Index

Index

Index

Lightning Source UK Ltd.
Milton Keynes UK
UKHW022305160522
403082UK00002B/23

9 781916 135901